GROWING LEADERS

GROWING LEADERS

Cultivating Discipleship for Yourself and Others

JAMES LAWRENCE

HENDRICKSON PUBLISHERS

Growing Leaders: Cultivating Discipleship for Yourself and Others
Hendrickson Publishers, Inc.
P. O. Box 3473
Peabody, Massachusetts 01961-3473
Published under arrangement with Bible Reading Fellowship.

ISBN-13: 978-1-56563-997-3
ISBN-10: 1-56563-997-9

Printed in the United States of America

First Printing — July 2006

Cover Art: Cover photograph by Eric Audras. PhotoAlto / Getty Images. Used with permission.

Library of Congress Cataloging-in-Publication Data

Lawrence, James, 1962–
    Growing leaders : cultivating discipleship for yourself and others / James Lawrence ; foreword by Bishop Graham Cray.
        p. cm.
    Originally published: Oxford, England : Bible Reading Fellowship, 2004.
    Includes bibliographical references.
    ISBN-13: 978-1-56563-997-3 (alk. paper)
    ISBN-10: 1-56563-997-9 (alk. paper)
    1. Christian leadership. I. Title.
    BV652.1.L29 2006
    253—dc22
                                        2006010721

*To all those who have patiently grown me as a leader,
too many to list, but all known to Him,
Thank you.*

*To Rob, friend and companion on life's journey,
thanks for everything. You're a star!*

CONTENTS

ACKNOWLEDGMENTS

As with any writing project, this is a joint effort. So many people have influenced and shaped this book, many without even knowing it. I think of the man who, when I was thirteen years old and terribly scared about reading a lesson in church, came up afterwards and offered a dozen words of encouragement. Because of you I preach today. I think of a well-known Christian speaker who gave a precocious nineteen-year-old ten minutes to discuss some finer point of theology, and, despite my arrogance, encouraged me to think deeply about the issue. Because of you I am still thinking. I think of the teacher at school who carefully guided me through teenage years and gave me my first opportunity to lead. Because of you I am a leader. To all who have grown me in faith and leadership, I dedicate this book with my deepest gratitude.

More recently, special thanks go to the team I lead and to my colleagues at Church Pastoral Aid Society (CPAS). I've learned so much through you all. Thank you to Miranda Adderley, Gareth Callam, Penny Frank, Simon Heathfield, Johnny Juckes, Rory Keegan, Andy Piggott, Chris Rogers, Rod Street, and Andrew Watson for reading the first draft and making such helpful comments. Without your help I shudder to think what would have appeared. Thank you to Naomi Starkey for her careful editing and constant encouragement to keep going. Thank you to my wife and children for continually supporting me and praying for me while I slaved away at this book.

Finally, thank you to Leighton Ford who kindly invited me into the Arrow Leadership Program and opened up a whole new way of seeing leadership. Because of you I've written this book.

FOREWORD

This book is published at a challenging time for the Church. Loss of confidence in historic institutions, a consumer culture in which religious practice is treated as a leisure option, a competing range of therapies, spiritualities and religions, and an increasing ignorance about the Christian faith all combine to create a substantial new missionary challenge.

In response the very shape of the Church is changing. We are in a new context and are exploring new approaches. It is a critical moment of opportunity. Any adequate response will involve renewed imagination, clear vision and the mobilization of the people of God. But under God, all of these are dependent on one supreme factor—the quality of leadership. A church that does not invest in developing leaders is incapable of responding to a changing culture.

As a result of the terrible decline in the numbers of young people in the church during the 1980s and 1990s, youth ministry had to reinvent itself or die! The extent to which it has been able to flourish again has been the extent to which it could change— not to adapt the gospel, but to restore contact with the everyday world of young people. The most significant change in the practice of youth ministry was this: we stopped providing programs to educate and entertain young people and began to equip young people to take responsibility for their own ministry. The results were dramatic.

It is no longer adequate to teach the emerging generation to do what we, their leaders, have done. We need to train them to think, act and lead in ways we could not otherwise have imagined.

This is why I am delighted to commend James Lawrence's book. Much of this material arises out of James' experience of developing young leaders through the Arrow Leadership Program, easily the best course of its type that I know. I value the emphasis on security in God, and on character and competence. This book will help the Church to identify, train and release the leaders we need.

+ *Graham Cray, Bishop of Maidstone*

INTRODUCTION

"I am the vine; you are the branches. If a person remains in me and I in them, they will bear much fruit; apart from me you can do nothing."

JOHN 15:5

Over the last ten years, four things have fueled my growing concern about leadership in the church. First, my own personal journey as a leader. I can't exactly remember when it started, but by the time I was a teenager I was leading a youth group in my home, completely untaught and without any real idea what I was doing. I longed for people to become Christians and, as there weren't many other Christian teenagers in the church I'd just started attending, it seemed the sensible thing to do. Then a couple of Christian school teachers began to mentor me, and by the time I was 24 I was ordained. I loved being a minister within a local church, made lots of mistakes, and learned a lot. In my early 30s I joined Church Pastoral Aid Society (hereafter CPAS) as an evangelist and I couldn't have been happier. Over the next ten years I was to experience the highs and lows of leadership, and the main struggles were to do with things that needed attention within myself. *Growing Leaders* is a personal reflection on what went wrong and God's gracious work in my life.

Second, in my role as an evangelist within two Christian organizations, CPAS and Springboard,[1] I've worked with churches throughout the United Kingdom (hereafter UK), and my experience has confirmed all the research I've read on church growth. One of the chief characteristics of healthy, growing churches is leadership. It isn't the only mark of a healthy church,[2] but it is a vital one. Leaders shape the church for good or bad. And sadly the initial research findings of the Natural Church Development Network indicate that "empowering leadership" is consistently the lowest-graded characteristic in English churches.[3] It's not that Christian leadership is an end in itself, or that good leadership will definitely lead to church growth, but leadership is a key factor in the spread of the gospel.

Third, as I started to read widely on the subject of leadership, I discovered authors saying similar things. Two examples will suffice. Leighton Ford, writing from a global perspective, says that "the world is undergoing a major leadership shift" with a corresponding need for "a new kind of leadership."[4] Chris Edmondson "takes the temperature" of the church and British society in his opening chapter of *Fit to Lead*, and concludes, "Fresh, imaginative leadership will be required and will need resourcing."[5] These conclusions resonate with many in leadership today. Models of leadership, church and evangelism that have worked well in the past are under question. Many are rethinking such models in order to engage with a rapidly changing world.

Fourth, I have had the privilege of working alongside younger leaders. In 1998 I attended a leadership development program in the United States called Arrow. It was a great experience. Arrow is an eighteen-month program aimed at leaders aged 25 to 40, seeking to help them to be led more by Jesus, knowing him and understanding his will; to lead more like Jesus, enabling his people to be a reconciling community; and to lead more to Jesus, serving his redemptive purposes in our generation. Since then, we've started an Arrow Leadership Program in the UK. We've completed three programs and have discovered that many of those who attend are grappling with similar issues. How do committed Christian leaders sustain their relationship with God, without succumbing to cynicism and disillusionment? How do they handle the demands on their time? How do they continue to grow as a Christian while encouraging others to grow? Where do they find resources to help them make sense of a changing world and changing church?

As a result of these four things, I am convinced of the need to resource leaders for what Chris Edmondson calls "fresh, imaginative leadership" within the Church. *Growing Leaders* is one small contribution to that task.

WHY GROWING LEADERS?

There are two main strands to my approach. The first is that we need to grow *more* leaders. As reflection on theology and financial restrictions affect the role of the ordained leader within the church, we will need more people to take on leadership responsibilities within local congregations. For this reason the book speaks of leaders rather than ministers, recognizing the diversity of leadership positions within local churches and Christian organizations. I also use male and female pronouns interchangeably.

Part of growing more leaders is to liberate the people of God to embrace leadership at every level. One of the common phrases I hear is "I'm not a leader. I just . . . take the children's group . . . run the youth club . . . coordinate the home meeting . . ." When I point out that they are indeed in a leadership position, they normally struggle to accept the term "leader." Why? Because the model of leadership reflected in the life of the local church is too limited, and not biblical enough. We need a church where people are helped to take up leadership roles, and equipped to carry them out with confidence and skill. We need a church where those in leadership in their Monday-to-Saturday lives don't feel they have to leave all that behind when they enter the church building on Sunday. We need a church where we grow more leaders of every age— children, young people and adults.

The second strand is a conviction that for us to grow more leaders, we need more *growing* leaders. This is the primary focus of the book. Growing leaders tend to grow others into leadership.

Christian leadership can be tough,[6] particularly at this time of change within society and church, when many leaders are unsure of their role and feel inadequately trained to fulfill it. Reports such as *Affirmation and Accountability*[7] and *Leaders Under Pressure*[8] highlight some of the current pressures experienced by church leaders.

- 3 in 10 have felt for a prolonged period like leaving Christian service.
- 3 in 10 feel that their family suffers because of their work.
- 4 in 10 feel pressured by inadequate income.
- Only 2 in 10 have received training in management or team building.
- 7 in 10 feel heavily overworked.
- 200 church leaders miss Sunday activities each week as a result of stress-related illnesses.
- 1,500 church leaders quit over a ten-year period.

Under these pressures it is easy to stagnate, opt out, or withdraw into what is familiar. I know from my own experience how easy it is to stop growing as a leader, and for that reason I've decided to be fairly personal in this book. This runs the risk of somehow suggesting that my way of coping with particular experiences is the only way of coping with them. I know that this is not the case. Each person is wired in a different way, with different gifts, experiences, and passions. Each reader of *Growing Leaders* will need to interpret it through his or her own personality and experience. There are places in the book where I think we are dealing with principles that cross cultures, personalities and times, and there are places when I am simply sharing something of my own story. When I do the latter, my intention is to be illustrative, not prescriptive.

AN OVERVIEW

The book is divided into six parts, based on the model for growing leaders at the heart of the Arrow Leadership Program.

Part 1: Leadership today explores the context for growing leaders today. Chapter 1 examines how we define leaders and leadership, with a particular look at the characteristics of *Christian* leadership. Chapter 2 considers some specific challenges for leaders today, and identifies a model for developing leaders that provides the framework for the rest of the book.

Part 2: Growing leaders know they're chosen considers the starting point for any Christian leader—discipleship. Unless we know we are chosen, the children of a loving God, we will lead from an insecure place, constantly twisting the privilege of a leadership position to meet our own needs. In this chapter we consider the cycles of grief and grace and how Jesus' life models for us the security of knowing who we are in him.

Part 3: Growing leaders discern God's call focuses on knowing what God wants for our lives. Chapter 4 introduces the concept of living in the "red zone," where we constantly overextend ourselves, damaging our relationships, health and effectiveness. Chapter 5 considers how God's call affects not simply the big picture of what he wants us to do with our lives, but also our daily decisions, thus helping us to move out of a "red zone" lifestyle.

Part 4: Growing leaders develop Christ-like character reflects on the place of character in the leader's life. Chapter 6 acknowledges that who we are communicates as clearly as what we do. Many of the problems in leadership do not come from a lack of skills or knowledge in a particular area, but from the underlying character issues that affect how we relate to people. Chapter 7 asks how we can grow more like Christ. How much change can we expect this side of heaven? What tools can help us avoid stagnation and disillusionment?

Part 5: Growing leaders cultivate competence looks at four essential areas of leadership competence: leaders lead themselves and those closest to them (Chapter 8), embody kingdom values (Chapter 9), discern, articulate and implement God's vision (Chapter 10), and develop people (Chapter 11). The first two are mainly inward-focused. Leading ourselves is one of the toughest challenges most of us face. Plenty of leaders pay lip service to certain values but then don't live them out; effective leaders embody their values. Without this, a leader lacks integrity, a fundamental quality of healthy leadership. The second two areas are mainly outward-focused. If we are to lead, we need to know where we are going, and ensure we get there. How do we discern God's way ahead with a group of people so that we can lead them well? Finally, the role of the leader isn't simply to achieve a task, but also to develop people. Taking Jesus as our example, we examine mentoring as a process in the life of the leader.

Part 6: Growing leaders lead in community considers the context for Christian leadership, the community of the people of God. Reflecting on the nature of God and his Church, we explore the corporate nature of leadership and look at the place of team as a reflection of this community.

As you read the book, you'll notice that each part varies in length. This doesn't reflect the level of importance of any one part, for each part builds on the previous one, with areas of overlap and distinctiveness. Each chapter starts with a scenario or poem, and ends with some questions or exercises for personal reflection. Questions within the chapters and a resources section at the end of the book provide additional material for discussion and reflection. You may like to use the questions in conversation with someone else. The difficulty with answering them on your own is that many of us are either overly negative or naively optimistic about ourselves; few of us are good at objective reflection. Leaders often struggle to find a mentor, so here is a simple way to establish an informal mentoring-type relationship. Invite a colleague or friend to read the book, and then meet after every chapter to discuss the content, using the questions as a starting point for your conversation.

A PERSONAL COMMENT

Any book that considers Jesus' leadership as a model for those who lead his people is going to be challenging. I want to stress at the outset that I can handle that challenge only by clearly understanding that God's call on my life as a leader is within the context of a number of theological truths. First, my baptism. Baptism is the inauguration of God's people into a lifetime of service for Jesus. In baptism I am assured that I am a child of God, and that my life in Christ is dependent on grace. If I am called to lead, it is as a child of God committed to serving Jesus, totally dependent on his amazing grace.

Second, the cross, which makes clear that sin and failure can be forgiven. I've made so many mistakes as a leader and struggle with many internal issues, yet at the cross I know the one who loves, forgives and offers a new start. The cross also reminds us of the place of suffering within the Christian life. The apostle Paul, reflecting on his faith, wrote, "I want to know Christ and the power of his resurrection and the fellowship of sharing in his sufferings, becoming like him in his death, and so, somehow, to attain to the resurrection from the dead" (Philippians 3:10–11). Christ suffered; we are called to share in the fellowship of his sufferings.

Third, the resurrection and the coming of the Spirit. I am not left on my own. Jesus is present with me through his Spirit, bringing about his transformation of my life. The process of change is not dependent solely on me, but on my willingness to be open to what God wants to do in my life. The good news is that he's been taking inadequate and ordinary people and using them in leadership for a long time. He is pretty good at it.

Fourth, Christ's return. This is the hope I have as a leader, that one day all will be well, that the tragedy and suffering of this life is not the end. "For the Lamb at the center of the throne will be their shepherd; he will lead them to springs of living water. And God will wipe away every tear from their eyes" (Revelation 7:17). God is sovereign of his world; he will return. Alleluia! Until then I seek to be faithful to God's calling on my life as best I can.

These four things keep me going. If I stray too far from any of them I collapse at the enormity of the task and the weakness of my character. Thank God that he is the one on whom I can depend, and thank God that he hasn't left me in this race on my own.

LET'S RUN THE RACE TOGETHER

A story is told of an event at the Special Olympic Games. It was late in the day, and the 400 yard sprint was about to start. Two young men lined up on the starting line, as all the other competitors had dropped out. A hard-nosed *Time* magazine reporter gave his commentary on the radio, describing the scene as "painful to watch." The gun went off. The two men, both with cerebral palsy, lurched off the line. One of the coaches ran beside the track, coaxing his athlete on. "Come on, Joey, you can win." At the first corner Joey was leading by 25 yards. A subtle chant came from the crowd: "Joey. Joey. Joey." Going into the last turn, Joey's lead had stretched to 40 yards. The other competitor was weary and losing heart. Twenty-five yards from the finish, Joey suddenly stopped. He turned to his coach and smiled, acknowledged the crowd, and then turned back to the other young man and said, "Come on, buddy." Joey held out his hand until the man was alongside him, and then they ran across the line together. The crowd went berserk. The reporter was heard to utter, "Make me more like Joey." The coach was heard to stammer through his tear-lined face, "Attaboy, Joey, you're a real winner."

As a leader, I am only half way though the race, so *Growing Leaders* is written looking ahead to those further on in the race, who will encourage me not simply to keep going but to develop and thrive in Christian leadership. It is written looking sideways at colleagues and companions, wanting to share the heady highs, the painful lows and the day-by-day endurance of Christian leadership. It is written looking back to those further down the track seeking to run the race set before them, offering a hand to help them run with verve, imagination and freshness. It is written looking around to the crowd who fill the heavenly stadium and cheer us all on the way; those who have completed their race, and have now received their crowns.

Above all, *Growing Leaders* is written looking up to Jesus, the one who is "the author and perfecter of our faith" (Hebrews 12:2) who alone is "able to keep you from falling and to present you before his glorious presence without fault and with great joy" (Jude 24). My desire is that this book may help you to keep growing as a leader, to be led more by Jesus, to lead more like Jesus, and to lead more to Jesus.

FOR REFLECTION

Father,
I abandon myself into your hands.
Do with me what you will.
Whatever you may do, I thank you.
I am ready for all, I accept all.
Let only your will be done in me,
and in all your creatures.
I wish no more than this, O Lord.
Into your hands I commend my soul.
I offer it to you
with all the love of my heart,
for I love you, Lord,
and so need to give myself,
to surrender myself into your hands,
without reserve and with boundless confidence,
for you are my Father.
Amen.

CHARLES DE FOUCAULD

PART ONE

LEADERSHIP TODAY

Part One explores the context for growing leaders today. Chapter 1 tries to untangle the web of how we define leaders and leadership, with a particular look at the distinctive characteristics of *Christian* leadership. Chapter 2 considers some specific challenges for leaders today, and identifies a model (see the diagram above) for developing leaders that provides the framework for the rest of the book.

NICK (18), WRITING TO HIS GODFATHER

Dear Joe,

Wow! Great Christmas present or what? Thanks! Exactly right. Thank you too for asking about what I'm doing when I finish school. It is all a bit scary.

Only six months to go and then what? Not a clue. Except for something interesting that happened a few days ago.

In the Sunday service there was a quiet bit during the prayers. I kind of sensed God speaking to me. Nothing has ever happened like this before. But it was as if God spoke, not with a voice, but it came across like that. He said, "I want you to be a leader in my church." Then, after the service, Dad came up to me and said he'd been thinking about my future and wondered if I'd thought about doing something in the church. It was kind of spooky. What if it was really God? What if he really wants me to lead in his church? What do you think, Joe? I hope you don't mind me telling you all this.

My friend Carol and I were chatting last night about the future. She thinks I should take up an offer with Youth for Christ, and get some more experience of youth work. A year on one of their teams sounds fun. I've learned so much from leading the junior youth group here, but I've also got loads of questions. Like, God may be asking me to be a leader—but, hey, what is a leader, anyway? And how do you become one? I feel a little on my own with all this. Carol is a good friend, but we're both at the same stage asking the same questions. Who's going to help me think this through? Any advice?

Anyway, gotta go. Stay cool. Thanks for the terrific gift—and for praying for me.

Nick

Chapter 1

WHAT IS CHRISTIAN LEADERSHIP?

Leadership for Christians is about God, not about us.
. . . We center our soul in the hand of God—only
then are we ready for leadership.

WALTER WRIGHT[1]

There is no shortage of ideas about leadership and images of leaders. Occasionally when I am exploring Christian leadership with a group, I'll start a session by asking them to draw a picture of a leader. The results are fascinating. Inevitably what they draw depends on their experience of being led and their understanding of leadership.

Some draw a picture of the typical "strong natural leader." We know the sort—jutting jaw, focused stare, determined brow. They walk with purpose, they talk with enthusiasm, and they thrive on action. Nothing seems to shake their resolve; problems are always opportunities. No one stands in their way; people are a means to a greater end. They have endless energy; sleep is for wimps. Yes, a caricature admittedly, but one that often comes to mind when people are asked to draw a leader. And . . . they are normally male. Such a caricature leads us to perceive leadership in a monochrome way. For if this is our predominant image or experience of leadership, we assume all leaders must look like, even sound like, this type of "strong natural leader."

Others draw pictures of ineffectual leaders. The media is very adept at caricaturing such Christian leaders. I was channel surfing the other night and stopped to watch a clergyperson on TV. I have no idea what the program was, or the storyline, but those two minutes once again reinforced the image so many have of ministers—weak, ineffectual, out of touch with reality, "nice," and unlikely to lead anyone anywhere. Those with this sort of image of church leaders often despair at what they perceive as the lack of leadership within the Church, and are in danger of looking for the stereotypical "strong natural leader" to fill the vacuum.

Other group members struggle to draw anything at all, sometimes because their experience is too painful. Again the media provide the caricature of the minister who leaves his wife and runs off with the choir director, or embezzles church funds for personal gain. More recently the high-profile cases of child abuse have heightened concern about those in leadership within the Church. When Christian leaders abuse their power, they not only damage those they lead, they destroy trust in leaders on a broader level.

Thankfully, others avoid the caricatures and draw a wonderful variety of people, all ages, both genders, different social and cultural backgrounds, leaders lay and ordained who've had a positive influence, shaping people's lives and providing support, inspiration and encouragement in the Christian life.

A mixed response to the exercise is fairly typical. The ensuing discussion tends to highlight a number of common themes. If we recognize that the caricatures are unhelpful, what is an appropriate model for a Christian leader? How do we respond to the challenges of leadership within a changing world and church? How do we help those in leadership grow and develop in a Christ-like way? How can we encourage more people to take up leadership within the Christian community and help them grow in confidence as leaders? These are the issues that Part I of *Growing Leaders* addresses.

WIDELY RECOGNIZED LEADERSHIP DEFINITIONS

Who or what is a leader? This is the proverbial million-dollar question, but I would like to suggest that it is the wrong one. It immediately limits the answer to a narrow definition that doesn't reflect the complexities of leadership. Instead, let's ask the question, "How might we define *leadership*?" Here are five categories, three of which are broadly recognized by writers on leadership, and two of which reflect a specifically Christian answer to the question.

Leadership is a function

Leadership is exercised whenever anyone influences another person. In this sense, nearly everyone exercises leadership, for good or bad. The older sibling who influences the younger one to do something naughty, the parent who helps a child to overcome a problem, the friend who encourages us to face a fear, are all exercising leadership. The employee who helps the employer to see a situation differently is exercising leadership, and so is the child who persuades the parent to tell the truth. Whenever and wherever we influence another person, we are exercising leadership. This simple approach to leadership challenges many of the assumptions behind caricatures of leaders. It highlights the importance of recognizing the huge impact our lives have on other people. Defining leadership as a function addresses the question "Am I a leader?" with another question: "Are you influencing other people?" But on its own, defining leadership as a function is insufficient.

Leadership is a position

Leadership is a position of responsibility given to an individual. Every organization, from businesses to social clubs, appoints people to positions of leadership.[2] Some of these positions are salaried, with clear job descriptions, limits of authority and lines of accountability—like the businesswoman with a job in a multinational consulting firm. Others are voluntary, but with clear expectations and lots of support—like the Sunday School teacher overseeing fourteen three-and four-year-olds. Still others are unclear and unsupported—like the coordinator of a local social group who didn't really want the role, and isn't sure what it is, but took it on out of a sense of loyalty to the group and gratitude for all that the group has meant for him over the last year. Each of these people is in a position of leadership, but with very different expectations.

Holding a leadership position doesn't guarantee the ability to fulfill the role. In business there is something called the "Peter principle"—promotion to the point of incompetence. Someone who makes a wonderful salesperson doesn't necessarily make a great manager of salespeople. When the person accepts promotion to a new position of leadership, they flounder because they simply don't have the talent or skills for the new role. In the Church it could be called the "recruitment syndrome." It is not unusual to find someone in a position of leadership that they accepted out of a sense of duty, or due to massive pressure brought to bear by the minister desperate to fill a leadership vacancy. I remember a children's group leader who'd faithfully led a group for five years. On getting to know me, he confessed that he didn't even like children. Every week it was a miserable experience for him, and it wasn't brilliant for the kids either. Just because a person has a position of leadership, it doesn't mean they are either competent for that role or called to that position.

Leadership is a talent

Research by the Gallup organization on leadership makes a distinction between knowledge, skill and talent.[3] *Knowledge* is something you can acquire, be it factual or experiential knowledge. For example, I gain more knowledge about the people I lead by asking good questions and listening carefully to their responses. A *skill* is something you can learn through training. For example, you can be taught the skill of good agenda setting. *Talent*, however, is a given. Gallup defines a talent as "a recurring pattern of thought, feeling, or behavior that can be productively applied."[4] It is not the same as skills or knowledge. Skills and knowledge are transferable from person to person, but they tend to be specific to the situation. Talents are transferable from situation to situation, but they are specific to the person. You can't give an adult a talent: it is either present or absent. Talents are developed at an early stage of life and are not dependent on gender, ethnicity, or background.

Gallup's research identifies twenty common leadership talents among exceptional leaders, but helpfully points out that no one individual has all twenty talents. Talents aren't just what you can do, but what you can't help yourself doing.

Lurking in the murky depths of leadership theory is a question we now need to address. Are leaders born or made? At a time when "genes" are found for every aspect of life, many believe there is a "leadership gene." You've either got it or you haven't, and if you haven't, you shouldn't waste your time trying to get it. Such "gene" theories have gained popular acceptance in a range of areas, but leadership research places them under question. "There is as much proof that the leadership gene exists, as compelling evidence supporting belief in the unicorn," writes Paul Simpson.[5] Part of the difficulty is in the breadth of characteristics that make up leadership. Attaching the full range of leadership skills to one gene is stretching the scientific theory to breaking point.

If there is a consensus, it is that leaders are born *and* made— born, because there are certain leadership traits that can be identified from an early age; made, because context and opportunity influence how a person develops. Talent is a combination of both. It is in the complex interaction of who we are (given to us through our gene code) and how we develop (given to us through our context and experiences) that leadership talents develop.

Each of these three aspects of leadership—function, position, talent—are like interlocking circles. When an individual has a leadership position that is aligned with their leadership talents, they will function best as a leader. Someone who leads well as a small group leader may not function as well at a different level of leadership. John Adair suggests that there are three levels of leadership within most organizations.[6]

- *Team/small group leader:* normally accountable for up to sixteen people—for example, home group/cell leader, youth group leader, children's group leader.

- *Area leader:* looks after significant parts or major functions of an organization or church—for example youth/children's coordinator, evangelism coordinator, associate minister, worship coordinator.
- *Overall leader:* the person who has ultimate responsibility for steering an organization or church—for example, minister, director of a parachurch organization.

Adair suggests that more people can lead well at the level of team/small group leader than overall leader. There are some who grow through the leadership levels, and others for whom this isn't appropriate. Bob was an excellent small group leader but, when asked to oversee the work of all the small groups in his local church, he said no. Slightly taken aback, the minister asked why. Bob replied, "The talents required to coordinate the groups are the very ones I don't have. My talents are ideal for what I do." He was right. Joan, also a small group leader, wasn't even thought of for the role. She was slightly shy, and rarely noticed. In fact, her talents were ideal for the role. She made a better coordinator than small group leader. What she needed help with was confidence, not competence.

ADDITIONAL PERSPECTIVES ON LEADERSHIP DEFINITIONS

For Christians, however, even this doesn't reflect the whole picture. We need to add two further insights into a description of leadership from the biblical tradition.

God gives a gift of leadership

In Romans 12:6–8, Paul writes, "We have different gifts, according to the grace given us. If a person's gift . . . is leadership, let them govern diligently." Listed among a variety of other gifts, leadership is one of those that Paul identifies as part of God's gifts to his people. The Greek word used can mean both "to lead" and "to care." This gift of "caring leadership" is not a trophy for the glass case, but a tool for the job. Gifts aren't intended to build a person up and make them look great, but are given through God's grace for the building of the body and the witness of the Church in the world. These gifts are given in the context of ongoing transformation into Christ-likeness (Romans 12:1–2), genuine humility about ourselves (Romans 12:3), and recognition that we belong to the body and therefore need each other (Romans 12:4). Paul urges Christians to use God's gifts with wisdom, a servant heart, and a desire for the common good.

The language of gift encourages us humbly to receive something rather than proudly boast that we have achieved something (1 Corinthians 4:7). This attitude is crucial to the way we use the gift of leadership. "Let them govern diligently" (Romans 12:8). The gift of leadership will benefit from hard work (zeal), ongoing reflection (earnestness), training (diligence) and maturity. As with all the gifts, disobedience, unresolved personal issues and immaturity will stifle it.

We need to be wary of building a comprehensive edifice on the foundation of a single verse that mentions leadership. What we know, however, is that leadership was exercised in the early Church, and that Paul speaks elsewhere of the gifts of the Spirit in terms of grace (1 Corinthians 12:4), service (12:5), workings (12:6), manifestations of the Spirit (12:7), and varieties (12:4–6). All these gifts are acts of God's power achieving his purposes and are the "tangible expression of the active leadership of the Lord Jesus in a congregation."[7] This is great news for the Church, for, unlike other contexts where leadership is dependent on natural talents, Christians recognize that leadership does not depend solely on the natural talent of a few exceptional individuals. God can give the gift of leadership to anyone. It is the expression of God's grace in ordinary people's lives. Often this is through the natural talents of an individual,[8] sometimes it is despite them, but always it is a sign of grace, so that no one may boast (1 Corinthians 4:7).

God calls people to leadership roles

The Bible shows us that God calls people into leadership and his choice is sometimes surprising. The disciples were a mixed bunch of ordinary men, many of whom wouldn't have passed the psychological profiles and assessment inventories of our day. Yet despite their obvious weaknesses, Jesus called these men to be with him and then to lead his Church. When God calls, the Christian's responsibility is to obey, however surprised we may be by his choice, trusting that he provides all that is needed for us to fulfill the role to which he has called us. This calling may be for a particular situation or for a lifetime's ministry.

As we've identified, God can call people and gift them for particular things he wants them to do, despite their background and experience as well as because of it. Unlike the behavioral psychologists and evolutionary biologists, we cannot close the "born or made" circle without reference to God. God does seem to work with who we are and how we've grown, but he also works despite these things. God's calling and equipping are as important as natural ability (born) or positive development (made), and all these things bring Christian leaders to a sense of gratitude, humility and dependence on God.

Leadership is therefore about function, position, talent, gift and call. When we restrict our understanding of leadership to just one of these areas, we automatically elevate one aspect of leadership above others, and create an unhealthy environment for leadership to grow. The five aspects of leadership need to be held in creative tension with one another. When you meet someone who is a naturally talented leader, with a clear call from God to a particular position, gifted by God with spiritual gifts to fulfill the call, and the maturity in personal development to continue growing in Christlikeness, it is a wonderful combination. There are leaders like that around, but not many. To grow leaders, we need to reflect a breadth of leadership understanding so people can see where they fit in, and identify how to move on in their leadership development. We need to release people to accept their leadership role at whatever level that is expressed, and through that grow more people into leadership at every level, constantly aware that God is the one who calls and equips.

DISTINCTIVES OF CHRISTIAN LEADERSHIP

If these five aspects describe what leadership is, what makes the exercise of Christian leadership distinctive?[9] I've been challenged by Steven Croft's[10] work on how much our leadership thinking is genuinely from a reflection on the Scriptures, and how much is simply a baptizing of secular theories within the Church. Of course there is much to learn from secular insights into leadership, but Croft is concerned about the tendency of the Church to respond to the latest fad or fashion. He suggests that truth is rarely found there, but rather in serious theological reflection. As the Church looks for ways both to grow the faith of those already Christian (deepening their "roots" in Jesus) and to help those outside the faith come to know Jesus (through a variety of "routes" to him), it is all too easy to abandon what the Christian tradition has to offer on leadership and embrace the latest "new thing" without a critical analysis of what is appropriate and what isn't.

Many ordained church leaders have an instinctive reaction to the word "leader." They sense that their calling was to be a minister, and are unsure how the roles of minister and leader link up. So is interest in "leadership" just the next fad to race through the church, attracting its few followers who will quickly abandon it for the following fad just round the corner? No. In a rapidly changing world and church, leadership is an important factor in helping the Church chart its way ahead.[11] It is also rightly reflected in the Christian world. The Church needs good leaders. The question is, what should shape the way Christians exercise leadership? I'd like to suggest several characteristics from the biblical tradition that mark out Christian leadership.

Christian leadership is founded in relationship with God as Trinity

Christian leadership depends on relationship with God as Trinity (see John 15). Without this fundamental relationship it isn't Christian leadership, yet it is easy to lose this relationship in the busyness and pressure of leadership. We'll explore this loss of relationship further in Chapter 3. Christian leadership is exercised out of the overflow of that relationship as an expression of the grace of Jesus, the love of God and the fellowship of the Holy Spirit.

It is a *result of grace*—Jesus' divine calling on our lives to follow him and lead others. We don't own this calling; we don't control where Jesus leads; we don't earn his blessing. He generously calls us out of love for people and a longing to fulfill his purposes in his world.

It is *shaped by God's love*—radical, risky, self-sacrificial, costly and forgiving. His love for us draws from us a love for him, and a love for people (1 John 4:7–12). This love goes the extra mile, takes a slap on the cheek, and gives away a garment (Matthew 5:38–42). It is prepared to listen to the thousandth person who isn't yet a Christian give their argument against Christianity, an argument we've heard so many times before we actually know it better than they do, yet genuinely engages with this person as if they were the first person to ask the question. This love receives unfair criticism or unjustified abuse and does not retaliate. It gives and keeps on giving, not demanding anything in return. This love aligns us with a young person who has just messed something up completely, rather than distancing ourselves through fear of looking bad.

Christian leadership is *dependent on the Holy Spirit* empowering and equipping individuals to play their part in the body of Christ (Ephesians 4:11–13). In his body, no one individual has all that is necessary for the body to function, but each person has their part to play, and is a valuable and vital part of the body. We are all "a chosen people, a royal priesthood, a holy nation, a people belonging to God" (1 Peter 2:9). It is the Holy Spirit who takes our strengths and weaknesses and transforms them, using them for God's purposes and for his glory.

Christian leadership is rooted in the Bible and directed by the Spirit

Christian leaders seek to be faithful to the Bible in all they do because it is God's word, "useful for teaching, rebuking, correcting and training in righteousness so that the godly person may be thoroughly equipped for every good work" (2 Timothy 3:16–17). Christian leaders seek to be open to the Spirit because the Spirit of Jesus within guides and leads us into all truth (John 16:13–15). Faithfulness to the Bible and openness to the Spirit of God are like the two spotlights at a theater. When they come together on one spot, they bring focused and brilliant illumination.

The Bible and the Spirit help us as leaders to *see our part in God's bigger story*, the salvation history of the world, the kingdom of God. This perspective prevents us from getting stuck in our own limited context. It reminds us of the wider world Church, and assures us that, no matter what we face, God is working his purposes out. The temptation to become cynical or disillusioned is countered by a healthy understanding of the bigger story of what God is doing, whose focus is on his kingdom. This will shape how we lead the local church, as an outpost of God's kingdom. If leaders focus anywhere else, they end up following something or someone other than Christ, and they end up serving an agenda other than the kingdom of God's agenda. Christian leaders are kingdom seekers, not empire builders.[12]

The Bible and the Spirit place a *willingness to follow* at the center of Christian leadership, for a Christian leader's priority is to serve the king. Discipleship is the constant journey of the Christian leader. All leaders must be learners, submitted to serving the king, following wherever he may lead. A Christian leader's allegiance cannot afford to lie anywhere else. This is a challenge, as Jesus' teaching doesn't allow us to retreat to where we are comfortable and stay there. The focus of his gospel constantly calls us to a daily practice of repentance and faith, to a concern for those who don't know Christ, and to the place of dying to ourselves and daily taking up our cross (Mark 8:34–38).

The Bible and the Spirit also help us to *take seriously divine sovereignty and human responsibility.* We will not be surprised by the constant mess the world is in and the rebelliousness of people or, if we are honest, the tendency for ourselves to be rebellious. As we daily confront the realities of a fallen world, we place ourselves in the hands of a sovereign God, who offers forgiveness and the possibility of change.

Christian leadership is marked by servanthood

Service is meant to be a normal part of Christian discipleship. Jesus expects those who lead to continue serving as a normal part of Christian leadership. This challenged everything about the accepted models of leadership in Jesus' day. It was utterly revolutionary, and I want to consider this particular distinctive in greater detail.

In Luke 22, Jesus shares the last supper with his closest friends. He has outlined his eagerness to spend these last hours with his friends before he suffers (v. 15) and then breaks bread and shares the cup (vv. 19–20). He speaks honestly about his impending betrayal by one of those closest to him (v. 22). At this moment of intense significance and personal vulnerability, the disciples start having an argument about who is the greatest. It is hard to imagine how Jesus must have felt, but his response embodies the very value he longs for them to adopt: "The kings of the Gentiles lord it over them; and those who exercise authority over them call themselves Benefactors. But you are not to be like that. Instead, the greatest among you should be like the youngest, and the one who rules like the one who serves" (vv. 25–26).

"You are not to be like that." Don't "lord it over them": don't make use of position or power to wield authority in an arrogant way. Don't think of yourself as a "benefactor": don't decide when to give and when to keep back. *"You are not to be like that."* The greatest should have an attitude of humility, a willingness to value others

above themselves. The one who rules should be like the one who serves, willing to help others fulfill their dreams.

Jesus isn't saying, "Avoid leadership." He is saying that the way we lead needs to be marked by servanthood: "But I am among you as one who serves" (Luke 22:27). Striving for greatness[13] was a mark of leaders of the day. Striving to serve is to be the mark of Christian leaders. Jesus says that it isn't about status or position, "For who is greater, the one at table or the one who serves? Is it not the one at table?" Yes, in the eyes of the people, those who sit at the table are "greater," but we are to see things differently. Neither success nor status defines Christian leaders, service defines a Christian leader. We may do a nice job of deferring to others, but all too quickly we are like the disciples disputing about who is the greatest. We may not do it verbally, but we do it internally in a multitude of subtle ways—concern with how we look, who we associate with, which jobs we get, who listens to us, who we know. *"You are not to be like that."*

Many years ago, the minister and I were once again the last people putting chairs away late at night after yet another church meeting. I made some quip about needing to be trained by a moving company, and he responded, with a smile, "Once a deacon, always a deacon." He was right. Steven Croft has developed this theme in *Ministry in Three Dimensions,* exploring the threefold nature of leadership in the early church: "Diakonia, the ministry of a servant, is the most important of the three dimensions if ministry and leadership are to be truly Christian and Christ-like . . . the principles of diakonia ought therefore to be the controlling and guiding principles of all Christian ministry."[14]

For many of us, this sets up a tension in our lives between being a servant and a leader. Obviously the word "servant" does not imply groveling servitude; nor does "leader" mean dogmatic dictator. However, am I called to give up my own agenda to serve others in fulfilling theirs? I've heard people debate on both sides, and am unconvinced by either, for surely the question involves a false assumption, that either my or the other person's agenda is the priority. The servant leader is called first to serve Christ. His agenda must be preeminent over all other agendas. That's why there are times when a servant leader must stand against the flow, prepared to challenge, confront and change things, because Christ's agenda is the priority. For example, if a congregation wants to maintain the church as an exclusive club for those who belong, the servant leader doesn't bow to their wishes and help them do a better job at excluding others. The servant leader knows that her first priority is to serve Christ. She goes before God before she goes before the people. But how she engages with the people will need to reflect a servant heart—a willingness to listen, a love for people, an ability to adapt, a humble attitude. The servant leader is a servant of God first, called to serve God's people in leadership. As Graham Cray reflects, "The controlling principle of local church leadership is that Jesus is the active leader of each congregation."[15]

External and internal expectations can easily undermine this fundamental priority. I was recently in a rural context where the pastor told me that he constantly heard, "Ah, pastor, our last pastor . . ." I asked him how long he'd been there, expecting an answer of a few months. "Twenty-five years" was the reply! External expectations can exert huge pressures, but many of us in leadership find the internal expectations even harder to handle. These can be fuelled by many factors, such as the need to be liked and therefore the tendency to try to please others. We'll explore this further in Chapter 4.

Rather than being molded by external expectations or internal expectations, shaped by secular leadership models, and formed by inappropriate experiences of leadership in the past, we need to be transformed by the Spirit of Christ and the renewing of our minds so that we accept Jesus' words, "You are not to be like that."

Christ served people; Christian leadership is marked by servanthood. As Stacy Rhinehart comments in his thought provoking book *Upside Down, The Paradox of Servant Leadership,* "Servant leadership is not an impossible ideal in our day. Rather, it should be the foundational cornerstone of our thinking about spiritual leadership. Christ lived, taught and modeled it for us, and it is our true distinctive as believers."[16]

Christian leadership is shaped by the cross and resurrection

The pattern of cross and resurrection, of suffering and new life, is the paradigm that will shape Christian leaders. I am amazed at how many younger leaders are surprised or even shocked when suffering comes as a result of leadership. Jesus teaches clearly that this will be the path for all who follow him (Matthew 5:11; Mark 10:38–39). This isn't suffering because we've been naïve or arrogant or plain stupid. This is suffering because we are engaged in "gospel ministry," and the gospel is offensive; it does divide people. In 2 Timothy, Paul writes of suffering in a variety of ways because he wants Timothy to understand the inevitability of suffering in leadership.

- Gospel-specific suffering that comes as a result of faithfulness to the gospel message (2 Timothy 1:8, 11–12; 2:9–10).
- "Hardship" of an ongoing nature (2 Timothy 2:3; 4:5).
- Suffering that comes at the hands of the church (2 Timothy 2:1–18).
- Suffering at the hands of Satan (2 Timothy 2:26).
- Suffering that comes from living in a fallen world (2 Timothy 3:1–9).
- Persecution from living a godly life (2 Timothy 3:12).

One of the keys to Christian leadership is therefore faithfulness rather than "success," and this is often most clearly seen by the way we handle suffering. The cross is central to our experience of suffering, as the place of comfort, forgiveness, empathy, reconciliation and a new start.[17]

We will also experience resurrection—glorious new life in the midst of doubt, decay and despair. We will witness the new life of a child deciding to follow Jesus, a young person deciding to resist temptation, or an adult breaking a destructive habit; the new life of a church slowly growing in confidence in God's love for them and his love for others, a community gradually being changed by the salt and light of God's people, a nation discovering that God's ways are best. We will experience the new life of personal transformation through death to self and resurrection to Christ. The reality of Christ's resurrection and return fuel hope in a world where hopelessness seems endemic. As I write, we are on the verge of a war. Standards in health provision and education seem to be on the decline. The suicide rate continues its relentless drive upwards, especially among young men, while church attendance continues its relentless drive downwards. Depravity is celebrated as freedom, consumerism as choice, self-fulfillment as spirituality. How does the Christian leader sustain a positive outlook at times such as this? Only through belief in the resurrection and placing our hope in God. Eschatology, the doctrine of the end times, reminds us that we live between the first and second coming of Jesus, in the "already but not yet" times of God's kingdom. This fuels our hope for the future and sustains us through the long dark nights of apparent hopelessness, drawing from us the prayer "Your will be done, on earth as in heaven."

Christian leadership is sustained by prayer

Prayer is central to the Christian life, and therefore central to Christian leadership. Prayer expresses our dependence on God in response to what he is doing in our lives, and is the spiritual energy of our relationship with God. Without it we shrivel and begin to exercise leadership in our own strength, utilizing only our own resources.

A healthy prayer life recognizes the following ingredients: it is more than language, but includes language; it is always conducted within the context of the universal family of God; it manifests itself in growing from being childish to becoming childlike; and it involves a right balance between structure and spontaneity. Patterns of praying vary from person to person, but without prayerful dependence on God we risk losing intimacy based on relationship, humility based on gratitude, wisdom based on God's perception, and courage based on his strength to keep going even when everything is against us. Other leaders may grit their teeth and keep going through sheer determination and self-belief, congratulating themselves when they succeed. Christian leaders will draw on God, and give him the glory for all that is good.

Christian leadership is lived out personally as part of the community of the church

One aspect of the incarnation that informs our understanding of leadership is the physical reality of Jesus entering time and space. We too are called to be fully incarnated in our context. We cannot operate as consultants for a people we don't know. Surely one of the great strengths of the Anglican church system (and I know it has many weaknesses) is that it invites ministers within that denomination to live this principle out. Talking with a friend of mine working in a very difficult area, I asked him what was difficult for him about ministry there. He replied, "Living here." I could see why. I'd had to take my car off the road and park it behind locked gates in the middle of the day, otherwise it would have disappeared by the time we'd finished lunch. The streets were unsafe during the day, and positively threatening at night. The school was struggling to cope with huge social problems. The burnt-out cars and squalor on the street reflected a far greater level of poverty and squalor in some of the homes. It was very tough.

I went on to ask him what was good about ministry in that context. He replied, "Living here"—for he was the only "professional" who did. All the others commuted in from outside to do their "jobs," returning home in the evening, whereas he shared something of the local life, and was present in his community. Ministry at a distance, be it physical or relational, is simply not an option for Christian leadership. Jesus became one of us; we are called to the costly work of integrating our lives with the people we lead.

It is possible to be physically present but relationally absent. My kids recognize this all too well. My middle one knows when I am not really present. When I am cooking and not really listening to what he is saying, he gets himself between the kitchen cabinet and my legs. He places his hands on my knees, his back against the cabinet and pushes with all his strength until I have to back up. He keeps pushing until he sees me looking down at him. When he gets eye contact he stops, smiles and continues what he was saying. Leaders too can be physically present but relationally absent. The constant knocks and nit-picking criticism, the betrayed trust, broken promises and failed dreams, the draining pastoral situations, the shredding gossip, all become bricks in the wall of defense that gradually builds through the years. Eventually the Christian leader becomes insulated from further damage, but also isolated from others. Understandable as this position is, Christian leadership is about being relationally present, not allowing the wall of protection to grow to the point where we are cut off from the very people we are called to serve.

Another aspect of Christian leadership lived out personally is a healthy embracing of who we are and how God has made us. Each of us is unique, wired up in different and specific ways, working in different contexts. Both our unique shape and our unique context will influence how we lead in any one place. Two of the crippling diseases among those in leadership are comparison and competition. Both can lead to pride ("I'm doing better than them") or discouragement ("I'm not doing as well as them"). Peter's question of Jesus in John 21:21—"Lord, what about him?"—is a good example of someone looking over his shoulder. Jesus responds, "What is that to you? You must follow me." Christian leadership involves accepting our uniqueness and celebrating the uniqueness of others. This is where research into leadership styles is useful, identifying the strengths and weaknesses of varying leadership styles, allowing us to recognize the effect our leadership style has on others and the importance of building leadership teams that reflect a variety of styles.[18]

Although Christian leaders are to live out their leadership in a personal way, they are not meant to be solo operators but part of a community. Not all the gifts are given to any one individual, so we need one another to exercise leadership within the Christian community. Accountability and vulnerability are a part of this process. For many of us, everything within us shies away from this type of leadership context. Pride says, "I can do it on my own." Protectionism says, "I don't want to get hurt." Power says, "I want total control." But the New Testament will not allow us this position; together we work for kingdom purposes, living out all those "one another" verses of the New Testament.[19] Viv Thomas, director of leadership development for Operation Mobilization, captures this well: "Great leaders are usually part of great communities."[20]

The six characteristics outlined above are some of the distinctive marks of Christian leadership. It is a daunting list, and one that challenges us to a deeper life of prayer and godliness. Thankfully, the golden thread that runs throughout these characteristics is grace. Without it we would give up in despair, but because of God's grace we dare to believe that he continues to call and equip ordinary people like us to take up leadership within the Christian community. How do we grow in this sort of leadership in a situation of constant change? What are the challenges we face? What are the practical tools that can help us? That is the theme of our next chapter.

For reflection

- What does it mean for me to be loved by God?
- How do I see myself as a leader? How do others see me?
- In what ways does my leadership reflect the six distinctives of Christian leadership? What one thing could I do for each characteristic over the next few months that would make a difference?

SONJA (22), YEAR-LONG ASSISTANT

Pulling up outside her apartment, Sonja relaxed. What a great weekend. She smiled as she recalled her anxiety about going. Rob had persuaded her it was worth a try, and he'd been right. A "Vocations Weekend" sounded such a big thing, and she thought she was going to be the only one of her age, and black. She was right about both, but it didn't seem to matter. Both the leaders made her feel so at home. The teaching on leadership and vocation hit the spot. So much resonated with her own questions, especially the stuff on call and character. It was good too to hear people tackling some of the issues she was struggling with in the church. The conversation with Simon on Saturday afternoon was exactly what she needed, and it was so helpful to get some personal coaching on "where to go from here."

Swinging open the car door, Sonja stepped on to the street and realized that this was what she wanted to do for the rest of her life. Like Rob, she sensed God's call to the inner city. And the weekend had clarified one crucial thing: she was a leader. Opening the door into her flat, Sonja spotted the card on the mat. Scooping it up, she read:

"Hi Sonja, welcome back. I hope you've had a great weekend. I just wanted to say what a privilege it's been to have you working in the church this past year. I pray that this weekend will have confirmed in your own mind that you are a leader, and that it has clarified a sense of God's call on your life. After nearly 25 years as a church leader, I can tell you I know no more challenging and exciting role. May God give you courage to follow wherever he leads. Love, Rob."

"Yesss!" breathed Sonja, dropping her keys—punching the air before bending to retrieve them.

Chapter 2

THE LEADERSHIP CHALLENGE

*One of the universal cravings of our times is a hunger
for compelling and creative leadership.*

JAMES MCGREGOR BURNS

There is a huge explosion of interest in leadership. Shelves groan with the weight of new books on the subject. Businesses are flooded with the latest seminars, conferences and training manuals, while Human Resources departments identify, promote, resource and monitor leadership development. Self-styled leadership gurus travel the globe explaining their latest insights. Even within the church, there is an increasing range of material on offer to help Christian ministers explore leadership today. Why this surge of interest? Many of those writing on the subject suggest that it is because of the huge changes in society and church over the last hundred years. Cultural analysts speak of an "era of unprecedented change," of "seismic shifts within the tectonic plates of culture," of "living through a period where worldviews are being reframed." While acknowledging the tendency for each generation to see itself as somehow unique, there is little question that the changes experienced within Western society over the last century have made a significant difference.

My grandmother recently died, aged 93. Through her life she saw not only massive shifts in industry and technology, but also in the social and religious fabric of England.[1] The minister of the local church who baptized her in a northern town in 1909 would hardly recognize the world or church today. Much is written on the causes and consequences of this change, detailing the shift from so-called modernity to post modernity, but my concern here is simply to register that, as a result of this change, people are looking for leaders to provide direction to help make sense of the changes that surround them. This presents particular challenges for those leading churches.

CHALLENGES TODAY

First, the place of change within the church is disputed. Some people within the church want things to stay the same as a way of buttressing themselves against the changes that affect them in every other part of their lives. The church is the one place that feels familiar, and any suggestion of change is met with under-standable resistance. Others feel a growing awareness of the need to change. Despite some encouraging signs, the church in England is still in decline. The latest statistics from an author of numerous research projects on the church, Peter Brierley, indicate severe losses among children, continued losses among young people, and a frightening absence of young adults. He notes that church atten-dance figures are alarming not simply because they are in decline but also because the rate of decline is increasing.[2] A number of Anglican dioceses are in severe financial difficulties.[3] The influ-ence of Christian thought and values seems to be diminishing. I don't mention all this to promote despondency, but simply to draw attention to what some people in the church already recog-nize: things have got to change. For change to take place, someone needs to discern the direction of that change, and that involves leadership. According to futurist Dr. Patrick Dixon, "Either we take hold of the future or the future will take hold of us."[4]

Second, generational expectations of leadership differ. The chart opposite reflects some of these changes across specific age ranges.[5] People respond to leaders in different ways, and this is part of what makes leadership more difficult today. We don't live in a monochrome culture; we now live in a vast kaleidoscope of in-terlocking cultures. In any congregation or organization, we may have a diverse range of cultures where people have very different expectations about how leaders should lead.

	YOUNGER LEADERS (age 13–35)	MIDDLE LEADERS (age 35–50)	OLDER LEADERS (age 50+)
Key question	How does it feel?	Does it work?	Is it true?
Expect leaders to . . .	Consult/understand me	Be competent and professional	Give teaching and direction
My first commitment is to . . .	People as people	My area of work	The company
Working together	I need a team to do anything	I see the need to work in a team	I'd prefer to work on my own
Disagreement	Get it out in the open and discuss it	Decide according to what is most efficient	Avoid confrontation
Description	Involved	Busy	Faithful
What counts is . . .	Ability to consult	Competence	Experience

Third, a result of the explosion of interest in leadership is that people's expectations of leaders have increased. What people experience in their working life creates expectations in their church life. At a time when people are looking to see leadership exercised in increasingly competent and professional ways, leaders within the Christian community are often poorly trained, and leadership is sadly lacking, both in quality and in quantity. Part of the reason for this lies with the change in society since World War II. With the decline in military service in the 1950s, the rise of the management era in the '60s, and the search for identity in the '70s, models for leadership diminished. It is also partly due to the perceived image of Christian leaders in the 1990s (and the erosion of trust in leadership in general across society), struggling to hold life together under the pressure of decline, or being pilloried by the press for misdemeanors. To reverse this trend, we need proactively to grow leadership, but not necessarily in the same ways as in the past.

These three factors present a challenge to anyone in Christian leadership today. Alongside these general challenges are specific ones that affect leaders within certain age profiles.

A challenge for younger leaders (age 13–35)

Today, many younger leaders start from a very different place both sociologically and emotionally than they did fifty years ago.[6] In an excellent article in the *Church of England Newspaper,* Pete Ward highlighted an aspect of this issue within the Anglican Church.

A growing number of theological students are looking for church internships which will train them in new ways of doing ministry. This is not surprising: many of the most lively and able students currently in theological education have come from a background in alternative worship, youth ministry, and church planting . . . But then there is a problem—the internship setting.[7]

The traditional training posts are often inappropriate for interns and assistant ministers whose calling is to develop new ways of doing ministry. They long to connect with the emerging culture, the very groups of people that inherited ways of "being church"[8] struggle to reach.

Our work alongside 25- to 40-year-old leaders in the Arrow Leadership Program confirms Pete Ward's findings. Younger leaders often struggle not only with the model of ministry offered by the churches they go to after leaving Bible college or seminary, but also with the model of leadership offered by the ministers leading those churches. The model of church, leadership and evangelism that so many ministers hold to is simply inappropriate for the younger leaders trying to engage with the lost generations of contemporary society.

I recognize that this isn't simply a generational issue. It is perfectly possible to be a 27-year-old assistant minister wedded to an inherited mode of church, or a 56-year-old minister reveling in the emerging mode of church. Yet it most commonly presents itself as a generational issue. As Pete Ward concludes, "This is not just a matter of pleasing junior clergy. Rather it makes sense for the mission of the Church." We need to release younger leaders to experiment with new models of church, leadership and evangelism, and ensure that we provide appropriate support, mentoring and accountability.

In this time of transition we also need younger leaders who are prepared to learn from older leaders and exercise self-control and submission; to understand before we judge, to be respectful before we criticize; and to be loyal before we speak out of place.

The discipline of submission is rarely taught, and is counter to the spirit of the age. In *Celebration of Discipline*, Richard Foster writes, "The obsession to demand that things go the way we want them to go is one of the great bondages in human society today."[9] His chapter on submission is a poignant reminder that "the call to live the cross-life is rooted in the cross-life of Jesus himself: "Be subject to one another out of reverence for Christ" (Ephesians 5:21).[10] He continues:

Modern men and women find it extremely difficult to read the great devotional masters because they make such lavish use of the language of self denial . . . we must underscore to ourselves that self-denial means the freedom to give way to others. It means to hold others' interests above self-interest. In this way self-denial releases us from self-pity.[11]

My first response when struggling with the way someone else is leading me is one of self-justification, followed, if I am not very careful, by self-pity. I never think of submission as my first option. Yet submission does not mean self-contempt or loss of identity, or giving up on wanting the very best. It means appropriate loyalty, respect and honor for those in authority over us. It means quietly reflecting on what are the real issues, graciously listening and learning before speaking and telling. It means asking the question, "What is God able to teach me through this time that I can't learn in any other circumstance?" For if we are to be good leaders we must first learn to be humble followers.

If we are working with a secure leader, honest and helpful discussion of the differences between us should be possible and fruitful. Such a leader is more likely to see us as colleague and partner. Where the leader feels threatened or is insecure, however, issues of control, power and authority are complex. Sadly, there are occasions where the breakdown of the relationship is so serious that real damage is done to those involved. In such cases external help should be sought, and it may be necessary to find an alternative position. But normally separation is not necessary, rather open communication and humble submission.

The challenge for the church is to provide appropriate opportunities and support for younger leaders, and for the younger leaders to be open to learning from those who've traveled down the track before them.

A challenge for older leaders (age 50+)

Alongside this "training trap" are the increasing numbers of older church leaders who feel ill-equipped for leadership in today's church. Perhaps trained twenty or thirty years ago, the ministry they were prepared for is no longer the ministry they find themselves called to exercise. This experience isn't unique to the church, but what may be unique is the lack of relevant ongoing training[12] for those who've been in overall leadership of churches for twenty or thirty years, and the lack of willingness to receive such training by some older leaders.

We need those who have been in church leadership for some time to respond positively to this challenge, to review existing practices and make changes where necessary. We need such leaders to invest proactively in the younger generation, as mentors and colleagues. Where such a leader is open to sharing their insights, not as a blueprint for the younger person to follow, but rather as a compass to help guide them through the uncharted territory ahead, they offer an immense resource. Years of experience, insight and expertise offer younger leaders wisdom, perspective and hope. In the Arrow Leadership Program we often struggle to find such mentors for participants. Yet the value of a wise, gracious, humble, older leader investing in a younger leader is incalculable.

I am grateful for older leaders who have put up with my youthful arrogance, loved me through failure, and offered me perspective in the difficult times. Leighton Ford is one such person. I've learned so much from him, but as I reflect on his mentoring of me, I recognize that one indispensable quality for older leaders investing in younger leaders is a willingness to learn from them. Rather than seeing the emerging leader as a threat, Leighton openly rejoices at the opportunity to look at things through the eyes of a younger person. When older leaders stop seeing younger leaders with very different insights into leadership, church and evangelism as a threat, but see them rather as a blessing, we strengthen leadership within the church.

The challenge is for the church to resource suitable leadership development for older leaders, and for these leaders to see investment in the younger generation as a priority.

A challenge for leaders in the middle years (age 35–50)

Those in the midlife years face a common issue in leadership: how to transition the middle years well. There is a well-trodden path that many follow. Gifted individuals in their twenties and thirties are often "recognized" and find themselves in significant leadership positions by their mid-thirties. The energy of youth, the excitement of ministry, the motivation of high ideals and the encouragement of others are an intoxicating combination. Consequently, they invest little time and energy in developing character, to match the pace of their gift development and increased responsibilities. If this situation continues through their late thirties and on to their forties, they are likely to encounter well-documented struggles, and if these struggles aren't handled well, they may prevent the person from reaching a point of maximum effectiveness in their fifties.

When I first came across this issue, it made sense of two things in my own life. First, it explained my experience as a 36-year-old leader, just becoming aware of a range of questions that I had about my own leadership development. Most of these questions were vague and peripheral but I could sense that if I didn't take time to work out what was going on, I could easily fall victim to one of the scenarios outlined below. Second, it made sense of my experience of talking with leaders in their fifties and sixties, many of whom described their experience of leadership in terms of one of the scenarios below, even if they didn't articulate it using this terminology. These are the classic struggles in midlife leadership.

- **Burn-out:** Busyness, over commitment and pressure take their inevitable toll. Often driven by either the external demands of success or the internal desire to please, the leader can be fooled by ongoing fruitfulness. Emotional, physical, relational and spiritual depletion eventually lead to burnout, a clinical condition with a long, hard road to recovery.

- **Drop-out:** Unfulfilled dreams, discouragement and disillusionment lead to the person either leaving their area of ministry to engage in a different occupation, or continuing in their ministry role but with little heart or energy for it, often finding personal fulfillment in a peripheral area of ministry that eventually becomes central. I recently met a church leader with responsibility for several churches who actually spent most of his time developing his psychotherapy practice. Statistically this person was still a church leader, but in reality he had long given up on that as his ministry.

- **Level-out:** The person reaches a plateau and, for whatever reason, stops growing as a leader. This may be due to an inability to resolve certain life issues and questions, circumstances preventing them from moving on, a loss of faith, or a number of other factors. They continue in ministry, but on a plateau. This is often subconscious, and the sense of disease is hard to diagnose.

- **Fall-out:** Fuelled by unmet emotional needs and over commitments, the leader succumbs to escapist sin in a desire to meet the increasing sense of hollowness within. Money, sex, power

and habitual substance abuse are the classic fall-outs. Sometimes such activities are exposed for all to see, and the person
leaves leadership in a blaze of destructive press coverage. Often
they remain undiscovered, hidden behind the well-polished
public image, but no less devastating in their impact as the
leader grapples with the increasing divide between their public
and private identities.

- **Spread-out:** With a growing uncertainty about the focus of
  their ministry, the leader dabbles in an ever-widening array of
  activities. Often gifted in many areas, they may be competent
  for most of the tasks, but the lack of focus leaves a rising sense
  of dissatisfaction. Rather than following a path to greater clarity about God's calling on their life as they enter their fifties,
  they spread themselves ever more thinly.

Of course, the list above is far too neat; the various scenarios are
often interlinked in one person's life, creating a complex web of
concerns fuelled both by unresolved character issues and life circumstances. But they do describe the symptoms of some midlife
struggles. Growing leadership involves helping midlife leaders
through these transitions, with a particular focus on issues involving character and call. Today I spoke on the phone with a
37-year-old minister. "James, I don't know how I am going to
survive. I am working 12- to 14-hour days, I don't see my family
enough, and I feel constantly on the edge of burnout. I don't feel
trained for the job I do and I don't know where to get help. I'm
wearing so many hats. The church is growing, exciting things
are happening, but if I look down the road of the next thirty
years I know I am not going to make it." If this was an isolated
incident, it would still be sad, but I've heard similar stories too
many times.

The challenge for the church is to invest in midlife leaders, to
prevent them from succumbing to any of the classic problems of
leadership at this stage, and for such leaders to widen their vision
to become leaders for the long haul.

A FINAL CHALLENGE

There is one final inescapable challenge I want to address at this point, that applies across all levels of leadership. What of those in leadership positions who don't have the necessary gifts or talents to lead? Sometimes the leader isn't aware of this inadequacy, but everyone else is; and on other occasions the leader is painfully aware but doesn't know what to do about it.

A wrong diagnosis

We need to be careful here, for there are those who come to a wrong diagnosis of their situation. Perhaps they read a book or hear a speaker, reflect on their life and ministry and, as a result, begin to question whether they have leadership gifts. In comparison to *that* leader, they doubt whether they are a leader at all.

This may be a result of "gift projection" rather than an actual lack of gift or talent. Gift projection occurs when a leader who is particularly gifted in any one area combines that gift with a passion for the subject and a track record of amazing results, and longs for everyone else to share their experience. They then write books, lead conferences, and teach on the subject. The danger is that they project their gift and unique SHAPE[13] on to everyone else, setting up the unhelpful idea that unless others lead in exactly the same way, they're not really leading at all. Thankfully, the body of Christ is made up of all sorts of people, and those with leadership talent will lead in different ways according to their SHAPE. We need to be wary of comparison: there are many styles of leadership and types of leader.

Right gifts, wrong context

Sometimes there is simply a mismatch of overall SHAPE in a particular role. One person may be good at leading in situation A but not in situation B. I remember meeting a church minister who was leading an Anglican church in a fairly tough area. He saw the congregation grow from twenty adults and a few children to 120 adults, forty children and twenty young people. The building was beautifully reordered, the giving increased, and the vision clear for the future. I asked, what next? His response stuck with me. "I've been here eight years. This is the third church like this I've worked in. The diocese keep offering me 'larger ships' to captain, churches of 300 or so, but that isn't me. I reckon I've got two more left in me." A short while after our conversation, he moved on to another struggling, difficult church with twenty or so adults. Three years later, I hear it is growing.

There was a man who knew his SHAPE and his call as a leader. He wasn't tempted by the offer of a "natural step up" to lead something bigger. He knew he was gifted to lead and grow small churches to medium sized churches. Knowing your leadership style is important.[14]

Square pegs, round holes

There are some in leadership who are square pegs in round holes simply because they are not leaders in the sense of gift or talent. To realize this is very hard, especially if they've faithfully committed a large part of their life to leadership, yet to avoid the reality of the situation is potentially even more costly. Most people in this situation struggle with their work, don't see much fruit for their labors, don't receive much affirmation and don't have many followers. To press on regardless is potentially an act of disobedience. Determination is a great virtue but stubbornness is a deadly vice.

The most likely reason for people to refuse to accept what everyone else can see is too close an identification between the person's role and their sense of self-worth. If the two are closely aligned, a gentle question or challenge about the person's ability in a role is taken as an assault on their identity. Understandably, he or she is likely to resist the question vigorously. How do we help such a person?

Start by being clear about whether we are the right person to address the issue. If it is our responsibility to do so, painful experience has shown me that avoiding the issue is nearly always the worst possible option. We're called to love the other person, recognizing that we don't have the right to change anyone, but we do have the responsibility to provide the best environment to make change a possibility. Love is costly: it sets its agenda by the other's needs, not my agenda and my frustration. Love is compassionate: it cares for the whole person and recognizes the impact of decisions on wider relationships. Love is patient: it not only waits for the right moment, but also identifies the right way to raise an issue. Love asks honest questions and listens carefully to the answers, to ensure that the entire picture is clear. And love is courageous: it will not avoid hard things because of personal insecurity or fear. It will rejoice in the truth that sets people free.

I'm not sure that anyone finds such conversations easy,[15] but without them people will continue to work as square pegs in round holes, and I know little else that so damages the person, the ministry and those they lead. One thing we ourselves can do to make sure that we are open to someone talking to us about how our role and SHAPE match is to ensure that our identity is "in Christ." When it is, we will be open to feedback, reflection and advice.

LEADERSHIP DEVELOPMENT

As we come to the end of this section, where we've explored in Chapter 1 what leadership is and what are some of the distinctives of Christian leadership, and then in this chapter identified some of the challenges facing those in leadership, I want to conclude by addressing the question of how we develop leaders. Why is leadership shortage the norm in our churches? There are several possible reasons.

We may have a *limited theology of leadership.* If we see leadership as restricted to particular people on the basis of age, gender, role or ordination, we will automatically select leaders according to our theological position. In the final section of the book, I want to argue that leadership is always plural in the New Testament, and the boundaries of who is included in leadership are not limited to age, gender, role or ordination.

We may have a *limited experience of leadership*. If our only experience of leadership, whether for cultural or theological reasons, is one type of leader—for example, a "type A" personality, strong natural leader, from a middle class white background—we may not see leadership talent in those who don't fit the mould. Throughout the rest of the book, I want to urge us all to look beyond our own experience, and I confess I don't find that easy. I am from a white, middle class, educated background. The mere fact that I am writing a *book* on leadership is an indication of my background and preferences. But I'm deeply grateful for the small glimpses I've had into other experiences of leadership in non-white, non-middle class, non-male contexts, and for being part of a worldwide church that isn't predominantly any of these things. Working in India opened new windows on to leadership for me, as has working with churches located in a diversity of contexts in this country.

There may be a *lack of opportunity* for leaders to develop. Some churches never provide the context in which people can grow as leaders because there is a personal blockage (an insecure leader who needs to maintain control), a cultural blockage (a critical atmosphere, a judgmental spirit, a lack of acceptance of failure or risk), a spiritual blockage (a lack of openness to the Spirit and his gifts), or a historical blockage ("the minister's always done it"). Without opportunity, as with any area of ministry, growth in leadership is stifled. Within Anglican circles one often hears stories of leadership growth in the time between one minister departing and the next arriving. It is not unusual for potential leaders to blossom when they move area and attend a smaller church, or when the larger church sends them out as part of a church plant.[16]

Finally, we may lack *a clear model* of leadership development. If we are not clear about how leaders grow, we either stumble along hoping that somehow a few leaders will emerge or we completely ignore the importance of developing leaders.

The model I want to outline in Parts 2–6 of this book is based on the model at the center of the Arrow Leadership Program (see page 19). It combines five elements to help grow those in leadership, which are summarized below.

Growing leaders know they are chosen (Part 2)

Christian leadership is centered on a relationship with God. Everything else flows from this center point. This relationship is not established through our own efforts, but in response to God's amazing grace. In a sermon, Leighton Ford once commented, "The heart of leadership is not in mastering the how to's but in being mastered by the amazing grace of God." The fact that Christ chose me is more important than my choice of him. This is at the heart of our model, providing a fundamental security, significance and self-worth based on who I am in Christ.

Growing leaders discern God's call (Part 3)

We are not on earth by chance. We are here for a purpose, and hearing God's call enables us to work out what that purpose is. This provides direction and insight that make a difference on a daily basis as we try to weigh up how to use our time and resources. As the 19th-century essayist John Ruskin wrote, "Blessed is the person who has found their vocation: let them ask for nothing more."

Growing leaders develop Christ-like character (Part 4)

All leadership involves influence. But will this influence be for good or bad? Will it grow Christ-likeness in others or destroy people's ability to trust? Character will determine the difference. It can be problematic when someone is "successful" before they are ready for success. Any model of leadership development that ignores character will risk producing people who grow in skills without the necessary character to support such skills. The roadside is tragically littered with those devastated by competent leaders whose character issues were never addressed. As theologian Peter Kuzmic put it, "Charisma without character leads to catastrophe."

Growing leaders cultivate competence (Part 5)

Leadership development considers the particular talents (those things that are a given part of who we are), skills (the how to's of a role), knowledge (both factual and experiential), and motivation (the desire to do something) a person needs in any given position of leadership, be it formal or informal. Even the most competent leaders need to take time to grow their talents, skills, knowledge and desire diligently.

Growing leaders lead in community (Part 6)

The New Testament makes it clear that leadership in the Church is plural: the model of one person leading a church would have been foreign to the early believers. Images of the body and our interdependence on one another form the backdrop to leadership and the growth of the Church. This community provides accountability, support, encouragement and mutuality. To meet the challenges of leadership today, we need to be honest with one another about the struggles and joys of leadership, and learn to depend on one another to provide the breadth of leadership required in our changing world. That's why community is the context surrounding all the other aspects of leadership in our diagram.

Any depiction of a model has its limitations, and this one neatly separates each element in a way that is unfaithful to the complexities of the human being. As we approach each section of this book, we need to recognize that each element influences and is influenced by all the others. Our experience through Arrow of working with this model over the last five years is that it combines elements of leadership that are often completely separated, leading to deep and lasting change taking place in leaders' lives. That is certainly my own experience, and I hope it may go some way to being yours as well, as we seek to be led more by Jesus, to lead more like Jesus, and to lead more to Jesus.

FOR REFLECTION

- Who has been a model leader for me and why?
- What are the particular challenges I face in leadership? Why?
- What limitations are restricting leadership development in my context? What can be done about them?
- With whom do I share my concerns?

PART TWO

GROWING LEADERS KNOW THEY'RE CHOSEN

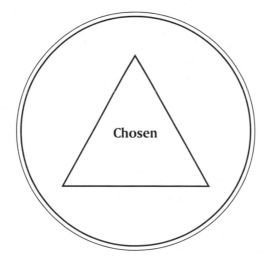

The starting point for any Christian leader is discipleship. Unless we know we are chosen, children of a loving God, we will lead from an insecure place, constantly twisting the privilege of a leadership position to meet our own needs. Knowing we're chosen is at the heart of leadership, and therefore at the center of our model. We consider the cycles of grief and grace and how Jesus' life models for us the security of knowing who we are in Christ.

JOURNAL ENTRY: SAM (38), MINISTER

1 January. Another New Year. Where did the last one go? Whoosh. It's going too fast. Sixteen years of ordained ministry—and I'm wondering, "What has happened?" Time for some New Year's resolutions? Yeah, yeah. Been there, done that. Too many times. I'm still asking the same questions. Am I the only one?

If I compare myself with what I was like when I first became a Christian, it's frightening. Then it was all vibrant and fresh. I would have done anything for Jesus. Now? Well, I know love changes, grows, develops. I know I can't expect it to be the same. But I've lost something. I'm tired, often grumpy, and yet I keep up the public face. I know you love me, Jesus. But—what? I long for renewal. I long for intimacy, for an encounter with you. Lord, hear me cry. I'm beginning to wonder if this is the normal Christian life, if this is how it is going to be until I die. Little change, and lots of commitments to keep going.

Lord, please come and do something in my life.
I offer myself to you with all of my
    Confusion
    Uncertainty
    Anxiety
    Longing
Please meet with me.
Please change me.
Please help me.
Amen.

FIRST LOVE

Beware of anything that competes with loyalty to Jesus Christ. The greatest competitor of devotion to Jesus is service for him.

OSWALD CHAMBERS[1]

It is easily lost. It is not so easily found.

Bill Hybels, Pastor of Willow Creek Community Church in Chicago, has a telling phrase: "The way I was doing the work of God was destroying the work of God in me." David Watson, Anglican church leader and evangelist, used to say, "Beware the danger of loving God's work more than loving God himself." Murray McCheyne, 19th-century minister and evangelist, said, "My people's greatest need is my own personal holiness."[2]

I'd heard them all. I still lost it.

William Temple, at his installment as Bishop of Manchester in 1921, said:

I come as a learner with no policy to advocate, no plan already formed to follow. But I come with one burning desire: it is that in all our activities, sacred and secular and ecclesiastical and social, we should help each other fix our eyes on Jesus, making him our only guide. . . . But pray for me chiefly, that I may never let go of the unseen hand of the Lord Jesus and may live in daily fellowship with him. It is so vital that you will most of all help me to help you.[3]

I believed it, passionately. I still lost it.

I lost my first love. And because of that, I began to lose perspective, joy, and hope.

I love what I do. I recognize that I am fortunate. I had a great church where I was given appropriate amounts of responsibility, encouraged to develop in the areas where I was gifted, and allowed to make a lot of mistakes. I had a great second job as an Advisor in Evangelism for an Anglican deanery, and opportunities to do one or two things further afield. I then got a fulltime post as an evangelist with CPAS. I remember reading the job description, thinking, "That is me," but not quite believing I would get the job. After a few years I was seconded to work for Springboard, the Archbishops of Canterbury and York's initiative for evangelism, following Michael Green. It was an enriching time, working with wonderful colleagues. In 1998 I attended the Arrow Leadership Program in the United States at the kind invitation of Leighton Ford.

As a result, I started up the program in this country. What a privilege! I was constantly learning, constantly growing, constantly being stretched and stimulated. On the surface, all was well. I loved my work, I loved God, and I loved sharing the good news of Jesus with others. Underneath, it was a different story.

It was so subtle that I didn't realize it was happening. Slowly, the way I was doing the work of Christ was destroying the work of Christ in me. I didn't stop praying, I didn't stop believing in God, I didn't succumb to escapist sin. I simply lost my first love. Year by year, the busyness of work, the fun of ministry, the changing circumstances of my personal life, the painful experiences and the emotional exhaustion slowly focused my attention elsewhere. While my head was stuffed with new and exciting ideas, my heart grew cool. While I led others to a place of finding new life in Jesus, my life in Jesus was decidedly stale. I can give a thousand reasons why this took place. I could speak of the blessing of having three wonderful children, and the demand of constant sleepless nights over six years. I could speak of the joy of endless opportunities to speak of Jesus, and the growing physical weariness. I could speak of the regular recommitments I made to a more disciplined life of prayer, and the nagging question about whether change was really possible. I could speak of numbers who looked to me as a model or mentor to follow, and the frightening awareness of the reality of my inner life. I could go on . . . but I won't.

The simple truth is that I lost my first love. I knew it was happening, and didn't know what to do about it. While I was attending Arrow, I heard Leighton Ford quote a colleague of his, Gerald Harrison: "Ministry is what we leave in our tracks as we concentrate on following Jesus." When we stop following Jesus so closely, or gradually allow our time with God either to erode away or degenerate into frantic activity, we lose three precious things—perspective, joy and hope. Why does this happen?

DRIVEN BEYOND THE CALL OF GOD

One of the common causes of this problem is a drive to achieve or perform, exacerbated by both the society we live in and the internal baggage we carry.[4]

One of the ways we find "status" in our society is through the work we do and what we achieve. We are what we do, and if we don't "do" then we are nothing. This attitude is reflected in the social niceties of how we engage in conversation with people we don't know—"And what do you do?"—and in the harsh reality of the addiction to success, prosperity and prestige that leads many to sacrifice relationships on the altar of achievement.

None of us escapes the early years of life without accumulating some baggage that we carry into the adult years. One word to describe some of this baggage is "drivers."[5] On the next page is a chart describing five common "drivers."

Each of these characteristics has strengths and weaknesses, which become problematic when they develop into "drivers," actually controlling the direction and speed of our lives.

Mary is a Christian leader in her forties. She's faithfully followed Jesus since the age of sixteen. She is outgoing, dynamic, full of energy, and very effective in ministry. Her driver is consideration for others, linked with a vision of God as a Father who

Dominant messages behind the driver, often picked up in early years	The driver's motto	What we value as a result
• "You can do better." • Little praise or affirmation. • Focus on what's wrong, rather than what's right. • Don't take risks or be child-like.	Be perfect.	Achievement, autonomy, competition, success.
• "You're not good enough unless you please me." • Don't be selfish or assertive. • Don't be different. • Be what you need to be for others.	Please others.	Cooperation, service, consideration.
• "You'll never get it done." • Can't waste time. • Don't think and plan, get on with it. • Don't be still or stop; keep going.	Hurry up.	Energy, speed, activity, efficiency.
• "You can't let them know you're weak." • Don't be weak or show weakness. • No permission to say 'I can't cope.' • Don't ask for help. Act as if "I'm fine." • Don't let people down.	Be strong.	Courage, strength, reliability, independence.
• "You didn't try hard enough." • Don't relax. • Don't succeed, because then you've nothing left to do. • Value input, not output; you can always do more.	Try harder.	Patience, endurance, determination, effort.

always wants more. Through the years of endlessly giving, she became depressed, desperately longing for her Father's approval, and earnestly trying to fulfill her motto, "Please others." She worked harder and harder but could never quite do enough. Her depression deepened, and she became ill.

Jack is an able evangelist, a good leader, thoughtful Bible teacher, and very focused person. His early family years valued determination and effort. Combining this background with a vision of God as a Father who always has time for everyone else but not for him, he tries to gain his Father's acceptance by working harder, staying focused. He was wonderfully appreciated by his congregation, yet his marriage fell apart.

When under the influence of drivers like these, Christian leaders work *for* acceptance rather than *from* it. This can be described as the cycle of grief.

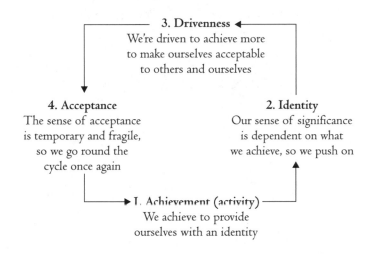

3. Drivenness
We're driven to achieve more
to make ourselves acceptable
to others and ourselves

4. Acceptance
The sense of acceptance
is temporary and fragile,
so we go round the
cycle once again

2. Identity
Our sense of significance
is dependent on what
we achieve, so we push on

1. Achievement (activity)
We achieve to provide
ourselves with an identity

Some of the symptoms of the cycle of grief are that our drive damages the relationships we value most; personal criticism rocks our sense of worth; we are unable to separate who we are from what we do; and whenever we achieve something there is only momentary relief and pleasure.

The cycle of grief erodes confidence in our position as children of God, and fuels unhealthy addictive patterns of living, to the extent that we become "driven beyond the call of God."[6] This sickness is often found in Christian leaders. Its roots are the sinful self-sufficiency and self-centeredness of most of our lives. Lodge them firmly in the soil of our early childhood experiences, add the fertilizer of life's messages, and the growing conditions are nearly perfect. Left to itself, the plant thrives on the very things so many people compliment us about: "Such a good preacher"; "She works so hard"; "Gets along so well with the young people"; "Wonderful to have a pastor who is always there for us"; "Great to see the church growing again." For this reason, maintaining a clear sense of who we are in Christ is the first priority for Christian leaders.

Anything less will place us in a dangerous position as a leader as the gap between the public image and the private reality grows. We become an increasingly unsafe person to follow, not only modeling unhealthy patterns of leadership but also at risk of allowing our unresolved problems to seep out in destructive patterns of behavior. Thankfully, there is an alternative.

THE DYNAMIC CYCLE OF GRACE

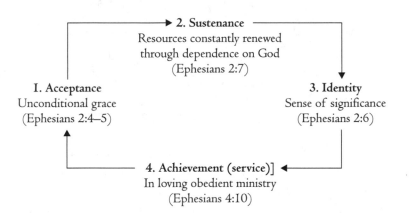

2. Sustenance
Resources constantly renewed
through dependence on God
(Ephesians 2:7)

I. Acceptance
Unconditional grace
(Ephesians 2:4–5)

3. Identity
Sense of significance
(Ephesians 2:6)

4. Achievement (service)]
In loving obedient ministry
(Ephesians 4:10)

Working within the cycle of grace,[7] we start from a place of acceptance rather than a position of achievement. Knowing who we are—a child of the loving Father—means that we start with grace. Adoption into God's family is not dependent on my worthiness, but on the love of the Father, Christ's generous self-giving, and the work of the Holy Spirit. Knowledge of our acceptance sustains and resources us for life and ministry. To be fully human is to acknowledge our absolute dependence on God, to embrace his sustaining presence.

Our identity is then clear—not determined by what we do but by who we are in relationship with Christ. I know that I am significant because God made and loves me, and has a purpose for my life. Our activity and achievement then flows out of our identity, as we seek to fulfill God's purpose for our lives. Our output flows from and reflects the input of God.

We see this at work when Jesus is baptized. He hears his Father say. "You are my Son, whom I love; with you I am well pleased" (Luke 3:22). These words commission Jesus for what he is to do. The combination of words from Psalm 2:7 and Isaiah 42:1 points Jesus to the path of the shepherd leader and the suffering servant. They also confirm Jesus in who he is. He is God's dearly loved child, the one in whom the plan for the salvation of human-kind resides. Through the years leading up to this event, Jesus has been growing in his understanding of who he is. Now, at this moment of "going public," God chooses to confirm his identity in a dramatic and powerful way.

It was from this place of secure identity as God's chosen child that Jesus "began his ministry" (Luke 3:23). The foundation of his public ministry is in his relationship with God as Father. That's why we hear of him constantly going off to a quiet place to pray (Luke 5:16). That's why, when challenged by Satan in the desert, "If you are the Son of God . . . ," Jesus was able to resist the temptation to confirm his identity through performance (Luke 4:9–11). That's why he could challenge the assumptions of the re-ligious leaders (Luke 11:37–54), speak with authority (Mark 1:27–28), embrace the outcast, despised, rejected, and associate with undesirables (Luke 8:26–39). He knew who he was. Chris-tian leaders, too, need that fundamental knowledge of who they are *in Christ.* When we lose it, we begin to work *for* God's love rather than *from* God's love, and start to travel round the cycle of grief.

Who are we in Christ? We are children made and loved by the Father, friends gloriously saved by the Son, and servants empow-ered by the Spirit to bear fruit. As Viv Thomas concludes:

The identity of Jesus is related to the identity of his Father. The initiative and execution of the whole salvation event was in conversation with his Father. If we are to lead well, our identity has to be shaped by similar forces; otherwise we will become victims of our own gifting, a liability to others and ourselves.[8]

As those chosen to be in relationship with Christ, but still struggling with personal sin and the effects of living in a fallen world, how do we grow in that relationship with all the many demands on our time? How do we sustain life and ministry as a response to grace? This is not only the age-old struggle for Christian leaders, but also part of the struggle for all in Christian discipleship. Thankfully, many have traveled this way before and have lessons to share with those of us following on behind. I want to highlight four ways to live in response to God's love rather than for it.

- *Live by Jesus' words.* Bizarrely, those of us who proclaim God's grace, love and forgiveness to others are often the very people who struggle to live by these things.
- *Exercise spiritual disciplines*—not fashionable, but essential for growth in the Christian life.
- *Resolve internal issues.* When internal problems hold us up in discipleship or leadership, it's time to sort them out.
- *Be clear about what we're aiming for.* Wrong understanding about aims often skews expectations in Christian leadership, and leads people to try to do far too much.

LIVE BY JESUS' WORDS

In John 15, Jesus creates a vivid word picture of the vine and the gardener. Jesus is the true vine and God the gardener. We are the branches, grafted on to the vine to bear fruit. Jesus urges his disciples to "remain in me," and offers us a number of insights into how to do that.

"Apart from me you can do nothing" (vv. 4–5). Do we really believe those words? Our experience is that we can do all sorts of things apart from Christ. We are often fooled by our apparent fruitfulness in ministry even when we don't "remain in Christ." So what did Jesus mean?

Without Christ we cannot bear *his* fruit. Good things may happen around us because of the Spirit's work in others, but the fruit of the Spirit cannot grow in our own lives if we don't remain in him. We may become very adept at growing counterfeit fruit—it looks good in a basket—but it won't be Christ's genuine, lasting, healthy fruit. Only Christ can produce that type. What does counterfeit fruit look like? Perhaps it is easier to describe from the inside—what it feels like.

- You speak kind words but lack genuine compassion for people.
- You teach with inspiring words but they have an increasingly hollow ring to your own ears.
- You patiently smile but inwardly doubt they will ever change.
- You laugh with abandon but wonder about opting out.
- You do good deeds but wish that someone else would do them for you.
- You gently encourage, but fear the day when the inner rage will escape.
- You exercise discipline but wonder why you bother.

The counterfeit stuff might win us applause, accolades, approval and appreciation, but at what cost? A diminishing relationship with Christ.

"If anyone does not remain in me, he is like a branch that is thrown away and withers; such branches are picked up, thrown into the fire and burned" (John 15:6). A tree in our garden is dying. Ten years ago it was healthy. Every spring it produced amazing blossom, followed by abundant fruit; but over the years it has gradually withered. It still produces amazing blossom (although even that is nothing like its former glory days), but year after year the amount of fruit dwindles. Even the fruit it does produce is unpleasant to look at, and inedible. The branches are brittle and break off with alarming ease. The kids love the bonfire.

We need to live by Jesus' words; apart from him we can do nothing that will last, nothing that will be genuine fruit, nothing that will honor the king and his kingdom. That's why Jesus is so adamant: "Remain in me."

He continues, *"As the Father has loved me, so have I loved you"* (v. 9). The nature of Jesus' love for us is the same as the Father's love for Jesus. Sadly, it is easy to preach about his love for others and struggle to receive it ourselves. God's unconditional love expressed so clearly in Jesus' death on the cross (v. 13) is "amazing grace." Many Christian leaders once knew it to be so, but have somehow lost it.

We play a game with each of our children to help them know unconditional love. From the earliest years, when changing their diapers, I would ask the question "Who loves you?" and then recite a litany of the people who loved them. As they began to understand what was going on, they said the relevant names. I'd then ask a second question, "Why do they love you?" The answer was simple: "because of who you are." In a small way, that reflects the love of God for us. In his book *What's So Amazing About Grace?* Philip Yancey defines grace as "Knowing that nothing you do can make God love you any more, nothing you can do can make God love you any less."[9] Does the way we live our lives reflect this truth? Too often our lives speak clearly of a lack of belief in grace.

I occasionally meet leaders who are confident in Jesus' love for them and confident that they will never lose their first love. Be warned: it happens so easily. It is behind the façade that love is lost. Live by Jesus' words, "so have I loved you." He's not looking over our shoulder at the person behind us. He's looking at us, into our eyes, deep into our soul. He knows everything about us, and still he says, "I love you." How do we receive his love? In myriad ways, but the two I want to focus on later in this chapter are by exercising spiritual disciplines and by clearing away the blockages that make it difficult to believe he loves us.

"Obey my commands" (v. 10). Once we've received Jesus' love, we need to remain in it, and to remain in him we are called to obey his commands—all of them. Why is this so crucial? Because Jesus knows that obeying his commands is the practical way of continuing in the path of faith. We become Christians by saying yes to Jesus, accepting his offer of forgiveness and a fresh start in life on the basis of what he has done for us on the cross, and by placing

our trust in him and turning from a way of life dominated by self, to a way of life dedicated to living as Jesus would want us to. We continue the Christian life in exactly the same way—by repentance and faith. Every time we try a different path, we set ourselves up as the one who knows better how to live life than God. His commands are not given to make life difficult or a drudgery. His commands are given because he loves us and knows what is best for us, and longs for us to live as he always intended us to live. We don't obey out of a solemn duty, but out of heartfelt gratitude and deep love: "If you love me, you will obey what I command" (John 14:15). Obedience again throws us back to the question: do we know his love for us?

Jesus illustrates such obedience with one command: "Love each other as I have loved you" (15:12). Do we obey this command? Genuinely? Comprehensively? Consistently? I am so clever at providing myself with excuses, rationalizing the command away, justifying my disobedience, robbing it of its simple clarity. We are called to live by Jesus' words: "obey my commands." We are foolish to do anything less, for obeying God's commands is how we remain in his love.

"My joy . . . in you" (v. 11). Jesus makes an incredible link in this verse: "I have told you this so that my joy may be in you and that your joy may be complete." The purpose behind these words is joy. An American friend of mine recently commented that he finds many of the younger leaders in the church in England "joyless." He put it fairly bluntly: "They whine a lot." I thought this unjust, and then I listened to the conversations among younger leaders. Even more sobering, I listened to myself. Not a lot of joy.

Joy isn't the frosting on the cake. Joy isn't dependent on circumstances. Joy is a result of knowing God's love, and remaining in that love through obeying Jesus' commands.

Jesus is saying here that a lack of joy is not the result of difficult circumstances. Paul surely confirms this as he recites a litany of afflictions and struggles he's confronted, culminating in "sorrowful, yet always rejoicing" (2 Corinthians 6:3–10). A lack of joy is not the result of an awkward bunch of people to lead. It is not even primarily the result of tragedy (we need to be real about our feelings and thoughts through all these difficult things). A lack of joy can be directly connected to wandering from Jesus' love. "The joy of the Lord is your strength" (Nehemiah 8:10) can seem like a pious platitude in the face of real suffering, but countless Christians through the ages have known it to be true in circumstances far worse than I've ever experienced. Joy is one of the distinguishing marks of the persecuted, suffering, underground Church. Why? Because despite (or maybe because of) the struggle, persecution and oppression, they remain in him. We are to live by Jesus' words: "I have told you this so my joy may be in you and that your joy may be complete" (v. 11). Without his joy, Christian leadership quickly becomes duty, duty becomes drudgery, and drudgery becomes deathly.

"You are my friends, if you do what I command" (v. 14). Here is the challenge that presents the appropriate response to God's grace—obedience. We have a part to play in this wonderful relationship with Christ; we cannot presume on grace, rather we are expected to respond to it with gratitude and obedience. That's why the little word "if" occurs five times in John 15:5–17. The flow is always from God to us, but he is looking for a response that enables him to fulfill his commitment to us. And the friendship he offers is extraordinary. We're not to be servants but friends, because everything he has learned from his Father he has made known to us (v.15). Those who think it is novel to call Jesus "friend" sometimes abuse the concept. Maybe they have misunderstood the nature of this friendship. This is not a casual acquaintance; nor is it even friendship on equal terms after years of growing close to someone. We can never be equal to Jesus. He is God; we are mortal human beings. He is the Creator; we are the created. He is without sin; we are sinful. It is only when we have fully grasped just how *other* Jesus is that this truth makes its full impact. Despite the total inequality, despite our persistent rejection of the sovereignty of Christ, despite our ugly sin, he calls us friends. This isn't novel; it is awesome. It leaves us on our knees humbled and grate-

ful, and raises us to our feet proud and strong. For if he has called us friend, whatever anyone else calls us is put in perspective.

"You did not choose me, but I chose you" (v. 16). I am chosen. My identity is not dependent on my ability to achieve great things for God, on the approval of others, or on the possessions I accumulate around me. I am a child of God, and he chose me—to respond to his love, to obey his commands, to know his joy, to be his friend. During a retreat, I meditated on John 15:16. Apart from the excitement of the privilege and blessing of being chosen, I recognized the enormous implications, both in terms of delight at who I am in Christ, and in terms of life change. I then wrote down an acronym:

Comforted
Held
Owned
Secure
Encouraged
Nurtured

An image of my daughter when she was 18 months old, curled up on my lap, came to my mind, and a sense of the immense security of a child chosen by God. I found myself drawing a picture of myself curled up in the presence of God, secure in the knowledge that I was chosen. Consistently throughout the Bible we see God choosing, and his choice encourages both humility and confidence. Without this knowledge we will wander from the Father's arms.

The priority of living by Jesus' words

These words of Jesus are vital—literally life-giving. We may want to press on to the higher slopes of how to lead effectively, but if we don't spend time at the base camp we'll never be in shape for the rigors of Christian leadership. We will never be a truly Christian leader unless we believe and act upon the words of Jesus, "apart from me you can do nothing." The fundamental priority of any Christian, leader or not, is to remain in Jesus. This is where I went wrong.

Through the years, I remained in many things. I remained in the Church, I remained in ministry, I remained in my marriage, I remained a reasonable evangelist, I remained a visionary leader. But I didn't remain in him. I believed in him, I followed him, but I didn't remain in him. There is no greater priority. Henri Nouwen, priest and author, says:

It is not enough for the priests and ministers of the future to be moral people, well trained, eager to help their fellow human being, and able to respond creatively to the burning issues of their time. All of that is very valuable and important, but it is not the heart of Christian leadership. The central question is, are the leaders of the future truly men and women of God, people with an ardent desire to dwell in God's presence, to listen to God's voice, to look at God's beauty, to touch God's incarnate Word and to taste fully God's infinite goodness?[10]

Jesus remained in his Father's love and obeyed his Father's commands, so how dare we do any less?

How do we do this? John 15 suggests that we must stay in the vine (Jesus) and draw sustenance from him (the sap that gives life to the branches). We can't do this without obedience and intentionality, and the single greatest help for me in fulfilling these two criteria is exercising spiritual discipline.

EXERCISE SPIRITUAL DISCIPLINES

Throughout history, disciples of Jesus have embraced spiritual disciplines as the way of growing in relationship with Christ. The very words have a strange, archaic sound to modern ears. We're free spirits, disciples of the new era, looking for the next thing to help us painlessly on our way. Isn't "discipline" rather old-fashioned, restrictive, legalistic? How the enemy must chuckle at the complete nonsense we've swallowed. Nothing could be more contemporary for our consumer-ridden church, more liberating for our self-indulgent lives, or more grace-filled for our shallow sense of holiness.

Richard Foster calls the first chapter of his classic text on spiritual disciplines "The spiritual disciplines: doorway to liberation." He writes:

Superficiality is the curse of our age. The doctrine of instant satisfaction is a primary spiritual problem. The desperate need today is not for a greater number of intelligent people, or gifted people, but for deep people . . . The purpose of the spiritual disciplines is liberation from the stifling slavery to self-interest and fear . . . They are means of receiving God's grace . . . The disciplines allow us to place ourselves before God so that he can transform us.[11]

Liberation, grace, transformation. Who doesn't need these things? Yet the disciplines are frighteningly absent from many Christian leaders' lives. Possibly as a pendulum-swing away from the legalism of the previous era, more probably because we have simply accepted the licentiousness of our era, few Christian leaders practice the range of disciplines. On the leadership development program we run, it is sobering to discover how many competent leaders don't have a structured way of reading the Bible, never spend time in reflective silence, rarely consider their consumption patterns, completely ignore fasting, and pray frenetically. Genuine fruit is not grown without the right conditions.

What are the spiritual disciplines?

Richard Foster identifies twelve disciplines. They are the inward disciplines of meditation, prayer, fasting and study; the outward disciplines of simplicity, solitude, submission and service; and the corporate disciplines of confession, worship, guidance and celebration. John Ortberg, in his book *The Life You've Always Wanted,* suggests that spiritual disciplines are "simply a means of appropriating or growing toward the life that God graciously offers." He defines them as: "Discipline: any activity I can do by direct effort that will help me to do what I cannot now do by direct effort. Spiritual discipline: any activity that can help me gain power to live as Jesus taught and modeled it."[12] The focus is on our effort helping us to be in a place where we can receive the gracious work of the Spirit to make us more like Christ. As Ortberg says, "Spiritual transformation is not a matter of trying harder, but of training wisely."[13] Godly living doesn't just happen, in the same way that running a marathon doesn't just happen. You train long and hard. Trying harder isn't the answer. You can try as hard as you like to run a marathon, but without training you are unlikely to succeed. Spiritual disciplines are the training manual for the marathon of Christian discipleship with our eyes firmly fixed on Jesus, the author and perfecter of our faith.

How do we exercise them?

In one sense, this is easy. There are excellent guides to help us set up a training program individually tailored to our particular needs.[14] There are people gifted and skilled at helping others to grow in their spiritual life.[15] There is God's Spirit longing to transform us if we would only make ourselves available to him. And that is the problem—not how we begin to exercise the disciplines but why we don't do anything about it. The following four reasons are fairly commonplace.

We don't actually believe what Jesus said. The words of John 15 are true, but we live as if we can afford to ignore them. We live as if doing for Jesus is more important than being with Jesus. We work as though everything depends on us rather than everything depending on God. We hide our insecurities behind impressive activities rather than allowing Jesus to strip us to the core and assure us he still loves us. We won't do anything about this unless we actually believe Jesus' words, "Apart from me you can do nothing."

We think we need more knowledge. "When I've read that book, attended that conference, or listened to that speaker, I'll be ready to get going," we say. Even worse, we substitute information for actual practice. For years, I longed to improve my prayer life. I read book after book, taking one or two key thoughts from each. I talked with others about praying. I listened to the words of wise leaders on prayer. The one thing I didn't do was pray more. Many spiritual disciplines are like a muscle: I don't need better food to make it grow, I simply need to exercise it. Even now I find it depressingly easy to set aside time for prayer and not actually do it.

We haven't got time. I've used this excuse often. Then I'd hear the quote about Wesley or Luther having so much to do that they got up even earlier to spend three hours in prayer before they started doing anything, and I'd feel even guiltier. What I've learned is that if we're too busy to spend time with God, we're too busy. Each person has a differing capacity for work and ministry. Each person has differing demands and responsibilities, that vary as we go through life. Wesley may have got up and prayed for three hours before he started his working day, but the lesson to take from this amazing fact is not "That is how it must be for me." Rather, it is the principle of dependence on God: "Apart from me you can do nothing."

Given who we are, what God has called us to, and how we function as a person, we need to ask, "What is an appropriate rhythm of life that reflects the priorities of the kingdom and a pattern for growth?" John Ortberg suggests that wise training respects the freedom of the Spirit, our unique temperament and our gifts, and will take into account our season of life, the inevitability of troughs and peaks. It also begins with a clear decision. "I haven't got time" is simply untrue. I would spend time watching mindless television rather than pray: it was more convenient. I would spend time working long hours for God rather than being with him: it was easier. I would spend time preaching about Jesus rather than praying to him: it seemed to gain more tangible results. We have time; it's a question of how we choose to use it.

We've lost hope of change. We become so used to the Christian life as it is that we think it can't be any different. We remember with fondness earlier days when there was vibrancy and excitement. Now we're waiting for heaven. It's quite a haul, but aren't faithfulness and discipline the marks of a mature Christian life? And as the hope of change erodes, so does our belief that God might change others.

I meet ministers who no longer believe change is a real possibility, either for themselves or for the people they lead, and that is where I was as a result of losing my first love. For Christian leaders, the harsh reality of seeing people apparently change and then return to their old ways slowly erodes faith. Quick to follow are despair, despondency, even hopelessness—unattractive qualities in anyone, but particularly unappealing in a Christian leader. These feelings seep out, and become a self-fulfilling prophecy as those around us begin to believe that change is impossible or move away to prevent themselves becoming "tainted" by the same attitudes. Idealism turns to cynicism; growth turns to decline; faith turns to doubt.

Change is possible, but only if we abide in Jesus. Spiritual disciplines help us to do that. Ortberg comments, "It is possible to live in such a way that when people see us, they will say to themselves, 'Wow! I didn't know that a life could look like that . . . ' But we will not drift into such a life. We must decide."[16]

One way of getting started is prayerfully to identify two or three spiritual disciplines to focus on, perhaps through conversation with others or through reading a book. Then take four to six months to practice one of those disciplines, working out practical, achievable ways to do it. Setting a target for the discipline can help (as long as we stick to it), as well as reflecting on anything that would prevent us from fulfilling the discipline. I've found it helpful to make myself accountable to a selected group of friends or colleagues, explaining what I am aiming to do and inviting them to pray for me. I also try to find two or three people who will join me in exercising spiritual discipline so that we can hold each other mutually accountable. Simple *memory devices* can prompt us to keep going. I create postcards that I stick in various places to remind me of what I am trying to focus on.

It is helpful to create a rhythm in our lives so that the discipline forms a natural part of who we are. Getting to that point is often painful, and involves hard work. It can also feel unnatural because we are out of practice, just like someone who decides that they want to run the marathon but hasn't run for a while. The first few days of training are agony, and the temptation to give up is overwhelming, which is why people often run with others. After a while, however, the benefits of disciplined training begin to show. We can't complete a marathon without training. Nor can we run the course of Christian leadership without the spiritual disciplines.

RESOLVE INTERNAL ISSUES

We all have them—issues that rattle around inside us affecting how we work, relate to God and others, and see ourselves. When those issues negatively influence our lives, so that we are no longer faithful to God's word and no longer bearing the fruit that he longs to grow in us, we have a choice. We either battle on, ignoring them, or we sort them out. Ignoring them normally means burying them, and they tend to come back with added venom. Often they can be resolved through prayer and the help of close friends. The sad reality is that Christian leaders often don't have friends they talk with about such difficulties; even some who are married rarely talk about them. I mentioned in the Introduction that you might use the questions at the end of each chapter as an aid to conversation with others. Maybe this is the time to open up some of the closed areas in our lives with our spouse or a friend.

If, for whatever reason, some sort of resolution isn't possible through these avenues, we may need more professional help. A mark of maturity is the willingness to face problems rather than avoid them, and to seek help if necessary. I've struggled with this. Am I being self-indulgent? Is it really necessary? What if it doesn't work? What will others think of me if they find out? Surely I'm meant simply to pray and trust God and get on with life? All of these questions contain legitimate and helpful insights, but none of them got to the core of my reaction, for that was pride.

A friend challenged me to think through my reservations, and to recognize the impact of unresolved issues on my life, my family and those I lead. Then she challenged me about pride. The point struck home. As I reviewed the situation over several months, I realized that pride was at the heart of a range of feelings. I am grateful for her challenge. So, I think, are my family, and those I lead.

I mention this because the combined effect of relational, psychological or emotional difficulties is a potent cocktail. Real change is possible, but sometimes we need help.

KNOW WHAT YOU'RE AIMING FOR

What is "success" in Christian leadership? The tendency is to grade success by outward results. The relentless drive to quantify everything encourages assessment on external criteria. This has its place, but can lead to more subtle and important criteria being sidelined. How do we quantify a child's happiness at school? How do we measure a patient's sense of being valued as a person rather than as a machine to fix? If we judge "success" in the Christian world by how many people come to our church or youth group, how many people applaud our preaching, or how many people come to Christ in a given year, we may aim for the wrong thing.

It is perfectly possible to have an apparently thriving ministry and actually be doing God's work in a way that dishonors God himself. It is also possible to appear a spiritually disciplined person and actually be full of self-righteousness, pride and inauthentic spirituality. Those were the marks of some of the most dedicated religious people of Jesus' day, the Pharisees. Jesus contrasts their outward show with the authentic spiritual life that is behind doors, in secret, where only the Father knows (Matthew 6:5–15). So what are we aiming at? How does Jesus help us define success?

Faithfulness

The first criterion is faithfulness to God's word and obedience to God's commands (1 Corinthians 4:1–2). It is possible to do God's work but not in God's way. Are we faithful to the commands of Jesus in the way we are leading and living our lives? Do we trust God's way of leading even when it seems foolishness? Are we growing in our knowledge of God's word and obedience to what he asks of us? Faithfulness frees us from identifying success as growth in numbers, amazing worship services, or more young people won for Christ. We still need to evaluate all these things and work out how to lead well in any given situation, but we are not dependent on numerical results for self-authentication. We've all heard the stories of missionaries who have faithfully served God in tough parts of the world, and in forty years of ministry only see a handful of people come to faith. My reaction whenever I hear such stories is to wonder whether I could have sustained ministry for that length of time without many tangible "results." They will not be judged successful by the world, but they will by God's standards. Faithfulness involves honest reflection on how we are doing, but it starts with a commitment to know and follow God's way of doing things. Without this there is no success.

Fruitfulness

Fruitfulness in leadership is more to do with character than it is with ministry success. You can have a growing church, lead people to faith in Christ, be a renowned Bible teacher or an amazing youth worker, and grow less fruitful as a leader. The more outwardly successful our ministry, the more vital it is not to be seduced by the outward trappings of success. Jesus does not offer external factors as the standard to assess things by; he offers fruitfulness. This is what he focuses on in John 15— "fruit that will last."

Are we becoming more like Christ? Do we love people more, or pretend to love them? Are we more joyful despite circumstances around us? When under pressure, are we known as a person of peace? How good are we at enjoying diversity rather than enduring it? Are small acts of kindness an increasing part of the way we treat people? Is it becoming more difficult to lie? Can we be trusted to stand by those we love even when they mess up? Do people increasingly feel valued in our presence, not for what they have to contribute but for who they are as a person? Are our fear, anger, or lust more under control than previously? And most crucially, are all these things increasingly an attitude at the heart of who we are rather than action stuck on to our lives to make us look good?

Knowing what we are aiming for directly relates to discerning God's vocation for our life (Part 3 of this book) and developing our character (Part 4). But if we are to avoid the cycle of guilt, and to live life in response to Jesus' words through the exercising of spiritual disciplines, it is helpful to build from an understanding of "success" as faithfulness and fruitfulness.

REGAINING FIRST LOVE

We are chosen to be in relationship with God as Trinity. Without this "first love," our leadership models a false center. We dare not allow this to happen, for those who follow will take their lead from us. If we've lost our first love, there is no greater priority than regaining it. Ultimately this is dependent on God's grace, for it is his gift to us, but our part is to put ourselves in the place where we are open to receiving his grace through believing and acting upon what Jesus said, through exercising spiritual disciplines, through resolving internal issues, and through knowing what we're aiming for.

Leading up to a sabbatical last year, I'd stopped practicing a number of the spiritual disciplines. Tiredness was one factor. Our three children aren't the world's greatest sleepers, and Sophie and I lived in a constant fog of exhaustion. Yet the real issue wasn't tiredness; the real issue was over-busyness, loving God's work more than God himself. I always found time to work; I didn't make the time to exercise the discipline of prayer. Along the way, I lost Jesus as my first love.

Thankfully, my wise spiritual director pointed out the flashing warning light over my life. I decided to take a sabbatical, and he urged me to take a sabbatical from doing and instead spend time just being. I am not wired to "be." I am an activist by nature, but I knew he was right. He suggested a silent retreat. I'd done retreats before, so that was fine. He suggested eight days. That was a novel thought, but I agreed. Two weeks into my sabbatical, I headed off to a retreat house for an individually guided silent retreat. As I entered the retreat house through the imposing gates, my heart sank. Surrounded by an industrial landscape, the house was a mix of slightly dilapidated old buildings and rather gruesome 1970s additions. My room was comfortable but located near the kitchens and on a main thoroughfare. The retreat house was from another spiritual tradition to mine, and there was much I couldn't connect with. The food was sufficient but not wonderfully appetizing. The introductory session was somewhat chaotic.

My journal entry that night is fairly desperate. It felt as though all my support mechanisms had been stripped away. I love my family, and they weren't with me. I love beautiful things, and it was rather an ugly place. I love reading, and I discovered that we weren't allowed to read books. I am an extravert, and I was expected to spend eight days in silence with my own company. I am "someone"—I have a small profile in the wider church as a speaker, author, and evangelist—and here I was unknown. I am a follower of Jesus longing for change in my life, and I was not even sure that I believed change was possible any longer. I felt very small, exposed and frightened.

What was going to happen?

I listened to the wise advice of my retreat leader. There was no money-back guarantee. He simply asked, "What grace are you seeking from God?" I responded, "Renewal in my relationship with Christ." And out of God's grace, that is what happened—renewal beyond my expectations, beautiful life-changing encounter with God as Trinity. As all my support mechanisms were stripped away, as I meditated four times a day on the scriptures, as I sat in deep silence, I met with Jesus—Beautiful Savior, Wonderful Counselor, Prince of Peace, Awesome King. My first love was restored.

FOR REFLECTION

- What does God's grace mean for me?
- How is my love for Jesus?
- What makes it difficult for me to receive Jesus' love?
- Which commands of Jesus am I struggling to obey at this time, and why?
- Which of the spiritual disciplines do I sense God prompting me to exercise at this time? How will I do it?
- With whom will I share the journey?

PART THREE

GROWING LEADERS
DISCERN GOD'S CALL

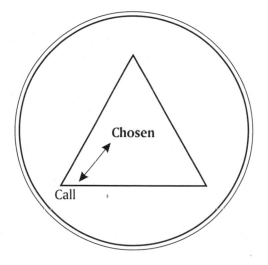

Once we know who we are (chosen), we need to know where God is leading (his call). In Chapter 4, I want to suggest that our sense of "call" is not simply about the overall direction of our life, but affects how we use our time on a daily basis. We'll focus on a diagnosis of the problem, and some definitions of terminology. Chapter 5 explores how we discern and live by God's call.

SALLY (32), YOUTH WORKER,
PONDERING AS SHE WALKS TO A MEETING

"Morning, Bob." He's looking better today. I must try and stop in and see him. So much to do. I'm certainly in the plate spinning business—and there seem to be more plates each month. When I started, my focus was very clear: invest in the youth leaders. That was five years ago. But as the work has grown, so have my responsibilities. Now I have the weekly youth leaders' training meeting, responsibility for thirty leaders, five youth groups to run, the after-school clubs, the monthly alternative youth service, liaison with the local authority youth officer, the church leadership team meeting, the "Time for God" worker to supervise.

"Hi, Joanna . . . Yup, see you tonight." When I write down my main jobs—well, yes, it looks doable. Not too much pressure. But the thing is, it's a people job and I'm a people person—and there are so many people involved, so many relationships. So many needing me and my time. The job seems to soak up all the time I give, and then some. Don't think there's much more of me left to give.

"Latte, please . . . no sugar . . . thanks." I feel bad about complaining. God has really blessed us. The groups have grown, we're seeing young people come to Christ, the leaders are motivated. But Lord, I'm not sure how much longer I can keep this up. Perhaps I ought to talk with Clare, but she's so busy herself, trying to lead the church. She's got even more plates than me—the last thing she needs is me asking her to help spin mine. Lord, what am I to do?

Chapter 4

LIVING IN THE RED ZONE

*Everyone was saying that I was doing really well, but
something inside me was telling me that my success
was putting my own soul in danger.*[1]

HENRI NOUWEN

What is the greatest challenge we face in leadership? How to build
an effective team that doesn't just share the task but also share their
lives? How to raise resources to keep things going? How to capture a
clear sense of direction that doesn't just reflect our own ideas and
hopes but is owned by the group we are leading? How to implement
vision so that it doesn't stay an interesting dream but becomes a vibrant reality? How to make hard decisions that leave people not
trampled upon but cared for? Some of these will be among our
toughest challenges, but I want to suggest that the hardest one for
most of us will be how best to use our time, faced with the many
competing demands on our time, energy and talents.

The pace of modern life, the multiple demands from people,
the pressures created by modern communications, the complexities of Christian leadership and the potential opportunities for
contribution to ministry leave many of us breathless. I don't meet
many leaders who are struggling to fill their time. I meet many
struggling to work out how to use it, and in the midst of this constant struggle, it is easy for the things that are most precious to receive scant attention. Two questions have helped me acknowledge
the reality of this in my own life. If we were to identify the three
or four things that matter to us most, what would they be? And
are these things really receiving the care, time and attention we
want to give them?

THE RED ZONE

We ignore this issue at our peril. Far too many Christian leaders struggle to balance their lives between competing demands, and live life in the red zone. If we look at a tachometer in a car, when the car idles the RPMs (revolutions per minute) hardly register— a mere six or seven hundred RPMs. The car wasn't designed to spend all its life idling, but to enjoy the variety of its performance range. There is an optimum speed for the engine, where performance and fuel consumption balance nicely and the engine is fulfilling the task it was designed for. This is normally around two-thirds of the capacity. Then there is the red line. Occasionally pushing the engine into the red zone is fine—exhilarating, even— but sustained operation in the red zone will damage the engine and shorten its life. Imagine that for each of us there are five gauges, representing physical, emotional, relational, intellectual and spiritual aspects of our life.[2] Each aspect is linked with the others. If we push ourselves into the red zone for too long, damage occurs. Inevitably there are going to be seasons of extra busyness, but problems arise when they become the norm—when the pace of life becomes frenetic and never returns to a sensible level. The results are outlined below.

The physical gauge

We become physically depleted and have little time for exercise. We feel constantly weary, drained or lacking in energy. Classic symptoms include stress targeting a particular part of the body. For some people it's their stomach, for others headaches, joints aching, lower back pain, or indigestion. Then, when we do take a holiday, we become ill within days of it starting. Colds or flu are the blight of many ministers' post-Christmas break.

The emotional gauge

We become emotionally drained, with no time to pay attention to our feelings. We become dispassionate about the plight of suffering people, and vulnerable to escapist sins. Temptations we are normally able to resist suddenly seem irresistible as our soul cries out for some emotional comfort. This is the path to late-night television, pornography, indulgent alcohol consumption, comfort eating, addictive exercise, and affairs. We also become surprised by escapist thoughts. We dream of leaving the role we have, of driving off into the sunset or simply jumping on a plane. We even think about leaving our spouse or family. We live for our holidays, our days off. The result is a shrunken heart, a hollow cavern where our heart used to beat. "Compassion fatigue" is a termed used by aid agencies when the public are asked to give to yet another humanitarian crisis. It applies equally well to Christian leaders who constantly respond to the emotional humanitarian crises around them, or are drained by constant overload.

The relational gauge

The greater our physical tiredness and emotional emptiness, the more likely we are to become relationally distant. Relationships become superficial, and those closest to us end up with the dregs of our time and energy. We're always apologizing to our friends, children or spouse for not being there. We hear ourselves saying, "Next time it will be better." We don't have time for friendships and slowly become more isolated and less accountable. It's a dangerous combination. As one minister said, "Nothing messes up friends more than ministry."

The intellectual gauge

We become stagnant, relying on past stimulation to resource us for present ministry. Our bookshelves reflect when we finished our training. The newspaper remains unread. We never quite make it to that stimulating conference we meant to attend. We rehearse old arguments, unsure whether they are still credible or if we still believe them. We find ourselves less and less open to new ideas and more cut off from the younger generation. We become bored with our own teaching and preaching. Our brain longs for intellectual food, but feels as though we've placed it on a hunger strike.

The spiritual gauge

We become spiritually disillusioned. Prayer is reduced to cries for help, worship reduced to thanksgiving. We lose our first love. We no longer exercise spiritual disciplines. We begin to rationalize misbehavior, and start skimming across the surface of important things. Sermon preparation becomes a hurried few minutes snatched throughout the week. Preparation for meetings takes place on the journey to the location. Pastoral care means a few quick words after the youth group meeting with a desperately hurting individual.

How are the RPMs for us at the moment—physically, emotionally, relationally, intellectually and spiritually? If we're not sure, we could ask those closest to us what they think. We may not like the answer (indeed, that may be why we don't ask the question), but if we continue to live in the red zone, problems lie ahead. Frenetic busyness leads to damage to ourselves, those closest to us and those we lead. We may be fooled into not bothering because we're still fruitful. Surely things can't be too bad if God is still blessing us?

When reflecting on this, most Christian leaders have an inbuilt response mechanism—more discipline. Reflect on the following question. If you were to fault yourself in one of these three areas, which would it be?

- The inability to prioritize
- The inability or lack of desire to organize these priorities
- Lack of discipline to maintain and tackle these priorities

People tend to respond with either "lack of discipline" or "inability to organize priorities." If only I could be better organized . . . if only I could discipline myself to do what I intended to do . . . if only I could sort out my time management. Yet these areas are normally symptoms of an even more fundamental issue, the lack of ability to prioritize. Leadership expert and life coach Stephen Covey says, "The greatest incentive to say *no* is having an even greater *yes* burning inside you."[3] Knowing our calling helps us to discern that greater "yes."

WHAT DO WE MEAN BY THE WORD "CALL"?

Os Guinness describes calling[4] as "the truth that God calls us to himself so decisively that everything we are, everything we do, and everything we have is invested with a special devotion and dynamism lived out as response to his summons and service."[5] Within this overarching call of God on our lives, I'd like to explore the simple distinction between our primary calling and our secondary calling.

Our primary calling as human beings is to respond to God's call, whose expressed intention is to bring all people within his saving purposes through the "call" on the life of the individual. The primary call is to faith and discipleship (Mark 2), from which we are called to grow and know Jesus (John 15) and to the work of the gospel (Romans 1:1ff). The appropriate response to this call is to love the Lord our God with all our heart, mind, soul and strength (Matthew 22:37).

Our secondary calling is to respond to God's particular purpose for our life. On the macro scale, we are all called to worship God, work for his purposes in the world and witness to our faith, but on the micro scale we are not all called to the same job, the same relationships, or the same responsibilities. Every human being is uniquely shaped to fulfill specific purposes that God has in store for their life.

Historically, the language of call came to be restricted to a few particular areas. People even speak of "fulltime" Christian ministry. This fuels the false notion that only if you are a monk, missionary or minister are you really in fulltime ministry, which is ridiculous. Colossians 3:17 tells us clearly, "Whatever you do, whether in word or deed, do it all in the name of the Lord Jesus."

There is no sacred/secular divide to suggest that some types of work are godlier than others. We need godly people in all sorts of work situations, recognizing that they are called to work out their discipleship in that context.

However, *Growing Leaders* is focused on those in leadership within the Christian community. The issue of discerning our secondary call is central. In a local church situation, a leader may have clearly discerned one aspect of God's secondary call. That call may have led them into paid Christian employment as a youth worker, or into the ordained ministry, or into leading a home group, but the issue of call is still relevant as they try to work out how to use their time day by day, and to discern what aspect of Christian leadership they are shaped to fulfil.[6] Every leader is called to faith in Christ, but not every leader is the same.

Recently I spent over an hour on the phone to a high-profile Christian leader. This is a man who has taught me much, whose life I admire. The reason for the call? He wanted to talk about how to balance the many demands on his time. Half way through the conversation I felt as though I must be saying things he already knew, so I asked him if it was any help. His response was, "Yes, because people rarely talk about this in detail. They mention it in generalities, either because they haven't actually managed to sort it out for themselves, or because they fear people will model themselves on them in an inappropriate way. Yet what people need is the detail, the practical how to's." Wise words. Let me respond to two issues he raised for me.

First, if we are to sort out how to use our time with any clarity and conviction, we need to know how God has shaped us and how he wants to use us. Generalities rarely help; people are looking for practical ideas. So in the next chapter we're going to take a look at Mark 1 and see what we can learn from Jesus about calling and life decisions.

Second, the leader highlighted the danger of individuals presenting their way of working as the way things should be done ("gift projection"). I mentioned this issue in the Introduction, but just in case you skipped the intro, I return to it here! Churches suffer from this disease. A particular individual dominates the leadership horizon and, unless they positively counteract this tendency, people begin to think that the way that leader does things is the way things must be done. I am in danger of doing the same thing in writing this book. I am male (just in case you hadn't figured that out), white, in my forties, an extravert-intuitive-thinking-judging Myers-Briggs type, with gifts in the areas of leadership, evangelism, teaching and administration. If you share a similar SHAPE to me, you'll automatically resonate with some of what I am saying. But if you are different from me, the danger is that you'll try to do things my way, and they won't work. Then, depending on your level of security in who you are in Christ, you'll either feel you've got it wrong (and perhaps feel guilty or stupid, or possibly both) or think I've got it wrong (and perhaps think I'm stupid or typically male, or possibly both).

So how do we explore this issue of calling in a detailed, practical way without imposing our particular SHAPE on others? By identifying the principles that apply to all Christian leaders, and the tools that some will find helpful and others won't. Too often, people focus on the method as if it was a principle.

A final thought before we launch into how we discern God's secondary calling on our life and live by it. Living life in the red zone can be exciting. The adrenaline flows, we achieve many things, ministry flourishes. But consistent living in the red zone leads to exhaustion, disillusionment and damaged relationships. Too many Christian leaders live in the red zone for too long, driven round the cycle of grief. It rarely glorifies God, and frequently glorifies us. Take a look at your gauges.

FOR REFLECTION

- How does the cross help you to face the reality of how you're currently living your life?
- What do you sense is God's secondary calling on your life at this moment?

- Ask someone you trust to read this chapter and to suggest where you are on each of the gauges.
- Take an average month and keep a really accurate record of your use of time (perhaps in 30-minute chunks). How does your use of time reflect your actual priorities in life?

MIKE (49), LEADER OF AN OUTREACH PROJECT

Nick and Tony completely got me this morning. I received a letter asking me to consider a position at a church in York. It was my dream job, and they were offering it to me. It didn't even cross my mind that it was a farce. Then Tony phoned up and asked if I'd ever considered moving. Then I heard Nick laughing in the background and it dawned on me what had happened. With friends like that . . .

Trouble is, it got me thinking. I'm not sure this job is "me." There is so much about it that I struggle with, and I can't work out if that is because the project is going through a hard time, or whether I'm a square peg in a round hole. With so many different demands, it is increasingly hard to work out my priorities. As usual, we're understaffed and under-resourced. I dream of someone leaving us a great chunk of money, but even then I am not sure it would resolve the issue. Is this what I should be doing? And how am I meant to work that out? Did I get it completely wrong three years ago? Back then I was much clearer about the gifts God had given me, but now I seem to use so few of them. I spend most of my time doing things I don't really enjoy and I'm not very good at. Is that the nature of Christian service? I know there is a large part of me that would love to escape, but is God actually calling me to stick at it?

Oh Lord, I don't know what to do.
Please help me to know your call and have the courage to follow.
Amen.

Chapter 5

FINDING GOD'S PURPOSE

There is enough time in the day to do everything
God wants us to do. So if you haven't got
enough time, what needs to go?

ANONYMOUS

Spending time is a daily occupation. Time is the most important commodity we have—irreplaceable, non-refundable, and portioned out equally to every person. How to use the time we have on earth is a quandary addressed by discerning God's call. Our primary call means that we give first allocation of our time to God through spiritual disciplines. Our secondary calling helps us work out how to spend the rest of our time. For those like Sally, for whom the "revs" are constantly in the red zone, being clear about what God wants us to do with our time enables us to make decisions that will help reduce the revs. When we're already working as hard as we can, adding more revs is simply not a viable long-term option, yet as we grow in leadership more options and demands for the use of our time come our way. Some take the drastic route and leave to take on another position, buying themselves a much-needed breather. But within a relatively short period, they are back to living life in the red zone. The problem travels with them.[1] The issue is one of calling, of discovering God's priorities.

In this chapter I want to consider the early days of Jesus' public ministry to see what insights we can gain from the narrative in Mark 1. Then I want to explore some tools that might help us work out some of those principles in practical ways as we seek to discern God's secondary calling for each of our lives. Some of the tools will connect with you, others won't, but I hope the range of ideas will inspire you to find a way to discern God's call. Only then, with the big 'yes' burning inside us, will we know where to invest our time.

EARLY DAYS IN JESUS' PUBLIC MINISTRY

Jesus knew his call

Mark's Gospel opens with a wonderful scene (Mark 1:4–11). The controversial, strident figure of John walks on to center stage, calling people to a baptism of repentance for the forgiveness of sins. Crowds gather in response, and among them an unknown Jewish carpenter submits himself to immersion in the river Jordan. As he comes out of the water, heaven is torn open, the Spirit descends and a voice speaks. The voice from heaven gives Jesus confirmation of who he is and a commission for what he is to do. In some senses this is his job description.

From early childhood Jesus may have reflected on the names given to him at birth: Jesus, which means "the Lord saves," and Emmanuel, which means "God is with us" (Matthew 1:21, 23). As a teenager he shows a growing awareness of who he is. When discovered by his anxious parents in the temple, listening to the teachers and questioning them, Jesus responds to their concern with "Why were you searching for me? Didn't you know I had to be in my Father's house?" (Luke 2:41–52). He knew that he was called to be about his Father's business, and here at his baptism this job description, mapped out in scripture, is confirmed and the Spirit is given to strengthen him to fulfill it.

Jesus knew his calling. He wasn't just passing through life, but pursuing a vision of what his Father wanted him to do. As the Son of God he did have an advantage or two, but the testimony of the scriptures is that we too are called. Knowing both that we are called and what our call is makes a difference. We are not on earth by chance; we are here for a purpose.

Jesus' call was tested

The drama continues (Mark 1:12–13). Freshly anointed by the Spirit of God, the first place the Spirit leads Jesus is into the desert. The language is strong: "*At once* the Spirit *sent him* out into the desert." Jesus goes from an amazing revelation of God as Father to the desert, alone. The same Spirit who descended on him as a dove drives him into the desert. Perhaps the story seems disjointed because we swallow the image of a pretty white dove, whereas the actual word used refers to a brown rock dove whose natural habitat was the desert. We picture a gentle dove descending lightly upon Jesus' head, but the actual words are that "he saw heaven being torn open" (Mark 1:10). We imagine the gentle voice of the Spirit whispering in Jesus' ear, whereas we are told that the Spirit "drove" him, literally "exploded" him, into the desert.

It is in the solitude of the desert that the call is tested. In the desert, in the place of hunger and solitude, we're told, Satan tempted him (v. 13). The reality of Jesus' temptation is enormously encouraging. As a younger Christian, I used to assume that the presence of temptation was a sign of my ungodliness. Now I realize that it may be exactly the opposite. As David Runcorn expresses it, "Temptation may be the evidence of a living, vibrant commitment to God. We are tempted because we are more alive, not less so."[2]

The three temptations relate to Jesus' passions, possessions and power (Luke 4:1–13). Each time, Satan subtly undermines his identity by offering another way to fulfill his commission. Jesus responds by bringing these things under the authority of God's word, to reclaim his identity as an inheritor of all that God has promised. In his resistance to temptation he gives us a model to follow as we seek to fulfill God's call in appropriate ways. Temptation to cut corners, pander to personal preference and use position for personal gain, all as a means to fulfill what we believe God is asking us to do, are likely to be part of any leader's experience. Response to such temptation in the public domain is largely governed by how we deal with temptation in the private world of solitude and silence.

We're told by Mark that "angels attended him" (1:13), marking the provision of God, even in the most desperate place. Starving after forty days, presumably cold at night, tempted by Satan, he was not alone. How exactly the angels attended to him we do not know, but that they did is a wonderful insight into the love of the Father. The next time we hear of angels waiting on Jesus, we are in the garden of Gethsemane, at his hour of greatest need (Luke 22:43). How much did the lesson of dependence on God in the desert prepare him for all those other occasions in his life when he could only throw himself on the mercy of his loving Father?

Jesus acted on his call

Some months after his baptism, "after John was put into prison" (Mark 1:14), Jesus senses that the time has come to act upon God's call on his life, and he walks into Galilee to proclaim good news. Jesus must have known a similar fate to John's might face him. I wonder if he was tempted to walk away into obscurity. This may not have seemed the ideal moment for him to go public, but Jesus declared, "The time has come" (v. 15). The Greek New Testament has two words for time—*chronos*, which is calendar time, and *kairos*, which is God's special moment for something. The word used here is *kairos*. All the previous years have prepared Jesus for this time. Fulfilling God's time may appear to be an unwise move. You can imagine some of his friends saying, "Not now, Jesus, give it a few months, let things settle down after John's arrest." But he obeys, and proclaims, "The time has come."

In the process of discerning our secondary calling, there will come a time when we need to act upon it. Sensing the right time is not easy, but when it becomes clear, we need to act. Speaking at a conference of predominantly younger leaders, I mentioned the challenge of acting upon God's leading in our lives and said, "A number of people here are sensing God's call and are fighting it.

Some of you are being called into ordained ministry. You're fighting it because you've seen what the Church sometimes does to its leaders and you don't want to be in that position. Some of you are being called to be a fulltime mom or dad. You're fighting it because the peer pressure is to continue your paid employment. Some of you are being called to work abroad. You're fighting it because you fear losing contact with your friends and family, of being isolated. Some of you are being called to leave paid Christian employment and to fulfill God's purpose for your life in another type of employment. You're fighting it because you're worried others will think you've gone soft on God. If God has called, don't fight, follow." I was surprised at the people who came up afterwards and spoke of the months, even years, they had been fighting God's call.

Discerning God's call is not enough. We need to respond and act upon it.

Jesus shares his call with others

Jesus then does something quite remarkable (Mark 1:14–20). He calls ordinary fishermen to work alongside him and ultimately to carry on his work. Simon, Andrew, James and John form part of the inner circle of disciples that he chooses to be "with him" (Mark 3:14). We know from the rest of the account of Jesus' life that he shared his whole life with them, not just his public ministry. He was committed to investing in others and sharing his Father's vision for his life, even though they struggled to accept it (Mark 8:31–33). I find this challenging because it speaks of vulnerability (seen clearly when the disciples let him down in his hour of need), interdependence (as the disciples provide for his needs), and recognition that others were needed to fulfill the next stage of what he came to do.

Bill Hybels writes, in *Courageous Leadership:*

I don't want to be a prophet of doom, but I am afraid that a steady stream of church leaders are going to disappear tragically from the rosters of kingdom lead-

ership unless they commit themselves to discovering safe people and leaning into those relationships. Our hearts were not built to handle the hardships and heart-aches of ministry alone.[3]

Finding God's central purpose for our life may be easier than fulfilling it. We need people we can share the vision with, those who pray, support and encourage us. We need people who will go on loving us even when we get it all wrong.

Jesus exercises his call with compassion

Jesus not only teaches in the synagogue, he has compassion on the man with the evil spirit, he heals Simon's mother-in-law, and he heals the many who are brought to his door who are suffering (Mark 1:21–34). I doubt that any of these things was on Jesus' agenda for that day, but all of them receive the loving attention of the Savior. Compassion is the mark of Christian ministry—to suffer with others, to be prepared for our agenda to be modified by the needs of those around us. Here is a reminder of this, loosely based on 1 Corinthians 13.

> *If I cast a vision with the tongues of people and angels,*
> *But lead without the love of God at my core,*
> *I am a ringing cell phone or worse,*
> *a clamoring vacuous corporate type.*
> *If I have the gift of leadership and can provide direction,*
> *build teams and set goals,*
> *But fail to exhibit Christ-like kindness or give Christ*
> *the credit for my accomplishments,*
> *In the eyes of God, all my achievements count for precisely nothing.*
> *If I give my tithe to the poor, my favorite study Bible to the new convert,*
> *or my team members' bodies to be burned*
> *But neglect to relate and work in a manner worthy*
> *of the one whose name I bear,*
> *In the final analysis, it all counts for precisely nothing.*

No matter how exciting the secondary call of God on our lives, it never takes priority over our primary call—to be good followers of Jesus, bearing his fruit. We see this in the way Jesus reflects his Father's perspective on time. Central to all his activity is relationships. "The practice of time management is actually relationship management within the arena of time."[4] People are always central to Jesus' ministry, and so must they be for us.

Jesus refocuses his call through prayer

After an exhausting day of ministry, when Jesus could have justifiably enjoyed sleeping in, we find, "Very early in the morning, while it was still dark, Jesus got up, left the house and went off to a solitary place, where he prayed" (Mark 1:35). Time spent with his Father was the priority. Time spent with our Father needs to be our priority, especially after a particularly successful period of ministry. For it is then that we are most vulnerable to other people's expectations setting our agenda, or our own pride obscuring the purpose of God in our lives. There are three marks of this early morning prayer time that strike uncomfortably at my approach to prayer.

"While it was still dark . . ." We don't know what time of the year this was, but in Jerusalem today the sun rose at 5.54am. Jesus woke up very early. Taking time out with God normally involves sacrifice. Are we prepared to make sacrifices to be with God?

"He got up, left the house, and went off to a solitary place." It is not enough just to wake up; Jesus got up. When my alarm clock goes off, there is a nanosecond in which I have to make a decision: get up, or lie there for just another minute or two, which invariably becomes thirty or forty minutes as I drift back to sleep. Then he "left the house." I imagine that everyone slept in the same area, so leaving the house was appropriate. My problem is that as I leave the bedroom to go to another room where I can pray, on the way there are a thousand distractions that tempt me to linger. Jesus took action. He went somewhere appropriate to pray. We need to be practical and take action as well. We need to be alone with God. For some,

that may involve going for a walk. A good friend of mine with five children used to load the early-waking baby of the family into the stroller and go for a long walk early every morning, praying on the way. Unless we come before God alone, we dare not go before God's people in public.

"And he prayed." I find praying incredibly hard work. I can think of so many other tasks to do at that moment, which is why it is sensible to clear all possible distractions from our place of prayer. As I've mentioned already, the most important lesson I have learned about prayer is to do it, however hard, however dry, however disjointed.

When I was attending university, everyone was concerned about a legalistic approach to praying. I am now equally concerned about license. I've done the legalism bit, and I've done the license bit. What I know now, to the core of my being, is that there is no substitute for time spent alone with God. It will involve making a sacrifice, being disciplined, and doing it.

I've also realized the importance of corporate prayer. I certainly find it easier to intercede when I am praying with others. In the organization I work for, we meet twice a day to pray together, and in all the busyness it is a great corporate discipline. Some church traditions have corporate prayer as part of the daily rhythm, and this is a helpful balance to the sometimes excessive emphasis on personal prayer.

Jesus reaffirms his call through hard decisions

"Simon and his companions went to look for him, and when they found him, they exclaimed: 'Everyone is looking for you!'" (Mark 1:36–37). Hear the disciples' frustration at being unable to find Jesus, and the pressure of expectation: "Everyone is looking for you . . . why aren't you there for them? There are more miracles to do, people need healing . . . wasn't it a blast last night, just think what might happen today . . . the papers will be down soon, probably a TV crew or two. In fact, Jesus, this could go out prime time and think what that will do for promoting the ministry."

Jesus replied, "Let us go somewhere else . . ." "What?" you can almost hear the disciples gasping. "You can't. What about the people? Why?" " . . . so that I can preach there also. That is why I have come" (Mark 1:38–39). The personal compass swings back to true north; Jesus knows where he is going. He will leave the crowds to continue his Father's priorities for his life. Time spent with the Father reminded him of who he was, a chosen one of God. Time spent with his Father helped him to pick up the maker's instructions for the day. Time spent with the Father reminded him whose approval he needed to seek—not that of the crowd, or even his closest followers.

This is the role of God's call on our life. It gives us clarity on how to use our time; it helps us make decisions that affect daily life. God's "yes" enables us to say "no." God's "yes" distinguishes the urgent from the important,[5] the pressing from actual priorities, mere distractions from divine calling. Without it, we enter the red zone, or we flounder around, incapacitated by a lack of direction to focus on anything. Growing leaders know God's primary call and discern God's secondary call, for his vision for our life shows us the way, spurs us on the way, and sustains us along the way.

Moving out of the red zone will take time. There are some practical steps that we could take immediately, but for most busy leaders the schedule is full, and canceling engagements is very difficult.[6] We are unlikely to have complete control of our own timetable, although most people in leadership within the church and Christian organizations have far more control over their diaries than our colleagues working in secular places.

Discerning God's secondary call takes time. The suggestions below may take six months to a year to implement, depending on how much time we can allocate them. If that creates a sense of panic in us, it is probably best to start straight away. To help make sense of the process, I've given an outline below of one way of doing this, involving five steps with related exercises and guidelines. (This is just one way, learned through personal experience, not the only way.)

STEP 1: IDENTIFY A STARTING POINT

Exercise 1: How has God SHAPEd us?

Os Guinness remarks, "Instead of 'you are what you do', calling says 'do what you are.'" Therefore it is helpful to know who we are, how God has made us and how he has used life to shape us. One model for this is the acronym SHAPE.[7]

S = Spiritual gifts
H = Heart's desire
A = Abilities
P = Personality
E. = Experience

What are the *spiritual gifts* God has given to us? Rick Warren defines these as "special God-empowered abilities for serving him." They are given only to those who know and follow Christ, and are given by the Holy Spirit as an expression of grace. For most of us, the regular use of a gift identifies that it might be a ministry area where God wants us to focus. There are a number of *Spiritual Gift Inventories* available.[8] They are of value, though somewhat limited as each one tends to define the gifts in particular ways, normally influenced by their theological stance on a number of related issues, but they can be a helpful starting point. See part 2 of the Resource Section for one way to explore what your spiritual gifts may be.

Rick Warren identifies the term *"heart"* as the Bible's way of describing "the bundle of desires, hopes, interests, ambitions, dreams and affections you have. Your heart represents the source of all your motivations—what you love to do and what you care about most."[9] Others align heart with passion. What are you most passionate about? What gets you out of bed in the morning? "Passion" is a very popular word today. I think we need to be a little careful, though. The contemporary use of the word refers to excitement and enthusiasm—what gives me a thrill—but the traditional

Christian use of the word is very different. It is used to describe the events surrounding the death of Jesus on the cross—the Passion narratives. It refers to suffering (from the Latin *passio*—to suffer), not excitement. That's why "heart" is a better word than the contemporary use of the word "passion": it refers to the deepest part of who we are, to those things that will invoke commitment to the point of inconvenience, suffering, even death.

Listening to our heart helps determine the area in which we can use our gifts. God may gift two people as evangelists, but one person's heart is for children, the other for senior citizens. They both have the same gift, but they will use it very differently because of where their heart is.

What are the natural talents and *abilities* we were born with? This means not the things we can do, but the things we can't help doing. I have always been an ordered person. I can remember, as a child, trying to copy out the complete works of Shakespeare by hand. If I made a single mistake on a page, I screwed it up and started again. Now some of you are seriously worried about my mental health, but this ability to bring neatness and order is a part of how God made me. Some people are naturally musical (although that doesn't necessarily make them good worship leaders), some are naturally creative, some love numbers. What can't you help yourself doing?

There are many tools available for gaining insight into our *personality type*—for example, the Myers-Briggs Personality Indices.[10] Such inventories can help us learn about how we are "wired," as long as we don't allow them to become prescriptive rather than descriptive. Excusing behavior on the basis "Oh, I can't help myself: I am an ESTJ or an INFP" is unacceptable. But knowing that I am an extrovert does help me to understand why I enjoy certain things and not others. It helps me to identify the sort of working environment that I will thrive in, and others that will stifle me. Rather than trying to become someone I am not, I can positively express who I am, how God has made me.

Everything that we *experience*, positive or negative, shapes who we are. Reflecting on our experiences and how we've responded to them gives insight into who we are. Aldous Huxley wrote, "Experience is not what happens to you. It is what you do with what happens to you."[11] Rick Warren suggests, "The very experiences that you have resented or regretted most in your life—the ones you've wanted to hide or forget—are the experiences God wants to use to help others."[12] This is hard for those who've experienced tragedy, brutality, or abuse; yet out of the negative experiences in life, God is able to bring his redemptive purposes. I confess, my life has been pretty easy so far—apart from the two years as a teenager where I wasn't able to walk, following an accident at school. Those two years shaped me; I still see their influence on my life today.

I like using the SHAPE analysis because it is fairly comprehensive. Its danger is that it may compartmentalize us into separate boxes, rather than integrating us as a whole. It is the combination of all these factors (and others) that goes to make up who I am. Understanding myself as an integrated whole helps me to be aware of my starting point and to identify the things I can change about myself and the things that are a given. I don't come to God to inquire about his central purpose for my life with a blank sheet of paper. A lot is already written there, if I take the time to decipher it. And once I've understood it, I won't waste time fighting those things that are a given, but rather work with them.

There is a tension here that we must not avoid. On the one hand, God seems to call us recognizing how he's made us. Too often I hear Christians say that if you identify something you definitely don't want to do or aren't any good at, be wary because God is bound to call you to that area of ministry. The image of God that lies behind this assumption is unhealthy, as if he capriciously deals out the very things we fear. God tends to use who we are and how he's made us.

On the other hand, we cannot avoid another aspect of call. There are times when God calls people who aren't in any way gifted for what he wants them to do. Oswald Chambers wrote:

*God can achieve his purpose either through the absence of human power and re-
sources, or through the abandonment of reliance on them. All through history
God has chosen and used nobodies, because their unusual dependence on him
made possible the unique display of his power and grace. He chose and used
somebodies only when they renounced dependence on their natural abilities and
resources.*[13]

Holding these two aspects of call in tension is how we discern the
truth of God's call as revealed in the Bible. If we are open to God's
call only in areas of strength, talent and giftedness, we exclude the
possibility of God's strength being made clear in our weakness
and inability. If we expect God's call only to be in areas of weakness, we deny something of how he has made us and longs to use
us. Ultimately the crunch is whether we are genuinely open to
wherever God may lead. Is he genuinely the king of our lives?

Exercise 2: What are our current responsibilities?

We don't do this exercise in a vacuum, disconnected from the daily
responsibilities of life. I am a father of three children, and I have a
responsibility to them. Once again here it gets tricky. On one occasion Jesus teaches that unless we hate our brothers, sisters, mother
and father, we cannot be his disciples (Luke 14:26), but on another
he challenges the Pharisees for their rampant disregard for the command to "honor your father and your mother" (Mark 7:9–13).

Generationally, the pendulum seems to swing back and forth.
Older Christian leaders are dismayed by younger Christian leaders'
unwillingness to take on tough jobs "because we're concerned
about how our children will cope." I once heard Billy Graham's sister speaking to a group of young leaders about the sacrifices she
and Billy Graham's wife made as young mothers, having to say
goodbye to their husbands as they went off on three-month missions abroad, without any of the modern-day communications
available to us. She challenged us to a life of sacrifice for the gospel. I also recall working in South India and reading tombstone
after tombstone of 19th-century Western women, children and

men who all died young as a result of disease or hardship while serving as missionaries.

On the other hand, younger Christian leaders are appalled at the apparently cavalier attitude to parenting that seems to have sacrificed children on the altar of ministry. I've heard people say that some of the great pioneers of the faith have left cynical, disillusioned and damaged families behind them.

The pendulum swings from self-sacrifice to self-fulfillment, from discipline to self-indulgence. Where is the appropriate place for it to stop? What does it mean to put Jesus before anyone or anything else? Jesus says, "Seek first [God's] kingdom . . . and all these things will be given to you as well" (Matthew 6:33). Our primary calling involves laying everything before God and placing God above all things. Yet our secondary calling must surely encompass the relationships that are part of being human, a glorious gift from a relational God. We were not designed to be on our own, but to be in relationships. The context for that is not as important as the content. God may call us as a family to go to what we consider a tough place. Suffering may be a part of that calling, as it is part of Christian discipleship. But within that context I cannot abdicate the responsibility to place my parents, siblings, spouse and children before my ministry. When considering our starting point we need to account for our current responsibilities—aging parents, young children, partners, wider family members, friends who need our loving care.

There are also our current work and financial responsibilities—a job to be done, a mortgage to pay. The pendulum swings, and where it stops will be highly individual. My concern is that in our time, it probably needs to be nudged more towards self-sacrifice and servanthood.

STEP 2: DISCERN WHERE GOD IS LEADING

One of my colleagues asks the question, "What is God calling you to be, become and do?" Our *being* is primary, and that relates to our sense of being chosen. Our *becoming* flows from our being. It relates to our character becoming more Christ-like day by day.[14] Our *doing* flows out of these other two, finding and fulfilling God's central purpose for our life. Central to this discerning process is prayer. It is God's will we're seeking. There is no substitute for spending time with God and with God's people to discern where he is leading, but there are some tools to help us as we reflect.

Exercise 1: Reflecting back on life

One way to do this is to write our own obituary. This might sound a little morbid, but it helps us get in touch with what we long for, deep down in our lives. The story is told of Alfred Nobel, a famous Swedish industrialist who'd made millions out of dynamite, sitting down one morning to eat his breakfast. Glancing through the paper, he was rather surprised to see his own obituary. Reading it, surprise turned to shock as he read a summary of his life. Despite his huge financial successes, the article spoke of him as a mean and unpleasant man. Horrified, because he recognized the truth of what he'd become, he changed his ways. As a result he established the Nobel Prizes, giving his huge wealth to benefit good causes in the world. The obituary was a mistake, but the perspective it brought was life-changing for Nobel. What would we like people to write about us when we die?

Alternatively, we can imagine we are attending our retirement party, where our best friend, who has known us for forty years, is giving a speech summing up our life and ministry. What would we like him/her to say about us? At the end of the speech another friend leaps up and asks if s/he can say a word. S/he begins with these words: "There is one vital thing that hasn't been mentioned that very few of you will know about . . ." If you can, finish this short speech about yourself.

The potential flaw with both these exercises is that they focus on human comment on our lives. We need to recognize that the most important reflection on our lives is, of course, God's. Imagine you've died, and are standing before our heavenly Father. As he looks at you, what do you long for him to say as he reflects upon your life on earth?

Exercise 2: Tackle some searching questions

A second way to discern where God may be leading is to reflect on a few searching questions. For example:

- If you were guaranteed that it was part of God's will, your friends would support you, you had all the resources required and it would succeed, what three things would you most like to do for God over the next five years?
- What do those who know you best think you should do with your life?
- What one thing could you do right now that would bring most pleasure to God as your heavenly Father?[15]

Each of these exercises is simply a way to look forward at what might be. We have no guarantee that what we come up with is part of God's secondary call on our life, but it might be. Why? Because God, as we've already noted, is not a spoilsport who, when we discern what we'd like to do, immediately asks us to do the opposite.

STEP 3: DEVELOP A PERSONAL LIFE STATEMENT

This next step brings together insights from Steps 1 and 2. A personal life statement (sometimes described as a personal vision statement) is a description of where we think God is leading us. It is likely to contain elements of both primary and secondary calling. It helps provide focus, discernment and direction, like a compass guiding us through the maze of decisions about how to use our time, pointing to God's priorities for our life.

A life statement isn't a substitute for the Bible, nor is it meant to subvert grace or be set in stone. The statement needs constantly reviewing (see Step 5) as God's word impacts our lives, and as we discern more of God's leading. But as a friend put it, "It is such a help to take time to think carefully and prayerfully about where God is leading. Knowing what he wants me to do, where he wants me to invest my time, means I am less reactive, less stressed, less confused. I know God's call, and now I have to follow where he is leading." Developing such a statement takes time, probably the best part of a year, so it helps to set a realistic timescale for what follows.

Guideline 1: Seek it through exercising spiritual disciplines

The life statement should reflect God's vision for our lives, so spend time praying, listening, fasting and reading, asking what God wants. Our task is not to dream up a vision for our life, but to see Jesus' vision, understand the Father's strategy for our life, and live it.

Guideline 2: Sharpen it by capturing it in detail

Vague thoughts in our minds are converted to concrete ideas and insights by writing the statement out, drawing it, singing it, talking it through with someone else. It is likely to have five main areas, loosely connected with the five dials from "living life in the red zone."

- Physical: how does God want me to take care of my body?
- Spiritual: how is God calling me to grow in my relationship with him?
- Relational: how does God want me to grow in my relationships with others?
- Personal/emotional: what areas of my character does God want to develop in me?
- Professional: what does God want me to do in my work?

Guideline 3: Test your call by submitting it to others

People who know us can bring a healthy external perspective on God's calling. It is best to choose people who know us well, who have God's best at heart for us, and who aren't afraid to tell us things as they really are. It may help to give them some good questions ahead of the conversation so that they can think about what to say.

Guideline 4: Develop your call through obedience

Are we really prepared to commit ourselves to this call of God on our lives? It is likely to be costly. If this is God's call on our lives, we need to submit to where he is leading. It is not enough to create a statement; we must act upon it.

We will probably go through several attempts at this before we have something faithful to what God is asking of us. At every stage, we need to be as open to God as possible, longing to discover his priorities for our life, prayerfully laying it before him, open to his prompting and correction.

STEP 4: IMPLEMENT YOUR PERSONAL LIFE STATEMENT

A good statement will make a difference to how we live. It will bring direction, clarify priorities, inform decisions, fuel motivation, strengthen perseverance and guide evaluation. Developing one isn't any help unless we actually use it. One leader told me that such an exercise was a waste of time. I asked why. He said, "I've got one of those things. It sits in my drawer, and I never look at it." Of course it is a waste of time if we don't use it. Here are six clues as to how it might be applied.

Guideline 1: Put "stones" in a year ahead

A philosophy professor stood before his class with some items on the desk in front of him. He picked up a large, empty glass bowl and proceeded to fill it with stones, about 50 centimeters in diameter. He asked the students if the bowl was full. They agreed that it was. He then picked up a box of pebbles and added them to the bowl, shaking it lightly. The pebbles, of course, rolled into the open areas between the stones. "Is the bowl full now?" "Yes," the students said. He picked up a bag of sand and poured it into the bowl. The sand slipped in between the rocks and pebbles. Once more he asked if it was full and, after some thought, they said that it was. The professor then took a pitcher of water from his shelf and, opening it, poured its entire contents into the bowl. The students roared with laughter at this demonstration. After the noise subsided, the professor spoke: "What is the point of the il-lustration?" One student responded, "Even when you think your life is full you can always squeeze more in."

"That would be one way of looking at it," replied the professor. "Let me offer an alternative. I want you to recognize that this bowl represents your life. The stones are the important things in your life—your partner, your health, your children—things with which, if everything else was lost and only they remained, your life would still be full. The pebbles are the other things that matter, like your job, your house, your car. The sand is everything else— the small stuff. If you put the sand into the jar first, there is no room for the pebbles or the rocks. The same goes for your life. If you spend all your time and energy on the small stuff, you will never have room for the things that are important to you. Play with your children. Take time to get medical checkups. Take your partner out dancing. There will always be time to go to work, clean the house, rewire the lamp. Take care of the stones first— the things that really matter. The rest is just sand."[16]

Put the stones in first. The busier our lives, the more important it is to put the stones in a year in advance. What are stones for Christian leaders? They are the things captured in our personal life statement. My statement has eight sections, only one of which is about work. The other seven are all relational. My first stone is my relationship with God, then with my wife, then children, parents, friends (both Christian and not yet Christian). If these things don't go in the schedule first, there will never be time for them. In my work, the stones include time for personal development. In my personal life, my stones include sport and leisure. These things are far too important to be relegated to sand. They are part of what makes me human. Stones take priority in the schedule, because they reflect what I believe God is asking of me, his priorities for my life.

Guideline 2: Identify your natural rhythms

Alongside this, it helped me as a Christian leader to reflect on the rhythm of life and to try to establish a way of living that works with how I am made and my current responsibilities.

Our bodies have a *daily rhythm*. I am a morning person, so getting up early to pray works for me. I am at my most creative in the morning, so creative preparation needs to happen before lunch. Yet my responsibilities mean that it is good to be around to help get the children up and ready for school.

Therefore, I pray at home before the children get up, I help dress and feed the children, get to work before most people arrive to spend time reading, and do an hour of administration from 9:00 to 10:00 am. Then I prepare talks until noon, when we pray as a group. Around lunchtime my body goes into decline, so I play sport, do administration, have a lunch meeting with someone, or take a 20-minute snooze. My brain comes back online about 2:00 pm so I can do meetings or more preparation. By 4:30 in the afternoon I am winding down again, so I try to file, clear up, make sure everything is ready for the evening meeting, and overview what I am going to do the next day. 5:00–7:45 is core family time. I know that if I am to survive I need to get to bed at a reasonable hour, so I'm heading for bed by 10:15 pm. Other people have completely different body rhythms. They structure their day in a way that wouldn't work for me. That's fine: the important thing is to know what our daily rhythm is and work with it.

It is also helpful to recognize our *weekly rhythm*. This involves identifying time off, space for leisure and sport. I need to take a day off each week, but a lot of that day is taken up with the kids and practical tasks, so Sophie and I blank out another night a week for us. We vary what we do—go out, talk about things, watch a film, read together—but it is part of the rhythm of the week. It is a stone. I need to play sport at least twice a week if I am to stay reasonably healthy—another stone. I love creative things, and the cinema and films are a particular passion. I come out of a good film feeling more alive, more human, more in touch with the divine. It is a stone.

With young children, our lives revolve around *semesters*, so this provides a further natural rhythm. I know I need to exercise the spiritual disciplines of solitude and silence, so I take a six-weekly quiet day to be still and silent. It helps me carve meaning into the previous six weeks, to spend time with God where the only agenda is to be with him. As a family, it helps to take two days off once a month, where we have a little more space to do some fun activities together.

Finally, we have an *annual rhythm.* In my work there are two periods of the year where things are slightly quieter. I am now proactive in keeping those times quieter. I refuse invitations that take me away from home, ensure the pace of life slows down, catch up with stuff, and plan ahead. In my yearly rhythm I make space for seeing a spiritual director, and for spending time with a small group of friends who meet for mutual support and encouragement. It is a stone. I find the winter quite hard as I am definitely solar powered, so I recognize that my creative juices flow better in the summer months and plan accordingly. I also know that I need a holiday every three months, so they go in the schedule well in advance. They are a stone, as are family anniversaries. Another aspect of the annual rhythm is the liturgical calendar. I try to ensure that my devotional life reflects the seasons of the Christian calendar, and as a family we try to do special activities together spiritually in the seasons of Lent and Advent.

I believe that these priorities are God's calling on my life at this time. Some of them will change as I move from one season of life to another, but my personal life statement helps me to identify them, and to shape my life accordingly. My quiet day, my night together with Sophie, holidays—in fact, nearly all the important things in life—get squeezed out easily. That is why it is vital to put them in the diary first, preferably a year in advance, and not to cancel them.

Guideline 3: Create specific targets from your personal life statement

It is easy for God's call on our life to remain unfulfilled. This will benefit no one. At the start of each year I prayerfully identify targets for the year ahead. The personal life statement is a long-term picture of where God is leading, like a guiding star. For that to become reality, I may need to break it down into smaller targets. I have a sheet of paper for the year ahead. Each month, on the first Sunday of the month, I sit down and work out the monthly tasks that will make God's call become reality—never more than six, rarely fewer than two—a mixture of very small things that will only take a few minutes, but don't get done unless I am intentional about it, and larger items that I need to work on each day that month.

This may all sound rather formal, structured and disciplined—and it is. If real change is to take place in our lives, if we are going to align ourselves more and more closely with God's call, then we need to be highly intentional. For years I'd tried to change, to move out of the red zone, and I didn't get very far because I wasn't sure where God was calling me (vision) and I hadn't worked out how to get there (training in accordance with targets). Those who are not SHAPEd like me will find other ways of doing this that will better reflect their SHAPE.[17] What I am convinced of is the need to be intentional. It won't just happen.

Guideline 4: Plan a week at a time

Stephen Covey points out if you plan a day at a time, you almost always give priority to the urgent rather than the important. If we look at life as a whole rather than breaking it down into little compartments, we gain a better perspective on the totality of how God is leading us. The key is to focus not on prioritization but on balance. Think about roles (child of God, daughter, friend, parent, spouse, and so on) and goals. Ask "What is the most important thing I can do in this role to have the greatest possible impact this week?" Before I started planning a week at a time, I always had a long to-do list and could never manage to get through it. Now, I start the week reflecting on my roles and goals, and then prioritize, spreading them across the whole week. Incredibly, it all seems to fit in, and I no longer have the pressure of this long list at the end of the day. This approach actually allows greater flexibility in use of time, especially if we follow the rule of not booking up more than 80 per cent of the day, and keeping one period of a day each week, and a day each month, blank for the unexpected—because the unexpected always happens. This gives us space to move things around so that we can be flexible and attend to the unexpected opportunity or emergency when it arises.

Guideline 5: Exercise integrity at all times

Inevitably there will be times when we have to reorder our schedule, when flexibility is necessary. Jesus somehow managed to react to those around him while keeping a clear focus on where he was going and what he was to do. If we regard our personal life statement as a compass, it will help us to realign our priorities in accordance with God's call. When Jesus drew aside with his Father, he was taking time to enjoy his Father's presence and to discover God's priorities for that day.

Guideline 6: Make yourself accountable to others

"Accountability" is a word with a dirty reputation. People shy away from it for fear of abusive control on their lives. Yet accountability correctly understood and practiced is life-giving and liberating. The best definition of accountability I know is "Helping me to do what I already want to do." I need people to help me, because I find it so easy not to do it. Invite a mentor, colleague, or friend to help you live out what you want to do.

These guidelines are things I've found useful in helping me actually do something about what I discern to be God's call on my life. I am amazed at how much effort it takes to realign the "revs" to a healthy level. I also know that it will be a constant struggle throughout my life to sense God's leading *and* follow. Yet my life is decidedly different from the way it was a few years ago. I work less and somehow seem to achieve more. I see more of my friends, children and wife. I find it easier to say "no." However, no one knows what is round the corner, and that is why the final step is . . .

STEP 5: REVISE YOUR LIFE STATEMENT REGULARLY

As I mentioned previously, our life statement isn't written in stone. We'll need to review it regularly in the light of what God is doing in our lives. I tend to do this once a year, and whenever something major happens in my life that helps me gain a different perspective on some aspect of God's calling. I find a quiet place for a couple of hours, and I prayerfully ponder the statement, asking myself, what have I learned about myself and God over the last year? What has changed in my personal, family or work life? What needs changing in the light of the answers to the previous questions, to ensure that my life statement continues to reflect where I sense God is leading me?

Without revision, our statement won't reflect the changing seasons of life. It will become stale, out of touch and blunt. Through revision, it is sharpened, alive to the breath of the Spirit blowing through it—a servant to help us live in accordance with God's call, rather than a slave to shackle us to one moment in time.

One result of this process may be that we begin to discern we're not in the right role. This is a very sobering position to reach, and one with long-lasting implications, but we won't be the first to discover it. A good friend of mine became a Christian as a young adult. He was very enthusiastic and dedicated. The only problem was his job as an accountant. He knew that he had never wanted to be an accountant and had simply chosen it as the path of least resistance. In his mid-20s he decided to get out, and became a fulltime worker in a local church. He assumed some leadership responsibilities, and committed himself wholeheartedly to everything he took on. But things didn't go very well: he struggled, and so did those he led. His role developed into a fulltime youth worker position. Things were a little better, but still not wonderful. After some years he realized that he had swapped one lot of pressure to conform (to be an accountant) for another type of pressure to conform ("really committed" Christians become church workers). Neither of these roles was God's calling on his life. It was a painful time, not helped by a naïve minister who wasn't a lot of help. I know; it was me! Eventually, somewhat disillusioned, he began to discern what might be God's leading, and took the brave step of moving home and family across the country to return to college to qualify as a social worker. He's brilliant at it, and more fulfilled than ever before as he lives out God's secondary call on his life.

Knowing that we are not in the right role may be the starting point of a journey of discovery that helps us to a new place. It requires courage, honesty, determination and a great deal of trust in God. But it is a journey worth making, even if for some that will mean leaving a leadership role within the Christian community.

A FINAL THOUGHT: BEWARE OF PESTS

PESTs are the things that most often seem to hamper people as they try to live out their sense of God's calling on their lives.

- **Pressures:** they will always be there. We fool ourselves if we think we are going to get life so sorted that it will be easy. Jesus didn't manage it, and nor will we. We need to resist pressures to go somewhere God is not leading. We need courage and boldness to say "no," and we need wisdom from God to help us discern things in accordance with his purpose.

- **Expectations** of others and ourselves: if we don't know who we are or where God is leading, others will quickly define our identity and direction for us. That is why it is so important to be sure of who we are in Christ (chosen) and where he is leading (called). People had very clear expectations about Jesus, and he regularly resisted them (see pages 95–102 on Mark 1:35–39). My own expectations of myself come from a weird mix of childhood influences, cultural pressures, personal insecurities and sin. That's why I so desperately need God's love and grace to help me see where he is leading, rather than listening to the mixture of voices from within.

- **Sin,** our own and others': we live in a fallen world, so life gets very messed up, confusing and complicated. I need daily to be forgiven and to forgive. But let's not fall into one of the enemy's favorite traps—the feeling that we've messed up so many times that there is no way back. God's way is always open, and he longs to offer a fresh start. Let's take him up on his offer.

- **Tyranny** of the urgent: we need to avoid succumbing to the urgent. The important things in life are rarely urgent. We can get by today without spending time with God, caring for those closest to us, making that hard decision, reconciling ourselves with that person, engaging in theological reflection, getting exercise. These things don't feel urgent, but they are important. We need to focus on the important things, prioritize them, and let everything else follow.

God has a purpose for our life. Finding and fulfilling it is one of the adventures of life. There are no guarantees that it will be easy or comfortable, but living life according to his call, discovering his priorities, is infinitely preferable to living life constantly in the red zone. Knowing what he wants us to do really is the best way to live life. He is the Creator, after all.

FOR REFLECTION

- How do I feel, knowing that God has a purpose for my life?
- What is the best way for me to discern that purpose? Who can help me in the process?

Rick Warren's book, *A Purpose Driven Life*, is a series of forty daily studies to help us reflect on God's purpose, and a most useful guide to reflection.

PART FOUR

GROWING LEADERS DEVELOP CHRIST-LIKE CHARACTER

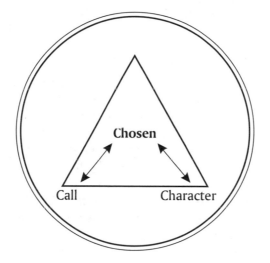

We've considered the central place of knowing we are chosen by God to be his children, and the importance of discerning God's call on our lives to help us out of the red zone. In Part Four, we address character. As the model shows, both call and character are the foundation upon which competence is built. Chapter 6 provides a description of character, explores aspects of a godly leader's character and asks how we handle our character flaws. Chapter 7 looks at godly change, and offers four resources to help change take place.

SIMON (29), ASSOCIATE MINISTER: AN EXCERPT FROM AN E-MAIL TO HIS FRIEND SURMEET LIVING ABROAD

OK, OK, so the sun shines and you go to the beach. Enough! The weather here is appalling. Glad to hear the new job is going well. What about friends?

Thanks for your interest and concern. When I trained, I remember one of the teachers talking about roles and how people perceive you. I thought it was a load of garbage at the time, but four years in I am beginning to see what she meant. My real struggle is with how I keep the public person and the private person in connection with one another. People see me in a particular way when I am leading a service or a meeting, but I realize that I operate in a role—I suppose you could call it a mask. If they really knew what I was like, the things I struggle with in private, the thoughts that assail me day by day, they'd be horrified. I'm sure they wouldn't want me as their associate minister, let alone as a friend. If I'm really honest, Surmeet, I'm even worried about how you'll respond to this . . .

I'm concerned the gap could so easily get bigger. I long to be a person of integrity, but I don't know how to make that longing a reality. Instead it feels like I'm traveling in the opposite direction. I find it more difficult to know how I'm going to react in any given situation, and my confidence level is slipping. With so little time or energy to think about this stuff, I sense I put the mask on with ever-increasing ease. I read in an article that character issues are often what scupper people in ministry. I'm worried that could be me in a few years' time if I don't do something about this. Maybe I need to see someone, talk to someone about it . . .

Must fly, sermon to prepare. I'm definitely coming to enjoy a bit of that sun when I can get some time for a holiday . . .

Chapter 6

CHARACTER DYNAMICS

*Be more concerned with your character than
your reputation. Your character is what you
really are while your reputation is merely
what others think you are.*

BASKETBALL COACH JOHN WOODEN

Character is foundational to everything. You can be a gifted person,
a talented leader, a natural enthusiast, an amazing speaker, but without godly character it all falls apart. I took a year out between school
and university and ended up sweeping floors in a factory. The
owner of the small company was a leader in a local church. Each
Sunday he would take part in some aspect of the service. Friday
nights the youth group met at his house. He regularly gave significant sums of money to charities. Many within the church and the
community admired him, but he wasn't admired within the factory—because his character was completely unpredictable, smiles
and jokes one minute and vehement anger the next. The first time I
saw him explode, I was frozen to the spot by the utter incongruity
of the situation. Sadly, it was a regular occurrence. He was a gifted
leader, but the flaws in his character meant he would never be a
great leader.

So what is character? Why is it foundational? And how do we
handle those flaws within us?

HOW DO WE DESCRIBE CHARACTER?

Character is notoriously difficult to define, especially in relation to
personality. The dictionary definitions are as follows:

- *Personality:* the sum total of all the behavioral and mental characteristics by means of which an individual is recognized as being unique.
- *Character:* the combination of traits and qualities distinguishing the individual nature of a person or thing.

The literature on the relationship between the two is extensive but not necessarily conclusive. So I want to focus on *character,* recognizing that it is intricately linked with personality, and try to describe it.

Bill Hybels describes character in a very simple phrase: "who you are when no one else is looking." That begins to get to the root of character because it is more than just the image we present of ourselves. We live in a world obsessed with style, image and presentation. We increasingly define ourselves by what we have and what we wear, far more than what we do or who we are. In this environment, style seems to win over substance. You can be anything you want to be in our designer world. But the substance of who we are, our character, is not so easily hidden. Who we are when no one else is looking not only affects us in the private moments; it also seeps out into the public arena. Character will shine through, and is often more clearly seen by those around us than by ourselves. It most clearly reveals itself in three ways.

- *In the small things:* How we treat people on a day-to-day basis—in particular how we treat those who can't do anything for us, we don't want anything from, or for whom we have no responsibility.
- *When under pressure:* "One of those days" reveals our character. On good days it is easy to keep the mask in place, but when someone unjustly accuses us, when there is simply too much to do, when we make a mistake and have to decide whether to own up, when the person we find it most difficult to get along with asks for something beyond the normal parameters, when we're tired and someone isn't pulling their weight, when God seems

far away, the mask slips and the real person surfaces. That's part of our character, and it isn't always very nice.

- *When in private:* The measure of a person's real character is what they would do if they knew they would never be found out. In private, when there isn't an audience to play to, when we can "get away with it," what are we really like? Sadly, many children of Christian leaders give up on the faith in their formative teenage years. One of the common reasons is that they can't handle the discrepancy between their parent as the public leader and their parent as the private family person. Hypocrisy stinks, and children and young people hate the smell.

WHY IS ALL THIS SO IMPORTANT?

We're called to a holy life. More important than any other reason, our character is supposed to be Christ-like to honor and glorify God. "But just as he who called you is holy, so be holy in all you do; for it is written: 'Be holy, because I am holy'" (1 Peter 1:15–16).

There are obvious benefits in terms of our personal fulfillment as we discover that is how life was always meant to be lived, and in our public witness as our lives more clearly speak of the God we serve, but these are not the primary motivation for the Christian leader. We long for Christ-likeness in our character first and foremost to please God.

People won't follow those they can't trust. I am constantly amazed and thrilled at the sacrifices people are prepared to make to further God's kingdom on earth. They give time, energy, money and talents to Christian work, and then give them all over again. Why? Normally for two reasons: they believe in the vision and they trust the leader. Sadly, I've also seen firsthand the damage that occurs when trust is shaken, even destroyed. People begin to withdraw their support and eventually their presence. In a local church, the giving goes down, motivation evaporates and eventually people move away. Without credibility, trust and integrity, a leader will have no one to lead. In Christian leadership, character determines how far people will follow.

Character issues nearly always lie at the root of leaders going astray. Not always, but nearly always. Christians are called to be holy people, and Christian leaders are no exception. When we don't grow in the fundamentals of holiness (for example, godliness, truthfulness, integrity, mercy, faithfulness) we leave ourselves open to grow in the opposite traits. These vices undermine Christian leaders and ultimately destroy their ministries. Self-centeredness, lies, in authenticity and deception destroy trust. It is of grave concern that people can have an outwardly successful ministry and yet be hopelessly failing on these character issues in private. Church history is tragically full of such occasions. The classic struggles are with money, sex, relational breakdown, substance abuse and power. As the rupture between the leader's public self (the part everyone sees), their personal self (the part those close to them see) and their private self (the part only they know about) widens, deception and lies increase. Some manage to justify their actions through the incredible ability of the "human personality to rationalize and compartmentalize its morality."[1] Others feel torn apart by the ever widening gap. Ministry collapse, personal breakdown, divorce, total escape and occasionally suicide aren't far away.

Character issues often drive us into the red zone. As we explored in Chapters 4 and 5, character flaws not only push people off track, they also fuel overwork and busyness. To reduce the "revs" involves clarity not only about God's secondary call on our lives, but also courage to face the character flaws that act as drivers.

People will model themselves on us. It is a scary thought, but true. Those we lead will consciously and subconsciously model themselves on us, unless the flaws are so glaringly obvious that they decide not to. Within churches the character of the minister is often reflected in the life of the congregation. I remember visiting one church where the prevailing atmosphere was one of encouragement. When I met the minister I realized why, as he constantly encouraged and affirmed people.

LIVING WITH A FLAWED CHARACTER

Jesus' command is, "Be perfect . . . as your heavenly Father is perfect" (Matthew 5:48), but we all know we're very flawed, and if we don't we've just identified our major flaw! Jesus knew that we wouldn't be perfect on earth, so why does he issue such an impossible command? It's both to set before us the ideal, the nature of God in whose image we're created, and to remind us of the constant need for God's grace and forgiveness. In the Old Testament, the people were to be like their father Abraham. Jesus says this is not enough: we are to be like our Father in heaven, to reflect his likeness.

This challenge to change is captured in Romans 12:1–2: "Do not conform any longer to the pattern of this world, but be transformed by the renewing of your mind." The Christian life is one of change—a constant call to become more like Christ, to grow in godliness, holiness, truth and love. That process of change can be seen in the context of the "now" (what Jesus achieved through his first coming), and the "not yet" (what Jesus will consummate through his second coming).

Christ's first coming brings freedom from what enslaved us in the past,[2] the gift of the Spirit to work change in our lives, and the support of God's people in the process. 2 Corinthians 3:18 reminds us that this process of transformation is the work of the Spirit: "And we, who with unveiled faces all reflect the Lord's glory, are being transformed into his likeness with ever-increasing glory, which comes from the Lord, who is the Spirit." Christ's second coming will be the day when the transformation process is completed, when we will be set free from the presence of all that continues to be sin in our lives.[3]

In the meantime, we live in the tension of between times, given the gift of becoming a "new creation" in Christ (2 Corinthians 5:17), and longing for the day when that new creation will be fully realized. Part of that tension is living with our character flaws, intentionally asking God to change us and handling things well when it all goes wrong. Christian leaders make mistakes—a moment of lost temper, an uncontrolled aside, a dismissive glance. Our character is flawed—lies told to protect oneself, disobedience to God's word, inappropriate use of power. Many in leadership know the danger of being placed on a pedestal, and the ease with which we accept the position. What can help us to be real about ourselves, protect us from inappropriate pedestals, live in the reality of the now and the not yet, and lead well with a flawed character?

Be clear about expectations

Expectations are a minefield. If we plot a path across it right at the start, we'll be less likely to detonate an explosion. Leaders have expectations about themselves, their conduct, their work and their lifestyle. Those they lead also have expectations about their leaders. Often the two sets of expectations are very different. Surveys show that, in a local church context, congregation members' expectations differ hugely from the reality of what ministers do. I've found it really helpful to talk about expectations, and then to agree them. Those we lead have a right to expect certain conduct on our part, but they do not have the right to expect perfection. They have a right to expect us to use our gifts for Christ's purposes, but not the right to expect omnicompetence. They have a right to expect that we will work hard, but not the right to expect omnipresence.

Establishing clear *agreed* expectations involves two stages—first, working with those who share in leadership with us, to identify clear expectations; and second, to communicate the agreed expectations to everyone who needs to know them.

Be honest about faults

We don't have to accept the pedestal: we can be honest about our faults. We should not be looking for affirmation or praise via the back door, or avoiding responsibility for apology or change, or constantly talking about our faults. But people need to know we're real, we're flesh and blood like them, and we're flawed and yet forgiven. Let's not hide our mistakes, but accept them and show how it is possible to grow through them.

Be open to feedback

Too many leaders never receive or ask for constructive feedback from anyone. The only feedback they do receive is negative and destructive, or from the weird and unstable. This is a totally unbalanced way to lead. Feedback helps to combat our incredible capacity for self-delusion, and provides some of the insights required to develop our character.

Two psychologists created a helpful instrument called the Johari window (their names were Jo and Harry).[4]

	Feedback
OPEN SELF I can see; you can see	**BLIND SELF** You can see but I can't see
CONCEALED SELF I can see but you can't see	**UNKNOWN SELF** You can't see, I can't see, but God can see
Disclosure	*Christian experience*

The Holy Spirit is at work across the whole grid, directly in us and through others, to help us understand ourselves a little better. Three other things can also aid the growth of self-understanding.

- *Disclosure* helps open up the *concealed self.* I choose to let you know something about me that you wouldn't know unless I told you. I'll develop this further under the heading "Be vulnerable" (p. 131).
- *God alone* can directly open up the *unknown self.* Thankfully, God doesn't show us everything all at once—we'd collapse. He reveals things about ourselves that no one sees, not even us. And when he does, it is not to crush us but to call us to ever greater

freedom in Christ. This may happen through reflection on the scriptures, in prayer, through dreams, or life's circumstances.

- *Feedback* helps open up the *blind self.* In every context, inviting feedback from those who know us, love us and want the best for us helps combat delusion and develop character, but we'll often need to invite it, especially in the area of our character.[5] Here are some questions to ask if we're feeling brave.

  - What do you see as my single greatest character strength?
  - What do you think are the blind sides I should be aware of?
  - What areas would you encourage me to grow in to prepare for whatever lies ahead?
  - What cautions do you have for me at this point in life?
  - What potential do you see in me that you think I don't see in me?

A final thought on feedback. Don't argue, even with critical, negative, unwanted feedback. Be open to the grains of truth that one can nearly always find in any criticism. I am learning to resist my natural tendency to argue, to want to justify myself, even when the feedback is harsh and unjustified. I've also learned, however, that if someone persistently gives negative feedback, I don't have to be a sponge. It is all right to say "enough."

I remember one Sunday when I was the guest preacher at a church. Afterwards, I was having lunch with a congregation member when the front doorbell rang. My host answered, and returned to say that it was for me. On the doorstep stood a woman who'd been in the service that morning. She smiled and said she'd brought a little gift for my three children. I was taken aback at such a lovely gesture, and offered my thanks. I'd never had that happen to me before—nor what was to follow.

Having handed me the gift, she let rip. She verbally shredded me on the doorstep, saying what an appalling preacher I was, how I'd manipulated and frightened people, and on it went. I just stood and took it all, and when she eventually left, I was internally in pieces.

I wish I'd known I could have said "enough" and, if necessary, closed the door on her.

Be vulnerable

There is a distinction between honesty and vulnerability. I am not bad at honesty, because it involves telling people about issues that are normally past and sorted—"I really struggled last week," implying that I'm not struggling any longer. It keeps people at arm's length. Vulnerability allows people into the issues I am struggling with now, and asking for help to get through them.

Recently I faced one of those days when it wasn't possible to do everything that needed to be done. As the morning hours ticked by, a rising sense of panic was making it harder to concentrate on what I was doing. Usually I would soldier on, but for once I stopped, went over to two of my colleagues and said, "I am not going to get through today. I feel overwhelmed with all that needs to be done. Would you please pray for me." They were a little surprised, but willingly prayed for me. It changed the day, and it changed the dynamic of my relationship with them. If the team leader could ask for help, so could they.

I hear so many leaders talk about the isolation and loneliness of leadership, and of course there is a real truth in that, but sometimes we make it worse for ourselves by not being vulnerable and allowing people in.

Be proactive in preparing for the worst

It may well happen. We get a decision completely wrong with horrendous consequences, and someone leaks it to the press. We act inappropriately towards another person, and someone accuses us of sexual abuse. We lose our temper publicly, and someone writes to the boss. One day it might just be us.

We can prepare by talking with those in leadership about what will happen when it all goes wrong, and agreeing a process that will carry us through a crisis, so that people don't simply react in panic but instead respond with prepared wisdom. As a charity, the organization I work for has to make "risk assessment." We need to do that as leaders as well.

A good friend of mine, Carson Pue,[6] who heads up the Arrow Leadership Program in North America, told me of an occasion when it all fell apart for him. He was accused of sexual misconduct. The church where he was a minister at the time handled it in perhaps the best way they knew how, but the denomination had no agreed way of handling such an accusation. As a result it was an excruciatingly difficult process. The lessons he learned through the experience are outlined below.

- Clarify roles. Who is responsible for doing what in a crisis?
- Establish boundaries. Who is allowed to do what in a crisis?
- Work out guidelines. What is the process for dealing with a crisis?
- Recognize that you can't rush the process. It will take time.
- Establish accountability relationships as a principle of life.
- Be more committed to people than yourself or your church's or organization's image.
- Identify the people you can talk to during a crisis, so that no one is isolated.
- Cut out idle chatter and always go direct to the person involved in the crisis.
- If any party has children, be honest with them and answer their questions. Don't keep them in the dark. Connect them with other close adults who can be stable for them when everything is falling apart for you.
- Take a "grace" stance rather than a legal stance (1 Corinthians 6).
- Respect the "power disparity." As a leader you have power: be aware of what you say, how you say it, and how you act.
- In an organizational context, "boards" or "councils" may not handle a crisis well because they are not set up to do it and are often too distant to be effective. Therefore, agree to a crisis management plan that utilizes an outside source.

- Create clearly stated procedures for a crisis, write them down and give everyone who needs one a copy. It helps create some objectivity.

Because of his advice, we have established an agreed and owned process for handling crisis. I hope we will never have to use it, but if we do, at least we've thought about what we will do, calmly and clearly.

Be proactive in preventing the worst excesses of our character flaws

All of us face the danger of succumbing to temptation. Billy Graham agreed a covenant with his close colleagues at the start of the Billy Graham Organization, that none of them would travel alone in a car with a person of the opposite sex (other than their family members).[7] Today this sounds rather quaint, but it has stood the test of time. What can we do to ensure that we don't put ourselves in a place where our character flaws could cause damage?

Our character will always be flawed this side of heaven. The six points above may help us to lead well, so that we are safe to follow, but we won't lead perfectly. It is good to remember Peter. Here is a man for whom everything went horribly wrong. He fled Jesus' side at the arrest, denied he knew Jesus three times, and ran from the courtyard abandoning Jesus into the hands of his enemy (Mark 14:50, 66–72). Yet Jesus went on loving him and, after the resurrection, in one of the most poignant encounters of the Gospels, he lovingly restores him. Jesus doesn't even ask if he is sorry, he simply wants to know whether Simon loves him. And as he hears Simon's response, "Yes Lord, you know that I love you" (John 21:15–19), Jesus commissions him to fulfill his calling, to be the rock on whom he will build his church (Matthew 16:18).

That same forgiveness and restoration is on offer to us every time our character lets God down. It is also good to remember King David, and the other fallible leaders of the Bible, who discover a God who forgives and restores. We are in good company if we know we're flawed. God is not surprised by anything we might do, and he longs to forgive and restore us.

As we saw earlier, however, he also wants to transform us more and more into the image of his Son. A colleague tells the story of a friend traveling in India who met a silversmith. As he watched the craftsman work, he asked him why he sat when he purified the silver. The silversmith replied, "Because I can get close enough to my work to see the impurities." The friend then asked, "And how do you know when it is purified?" "When I can see my face in it." What might the face of the Creator look like in our lives as he refines us to be more like him?

MARKS OF A GODLY LEADER'S CHARACTER

I want to end this chapter with a brief consideration of some of the aspects of Jesus' character that we are called to emulate.[8] They are listed not to depress us but to inspire us and fill us with hope, for this is what the Spirit is transforming us into.

Jesus, a man of love, looks for leaders of love

God is love, and showed his love for us in that while we were still sinners he sent his Son as "an atoning sacrifice for our sins" (I John 4:8–12). His love is for the whole world, and one of the primary ways he can show that love is through his body, the Church. Perhaps the single greatest character trait to ask God for is love for people—costly, self-sacrificial, generous love. As Paul writes, "Do everything in love" (I Corinthians 16:14).

Jesus, a man of integrity, looks for leaders of integrity

Jesus was "tempted in every way, just as we are—yet was without sin" (Hebrews 4:15). Integrity exists when habits are congruent with values, deeds are consistent with words, and expressions are in harmony with feelings. The most attractive people I meet are old people who have spent their lives following Jesus, being transformed by him, and whose lives are so integrated that you sense Jesus at the very core of their being.

Jesus, a man who served, looks for leaders with servant hearts

Jesus constantly surprised his disciples by his willingness to go against all the customs of the day and serve, most clearly demonstrated in his willingness to wash their grubby feet, which was a portrayal of his entire life of servanthood. "For even the Son of Man did not come to be served, but to serve, and to give his life as a ransom for many" (Mark 10:45).[9] The goal of the Christian leader is to be a servant of all. When we allow the desire to become a leader to be our focus, "servant-heartedness" quickly diminishes.

Jesus, a man of compassion, looks for leaders of compassion

Jesus was no emotionally repressed, stiff upper lipped Englishman. He was a man of passion, and huge compassion. He wept over the death of a close friend (John 11:35), "his heart went out" to the grieving widow who lost her only child (Luke 7:11–17), he stopped a crowd for the sake of one despised blind man begging at the side of the road (Luke 18:35–43). Leadership needs to be characterized by compassion, an ability to embrace the tragedies and sinfulness of people's lives, to weep with those who weep, to suffer with them without the need to "fix them."

Jesus, a man of truth, looks for leaders of truth

Jesus commands, "Let your 'Yes' be 'Yes,' and your 'No,' 'No'" (Matthew 5:37). In a world where spin is commonplace and where the credibility of leaders is low, truthfulness in all circumstances is a rare virtue. Yet as followers of the one who is truth, we should be marked by our willingness to speak the truth, to avoid exaggeration, "white lies," half-truths and gossip.

Jesus, a man of faith, looks for faithful leaders

Jesus consistently obeyed his Father's commands, only seeking to do what he saw his Father doing. He was faithful to the end as he uttered, "Not what I will, but what you will" (Mark 14:36). If we are to be faithful leaders, we will need to hear God's commands and obey them. "Now it is required that those who have been given a trust must prove faithful" (I Corinthians 4:2).[10] Such faithfulness will involve sacrifice. It did for Jesus and it will for us. Hard work and sacrifice are part of Christian leadership.

Jesus, a man of forgiveness, looks for forgiving leaders

I leave this until last deliberately, because unforgiveness is such a problem within society, and among those in leadership within the Church. I don't think anyone in leadership avoids hurt, and the temptation to harbor hurt, nurture anger and build defenses is great. Jesus forgives, and asks us to forgive as well. Most of us are familiar with the phrase from the Lord's prayer, "Forgive us our sins as we forgive those who sin against us." What we may not know so well are the tough words that follow just a few verses later. "For if you forgive people when they sin against you, your heavenly Father will also forgive you. But if you do not forgive people their sins, your Father will not forgive your sins" (Matthew 6:14–15; see also 18:21–35). Unforgiveness is not an option. Not only will it destroy our character, eating away like a cancer, but it will also destroy our relationship with our Father. We cannot avoid forgiveness as one of the crucial marks of a godly leader.[11]

To meditate on Jesus is one of the privileges of Christian leadership, and the more we meditate on him, allowing his Spirit to dwell within us bringing about change, the more we'll be captivated by his flawless character, and see his refining work purifying us to become just a touch more like him.

CHARACTER BEFORE COMPETENCE

People are longing for leaders of godly character. In his introduction to the 1994 version of his book *On Becoming a Leader*, Warren

Bennis suggests that, in the light of the seismic changes in the world, "followers need from their leaders three basic qualities: they want direction; they want trust; and they want hope."[12] He argues that the "trust factor" is the most pivotal of the three, and that trust is like a tripod where one leg is ambition, another competence, and the third is integrity. He comments, "I've seen too many leaders who have that formidable combination of competence and ambition but lack integrity and they succeed only in the short term, if that. I call them 'destructive achievers' and they are dangerous."[13] How do we avoid the wobbly tripod? How do we become leaders of godly character, of integrity? That's the thrust of the next chapter.

FOR REFLECTION

- Meditate on Jesus' life through one of the Gospels, or select one encounter there. What one aspect of his character do I sense that God is longing to form in me?
- If there is unforgiveness in my life, what am I going to do to resolve it?
- Who could I ask to give me some honest feedback on my character?

RANVIR (25), CHILDREN'S LEADER,
SITTING IN A RETREAT HOUSE CHAPEL

9:15 am. I've made it. And now I'm here, I'm not sure what to do. It's a beautiful place. The sun is out and it's all so quiet and green here. Makes a change from home. A whole day to spend with God on my own without any distractions. The difficulty will be switching off from all the things I need to do back at the church.

11:30 am. I've been reading 2 Peter 1 and I'm challenged by the need to grow some of the qualities he mentions in my life. At the conference last week, one of the speakers mentioned the importance of being a "safe person to follow," and it struck home. Am I a safe person to follow? What if the kids I lead model themselves on me? What are the qualities they are going to pick up? I know I lack self-control, and can easily lose it with one of them when they are playing up, which is most of the time. I can't blame them, given some of the home situations they come from, but how I respond to them when they attend the after-school club is my responsibility. Lord, please forgive me.

3:30 pm. I fell asleep after lunch! The only way I could keep awake was to go for a walk. I think I need to give some time to this process of change that Peter outlines. The last few years have been great for learning more skills in working with children, but what I really need to do is grow my character so I reflect Jesus more clearly in the way that I lead. I don't think that is going to be easy, but I do want to be a safe person to follow, and I know that means change. Lord, please help me to become more like you. And how about showing me how that can happen?

Chapter 7

GODLY CHANGE

Everybody thinks of changing humanity and nobody
thinks of changing themselves.

LEO TOLSTOY

Given a choice, will we follow a highly competent leader whom we don't trust, or a less competent leader whom we trust implicitly? I know my answer. That's why character development is so important, yet growing in godly, mature character is not easy. In this chapter I want to reflect on four things that have helped me as a leader who longs to become more Christ-like. Then, to end this section on developing Christ-like character, we'll consider some insights from 2 Peter 1:1–11.

THE LOST ART OF REFLECTION

Apparently, Socrates said, "The unexamined life is not worth living." An unreflective life is often an uncritical life that leads to little change. Part of the psyche of English people is that we seem fairly poor at reflection. Perhaps it is connected with that wonderful English reserve—not wanting to think too much of ourselves or promote ourselves above others. Certainly when I travel and work in the United States, I find fewer of these inhibitions when it comes to self-reflection.

Without a critical approach to life, there is little change. This is true for a society as a whole. Someone had to stand up and criticize slavery before it was eventually abolished in England. It is also true for character development. People rarely change for the better without healthy reflection, but they do change for the worse. "No change" is rarely an option. If we don't grow, we normally shrivel. Change is going to occur, and the real question is whether we are going to allow it just to happen, or whether we are going to play our part in allowing the Holy Spirit to direct his change in us.

Such reflection is not about an unhealthy introspection, self-absorption or in-depth self-analysis. It is a means of being open to the Holy Spirit as he convicts us of sin and gives greater self-awareness. It is not about self-reformation, but Christ-transformation.

Two strands of the biblical tradition encourage us to a life of reflection more than any other—the Psalms and the Wisdom literature. The Psalms are primarily songs reflecting on living life as the people of God in the world. They offer us a number of models for reflection, through meditation on the scriptures (for example, Psalm 119), through meditation on life (for example, Psalm 77:12), and through taking time out (for example, Psalm 37:7). The Wisdom literature also points us to the role of close relationships in aiding personal development (Proverbs 27:6, 9; Ecclesiastes 4:10). Each of these can lead to godly change.

Godly change through meditation on the scriptures

"How can a young person keep their way pure? By living according to your word" (Psalm 119:9). The scriptures provide us with a looking glass to see ourselves, and what may need to change in our lives, in the light of God's revelation. Many of us have had the experience of God's word cutting deeper than any two-edged sword. Sadly, however, just as it is easy to stop praying in any structured way, so too it is easy to stop meditating on God's word. Personal Bible study is restricted to what we need to do for talk or sermon preparation, and is often focused on what we can get out of the text, rather than allowing the text to get into us. Group Bible study is hampered by the pooling of ignorance, and is often used to buttress already held views. Public study of the Bible is limited to ten minutes on a Sunday, and is often little more than a blessed thought. I caricature, but there is truth within the caricature.

As Christian leaders, we need to ponder, meditate upon, and pray over the Bible not simply for things we are going to do, but as a way of developing intimacy with God and allowing him to mould us ever more into the likeness of Jesus. I once heard that the root of the Hebrew word for "meditate" is the same as the word used for a cow chewing the cud. I like that image. We take time to chew the same bit over and over again, coming back to it to extract every bit of goodness from it. Psalm 119 encourages us to "chew" in a variety of ways. We hide his word in our hearts that we may not sin against God (v. 11), we ask him to open our eyes so that we may see wonderful things in his word (v. 18), we bring to him our weary soul and seek strength through his word (v. 28), we find delight in obeying his commands (v. 35), and we turn our eyes from worthless things, discovering our life is preserved by his word (v. 37). Without such reflection, our horizon shrinks to the limits of our own understanding. Through such reflection our eyes are raised, our hearts are warmed, our hurts are healed, our troubles are comforted, our sin is revealed and our character is changed.

Godly change through reflecting on life

The Psalms in themselves reflect on life. They are a record of the insights of God's people through personal and corporate experiences, helping them to find meaning and orientation. They are brutally honest, full of very human emotion and a great encouragement for those of us looking for godly change.

Drawing on this tradition, throughout Christian history, people have found ways to reflect on life through song writing, poetry, painting, and journaling. Not being very artistic, the method I've found most accessible to me is using a journal to help prayerful reflection.

A journal isn't primarily a diary of events, but rather a personal tool to aid reflection. Through journaling we monitor what is going on in our lives. Like all tools, it helps to find the one that best fits our purposes. I keep a journal on a daily basis, but others do it weekly or monthly, or when they have their quiet days. I write mine by hand in a spiral unlined notebook with occasional sketches, poems and prayers. Others use their computer and create a template to fill in each time they journal, write poetry and songs, work with PowerPoint, or sketch. I have a series of questions that help me to reflect; other people simply download whatever comes to mind. I like to keep my journal private; others share it with those close to them.

Here are some suggestions of what to cover in a journal:

- A personal record of what I've done—people I met, decisions I made, how I used my time, how I served people and fulfilled my personal life statement.
- Self-reflection on my mood, attitudes, feelings, health, stress, dreams—what I've thought and felt, the highs and lows of the day, ways I've experienced change within myself.
- A record of spiritual experiences—ways I've been aware of God's presence, and what these experiences might mean.
- Working through relational issues—how to engage with a particular person, why I struggle in particular relationships, coming to terms with a bereavement.
- Saying things to God—hopes, longings, dreams, worries, fears.
- Pondering problems—decisions I'm concerned about, discerning God's perspective on life and seeking his will for the future.

Looking back over the years, I've spotted patterns of unhealthy living that needed to be changed, encouraging signs of where change has taken place, particular things that cause me to react badly in certain situations, and incredible ways I've seen God at work. To this day I am grateful that, soon after I came to Christ as a teenager, someone suggested I wrote down my experience while it was fresh. Occasionally I read this account, and am reminded of the joy of discovering God's existence and his love for me. Now I can read back on nearly thirty years of following Jesus and be thankful for what he has done. I may not yet be what he longs for me to be, but I am certainly not what I used to be.

I also use the following four questions to help me discern where God might be leading me at any point in time.[1]

- What is the next step in my relationship with God?
- What is the next step in the development of my character?
- What is the next step in my family life?
- What is the next step in my work?

Reflection through meditation on life has been a great way to see where God might want to bring change, and journaling is one tool to do this.

Godly change through taking time out

Taking time to be with God is a priority for any leader. Sadly, in the busyness of ministry this easily gets squeezed out. Time each day is vital, but many also find that practicing the spiritual disciplines of solitude and silence is a helpful way to maintain a vibrant relationship with Jesus. "Chunky time" with God, as one friend calls it, is about unpressured time to be, to reflect, to leave behind other more pressing demands and pay attention to God. The following guidelines are offered in the hope that they may provide some insights into how to use a day set aside to be with God. There are many ways of doing this, and many resources available to help but, as with prayer, the most important thing is to do it.

How often? For most people, establishing a regular pattern is a real help. This may involve taking a quiet day once a month, every six weeks, every two months, three times a year. The key is to establish the pattern, put it in the diary, and stick to it. Be warned, there will always be a hundred good reasons why we haven't got time to take our quiet day.

Where to go? It's important to find somewhere that helps us relax, be still and be quiet—a retreat house, a friend's home if they are not using it during the day, or a particular spot of natural beauty (although ideally we need a place we can use in all seasons). It helps if it is relatively nearby so that we don't spend the whole day traveling.

How long? This will depend on our personal circumstances. Some find it helpful to go away the previous evening to relax and unwind before the day. Others go for the day itself. It helps if we make sure that we don't have any work planned into our diary for the evening of that day, and preferably nothing major planned for the next day, otherwise we spend the whole time with our mind on what we've got to do.

What do we do? Be clear about the purpose of the day. A quiet day set aside to spend time with God is different from a prayer day or a study day. A prayer day is important, but normally involves us going with a set idea of what we want to do—for example, to pray specifically for some aspect of our life or ministry. Nor is it a study day where we take loads of books to learn more about God or the work we're doing. The whole focus of a quiet day set aside to be with God is simply to meet with him, and in that sense we allow God to set the agenda. It is a day of abandoning ourselves into his hands. We are saying, "Here I am, Lord. Please meet with me in whatever way you think fit."

How can we best prepare? I try to make sure I don't enter the day exhausted. I get a good nights' sleep and identify what I'm going to do over days and weeks leading up to it. Before the day, it helps to have a clear outline in my mind of Bible passages I might read. I also ask other people to pray for the day, that I meet with God afresh. The night before, I offer myself to God in prayer, handing over the day to him and asking for his blessing.

How might such a day be shaped? This is, of course, entirely up to each individual. It helps if we don't overfill the day, and allow space for relaxation and something recreational. Here is the pattern that I currently use.

What do we do if the day is a real struggle? We need to recognize that by placing ourselves entirely in God's hands we cannot govern the outcome of the day. Just because we have set aside a day to be spent in quiet with God, it won't necessarily be a spiritual high. That is why this is a discipline. God may well decide to hold

9–9:15 I take time to be still by acknowledging God's presence, offering myself to him, and writing down any matters that come crowding in that need noting but are not part of this day.

9:15–10:00 I read a predetermined passage of scripture in a meditative way (I've found the *Lectio Divina* method pioneered by Ignatius really helpful).[2] The aim of this time is not to prepare my next sermon or talk, but to ask God to meet with me and speak to me through his word.

10:00–10:30 I journal on the meditation, reflecting on what God has said. I use some of the questions outlined in the journaling section above. During this review I thank God for his favors and ask forgiveness for sin, and throughout I ponder what God may want me to do in response to what he is saying.

10:30–11:30 I try to do something relaxing or creative. I might go for a slow walk, taking notice of creation and expecting God to speak to me through it. I might paint (absolutely hopeless), write poetry (even worse), compose a song, make something, write a psalm or take photographs. (Find a way that works for you of being creative, expressing something of what is in you to God, or allowing him to continue to feed you.)

11:45–12:15 I meditate on my second predetermined passage.

12:15–12:45 I journal on my meditation.

12:45–1:45 I have lunch or, if I am fasting, pray for the disadvantaged of the world.

1:45–2:15 At this point I often take a nap! Alternatively I get some gentle exercise.

2:15–3:30 I meditate on a third predetermined passage.

3:30–4:00 I journal on my meditation and on the day as a whole, perhaps asking, "What do I sense God has been saying to me through this day? What might I need to do as a result of this day? How might I shape my daily life as a result of this day?"

4:00 The day ends. If at all possible, I do something I really enjoy in the evening, for example go to see a movie, have a meal out with someone I love, go bowling, go to a concert—basically have fun.

himself back because there are issues he wants us to grapple with. Quite often I find that my quiet days are not much more than hard work. That is why it is really important prayerfully to plan the day in advance and then stick to it, not allowing our feelings or tiredness to govern the agenda. It can also be really helpful to have a wise and godly spiritual director with whom we meet two or three times a year to talk through our spiritual life, and perhaps share something of what happens on our quiet days.

Where can we find out more? Older, wiser Christians often have insights from their own experience worth sharing. Of greatest use may be those outside our own spiritual tradition. We won't agree with everything they say, but we will gain valuable insights into how to spend time with God. I've also listed some books in the endnotes that may be helpful.[3]

Taking time out is not a luxury but a necessity in the fast-moving pace of life today. The style of life in Jesus' day meant that space was much more naturally built into an ordinary day. It took time to travel from one side of Palestine to the other. The walks afforded opportunities for quiet as well as time with people. Even so, Jesus still took "chunky time" with God. Many Christian leaders may not be able to make it away for a whole day because of personal reasons, in which case finding an hour or a morning/

afternoon/evening is an alternative. One of the ways we can support one another is to take on other people's responsibilities to enable them to take time out. As leaders, we can model servanthood by caring for someone else's kids to give them time out.

Godly change through relationships

Proverbs 27:6 says, "The kisses of an enemy may be profuse, but faithful are the wounds of a friend." Good friends are prepared to tell us the hard truths about us that we'd prefer not to hear, yet Christian leaders regularly find themselves without such close relationships. This can be a particular struggle for those who are single. Inappropriate expectations about single people in leadership heighten the problem. Some people seem to think that an unmarried leader has nothing else to do with their time, and expect them to give every moment of every day to the job. Single people need close relationships too, and may have to fight even harder to maintain them.

For those who are married, a close relationship with our partner will bring support and self-awareness. I thought I was a reasonably nice person until I got married! So much godly change has come through the inevitable closeness of Sophie and her ability to strengthen and support me through difficult things that I didn't want to face about myself. The kids are pretty good at that as well. I often ask them to pray for something I am struggling with, and regularly need to ask their forgiveness for how I've acted towards them. God uses these closest relationships to bring change in me.

It also helps if married people develop close relationships outside their marriage. Friends nurture us, encourage us and provide us with perspective, and sometimes we need that for our marriage. I have a great friend, called Rob. We've known each other for years, and although our friendship was initially strong and close, we drifted apart through the busyness of life and it became weak and distant, until eight years ago. I realized that my busyness meant I didn't take time to nurture friendships. Rob and I agreed to meet a couple of times a year just to be with one another and talk about deep things. In a sense, we formalized our friendship. We continue to meet outside these times as two families, for fun and holidays, but we meet to develop our friendship in this particular way. Alongside my wife, Rob knows me better than anyone else in the world. He is a best friend.

We also have friends we regularly go away on holiday with, friends we share as a couple, and friends we individually relate to. All of these close relationships help to provide perspective on my life. Author and satirist Mike Yaconelli, reflecting on his own life, concluded, "If we are too busy to have friends, we are much too busy."[4]

One way of proactively developing close relationships is through small cell groups. Ten years ago I read a helpful book by church leader Gordon MacDonald. In *Renewing Your Spiritual Passion,* he speaks of gathering around you a team of people. I remember thinking that if I was to get through the next thirty years of ministry, I needed to think about that, so I invited three other men to discuss the possibility of meeting regularly to hold ourselves accountable to one another. I didn't really know any of them that well, but I knew enough about them to see that we shared a similar concern, and were of a similar age. One of them suggested another man, so we met as five men in our early 30s. Four of us were married, one single. Three had children, two didn't. Three were based in local churches, two had a more itinerant ministry. Over the last ten years we've laughed and cried together. Meeting with them four times a year has kept me going, kept me faithful to Jesus, and given me a place to be real.

Such cell groups can be of likeminded people, or people who are very different in age, background and life experience. For them to work, everyone must be committed to developing close relationships and clear about the purpose of meeting. The following guidelines are drawn from the experience of establishing my peer group, and also the experience of establishing peer cells for the Arrow Leadership Program.

- *Getting started:* Identify the people you'd like to meet with, and then ask them all to an initial meeting with no further commitment, explaining what you are hoping to do. At that meeting, address some of the issues outlined below, and allow people time to reflect on whether they would like to be a part of the group. If it doesn't work out with this group, seek another group and keep trying. It is worth it.
- *Be clear about the aim:* When groups go wrong, it's normally because people come with different aims and expectations and the group never clarifies why it is meeting and what it intends to provide. Once you've identified your aim, and the way you are going to address some of the issues below, you may even consider drawing up an agreement or covenant.
- *Size of group:* This should be ideally between three and six. This enables the maximum amount of interaction without being so small that one person's absence from a meeting renders the group inoperable.
- *Frequency of meeting:* This will depend largely on your aim, and where the members live. A minimum of twice a year and a maximum of six are good parameters, although if you are meeting for a very focused reason you may need to meet more often.
- *Commitment or chemistry:* A good peer support group does not have to be made up of people who already know each other well; nor does it depend on close friendships developing. Commitment to one another is vital, and being clear about what that commitment means. Chemistry does play a part, however, for if you struggle to have fun and be relaxed with one another it will restrict the effectiveness of the group.
- *Confidentiality:* Agree what you mean by confidentiality. Be clear about whether things shared in the group can be shared with anyone else at all, for example, spouses.
- *Format:* Identify a clear format for your meetings. In many ways it doesn't matter what this is, as long as it is agreed by everyone and people's expectations are clear.
- *Leadership:* It might help to have someone "lead" the meetings— to be responsible for coordination of venue, time and so on,

and for guiding the day together. This responsibility can be shared around the group, perhaps each person doing it for a year.

- *Maintaining contact:* Identify what level of contact you want between meetings. There is no right answer; you simply need to be sure about expectations.

Once the cell is established, the following guidelines may help people contribute to the life of the cell in the most beneficial way.

- *Be honest.* It is amazing how easy it is to hide, even within a group designed to help us talk about the real "me." No one will force anything out of you, so choose to be honest.
- *Be vulnerable.* There is always the danger of being hurt when we are vulnerable, but the benefits are extraordinary.
- *Be committed.* Everyone in the cell is likely to be a busy person, and there will always be the temptation to cry off from the meeting because of busyness. *Don't.* The cell will work best when everyone is committed to attending.
- *Be prayerful.* Try to pray regularly for the other members of your cell.
- *Be aware.* Most groups go through an initial period when all seems well, and then hit some difficulties. Working through these can be one of the great lessons of the cell. After some years, the setup will need revising, and occasionally someone may decide to move on from the group. Reviewing the cell's life and recommitting to the next phase of its life is part of the ebb and flow of any group.
- *Be caring.* Look out for the needs of one another—practical, emotional, physical, spiritual. Be prepared to go the extra mile.

Close relationships bring useful insights into who we are and how God may be at work in our lives. I also want to affirm an obvious truth here: relationships are to be enjoyed. They are not all about hard intense work, but we do need to recognize their place in helping to bring about godly change.

Does a leader who reflects in these ways ever have time to work? Some people could spend all their time in unhealthy self-reflection, but my experience is that most leaders spend far too little time in reflection. That is one of the reasons why many leaders see little change in their character; all too quickly they enter the red zone, and all too easily lose their first love.

One way of encouraging myself to keep going is by looking at those who are changed by God in the Bible, so I want to end this chapter with a brief look at Peter and the change God brought in his life.

FROM SIMON TO PETER: A CASE STUDY IN CHANGE (2 PETER 1)

2 Peter 1 begins with the words, "Simon Peter, a servant and apostle of Jesus Christ" (v. 1). The man who knew what it was to fail writes this letter. Jesus may have renamed Simon "Peter," but he was anything but a rock at the crucial moment when Jesus needed him to be firm—denying Jesus three times. Wonderfully reinstated by Jesus after his resurrection (John 21), Peter goes on to lead the early Church. His own character development was a painful path, but it led him to godliness. There are five insights in this passage that have helped me reflect on my own growth.

Know who we are: Peter's acknowledgment of who he is—"a servant and apostle of Jesus Christ"—is a wonderful combination of his primary and secondary calling. He also affirms his readers in their relationship with Jesus, acknowledging the initiative of God in establishing this relationship: "To those who through the righteousness of our God and Savior Jesus Christ have received a faith as precious as ours" (v. 1). All growth in character is dependent on this starting point—knowing who we are in relationship with Christ.

Receive God's power: Incredibly, "his divine power has given us everything we need for life and godliness through our knowledge of him who called us by his own glory and goodness" (v. 3). This is great news indeed: God in his grace has given us *everything* we need for life and godliness. There is no shortfall, where somehow God's power runs out and we need to supplement it from our own meager store. Everything we need for life and godliness is supplied by God. Therefore, change is not primarily something we do, but someone we receive. It is all God's initiative. He invites us to stay close to him and receive his power.

Accept God's promises: God has given us his "very great and precious promises, so that through them you may participate in the divine nature and escape the corruption in the world caused by evil desires" (v. 4). At times when we are overwhelmed by the cynicism of the world, or bitterly disappointed by someone letting us down, or struggling to believe we can really change, this verse offers hope. Through God's promises we participate in the divine nature. God brings profound change as he turns us into the likeness of his son Jesus. This change involves escape from one thing (corruption in the world) and participation in another (the divine nature). It is complete and total.

Hold on to God's priorities: "For this reason, make every effort to add to your faith . . ." (vv. 5–9). God does the work of transformation in our lives, and we then have a part to play in growing Christ-likeness. We are to play our part with vigor, determination and diligence. These qualities are not mass-produced at great speed, but handcrafted over time, requiring great effort. God is not interested in surface change but in deep, lasting change. "Faith" is a given (see v. 1), but all the rest can be added to it— goodness (or virtue), knowledge, self-control, perseverance, godliness, kindness, love. The challenge comes in verse 8: "For if you possess these qualities in increasing measure, they will keep you from being ineffective and unproductive in your knowledge of our Lord Jesus Christ." What struck me when I read this verse was the *possibility* of being ineffective and unproductive. We may know Christ and yet not grow in that knowledge. Verse 9 confirms this: "But if anyone does not have them, they are shortsighted and blind, and have forgotten that they have been cleansed from past sins." These qualities are a priority, and we need to make every effort to add them to the faith already given us. How? Through spiritual disciplines, through reflection, through determined effort, all of which help us to grow in Christ-likeness.

Relish God's welcome: In calling us to "be all the more eager to make your calling and election sure" (v. 10) Peter reminds us of what is to come: "For if you do these things, you will never fall, and you will receive a rich welcome into the eternal kingdom of our Lord and Savior Jesus Christ" (vv. 10–11). What an incentive! When I've been away for a while, I relish coming home. I know that, as soon as I put my key in the lock of the front door, three lots of ears prick up. As I swing open the door, six little legs begin running in my direction. As I close the door behind me, three bodies launch themselves at me, and three voices say, "Welcome home, Dad." Yet even this wonderful welcome will pale in comparison to the welcome that awaits us in heaven. If we want to make sure of our election and calling, if we want to prevent ourselves from falling, if we want the rich embrace of Jesus himself, remember these things, says Peter (vv. 12–15).

Peter knew what it was to fail Jesus. He also knew Jesus' incredible forgiveness and restoration. Peter worked on these qualities, and urges us to do the same. Growing leaders develop Christ-like character, and for this to happen growing leaders lead themselves—the subject of our next chapter.

FOR REFLECTION

- What does it mean for me to know that one day God will welcome me into his heaven?
- Of the four areas (meditation on the Bible, reflecting on life, taking time out, developing key relationships), which one might I give attention to at this time? How am I going to do that?
- What godly change do I sense God may want to bring into my life at this time?

PART FIVE

GROWING LEADERS CULTIVATE COMPETENCE

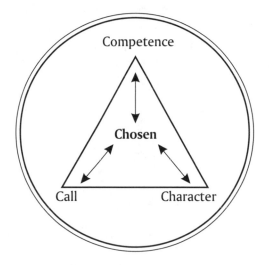

In Part Five, we consider four essential competencies of leadership. If leaders don't first lead themselves and those closest to them, they have limited authority to lead others; if leaders don't embody their stated values, they lack integrity; if leaders don't discern, articulate and implement vision, no one will know where they are going or how to get there; and if leaders don't develop people, they will leave no one behind able to carry on after them. All of these are built on the previous parts of the model and are intimately related to them.

JUDE (11), IN HER DIARY

Dad, you are so brilliant. NOT. He did it AGAIN. He promised mom he'd be back in time to take us to the movies, and he was late. We only just made it, and mom was all upset. I don't know why he has to work so hard. I know Jesus is really important, and it's good if more people get to know about him, but why does my dad have to spend all his time working for Jesus at the church—and like thirty seconds a week with us? Not fair. He keeps saying sorry, but things don't seem to change. I think that's why mom is fed up. I caught her crying the other day. It makes me sad. Hey Jesus, how about sharing Dad with us? We like him too.

Chapter 8

LEADERS LEAD THEMSELVES AND THOSE CLOSEST TO THEM

*Self-leadership. Nobody—I mean nobody—can do
this work for us. Every leader has to do this work
alone, and it isn't easy. In fact, because it's such tough
work most leaders avoid it. We would rather try to
inspire or control the behavior of others than face the
rigorous work of self-reflection and inner growth.*

BILL HYBELS[1]

Mention the word "leader" and what pictures come to mind? Images of commanders leading their troops into battle, politicians leading their people through turbulent times, heroes leading their followers out of danger may fill the imagination. Christians may also think of Moses leading the people out of Egypt, David leading the people into battle, and Nehemiah leading the rebuilding of Jerusalem. But we cannot allow this to be our first thought. So eject the videotapes, and let's play a different series of images, for surely the pastoral epistles, and much of the New Testament, remind us that leaders must first lead themselves, then those closest to them, before they lead others. A reporter once asked evangelist and minister D.L. Moody which people gave him the most trouble. He answered immediately, "I've had more trouble with D.L. Moody than any person alive."[2]

In the excitement of what God is doing, the pressure of busyness and the tiredness of over-activity, we often give least attention to leadership of ourselves and those closest to us. Surely that is why Paul strongly encourages Timothy to pay attention to these things, and that is why the first two leadership competencies continue our exploration of character-related issues.

LEADING OURSELVES

In writing to Timothy, Paul urges him, "Watch your life and doctrine closely. Persevere in them, because if you do, you will save both yourself and your hearers" (1 Timothy 4:16). This isn't just about a concern to save ourselves, it is about honoring our hearers—those we lead.

Earlier in the letter, Paul gives advice to Timothy about what to look for in potential leaders (1 Timothy 3:1–13). This list is an excellent starting place for anyone who wants to do a leadership check-up, for we need to steer ourselves through these areas to avoid succumbing to tricky and subtle temptations. Whole books are written on most of these subjects, so in a few paragraphs I can't go into great detail. Instead, my aim is to allow this part of the Bible to remind us of those areas where we're called to lead ourselves and, where necessary, to prick our conscience so that we might be reminded of where God may want us to change. In the endnotes, I've listed further resources in case you'd like to explore any area in greater detail.

Above reproach

The word "reproach" (v. 2) means "blame, rebuke or censure." If a person is "above reproach," there is nothing in his or her life that an enemy can seize upon to attack or condemn. The thrust of the word used here is in the present: it is about how we are living *now*. Are we above approach? Is there currently anything in our life that our local newspaper could use as a headline to scandalize our community? Experience of working with leaders tells me that, more often than we might expect, the answer to this question is "yes." Hidden skeletons are often unknown by anyone other than the person concerned, and they live in daily fear of someone finding out. What can we do if we are in that position? We can tell someone.[3] Part of the power of hidden skeletons is in the enemy's ability to twist around them deceit, lies and isolation. Naturally we need to be wise about whom we tell, but someone needs to know, and help us work out what to do. I cannot emphasize this too strongly.

Many excellent leaders have something hidden, believing they can handle it on their own, and then one day someone finds out. The scandal that ensues not only damages or even destroys the leader, but it damages relationships, Christian communities and the name of Christ. Battling on alone is not a safe option. However large or small the issue might be, finding someone we trust and finding a way forward is crucial. Sometimes, in extreme cases, this may mean that a leader steps down from their position to work matters through. Better that, though, than bringing disrepute to the name of Christ and damage to those we care about most. Normally, however, it involves receiving the wise advice of a Christian friend, colleague or counselor, and placing ourselves in a safe place of care and accountability.

The husband of but one wife

Much has been written about this controversial phrase from verse 2. Some argue that it clearly shows that Christian leaders must be men, married and not divorcés. Others argue that Paul is writing to Timothy about the church in Ephesus, where his instructions are for a specific situation of breakdown in the normative leadership practices of the New Testament.[4] My own position is that whatever we think this verse is saying, we must be faithful to it in its entirety and not just selectively. Therefore, to say that it prevents women from being overseers within the church, without also excluding single men, is not an option.

Given the presence of polygamy in his society, Paul's injunction is literally to be a "one-woman man." Are we utterly faithful to our spouse, not just in deed but also in thought and word? How are we handling adulterous thoughts, affairs in the mind, lustful behavior, inappropriate flirting and pornography? I know few men who don't struggle with some of these aspects. I've also learned that they are a struggle for many women as well. Here is another crucial area in which we need to lead ourselves, rather than filling our minds with thoughts that will lead us astray.

For most people, this will mean taking our thought patterns captive, being transformed by the renewing of our mind (Romans 12:2), and not allowing ourselves to indulge in inappropriate thinking. I've found it helpful to identify when I am most likely to be tempted, and build in extra safeguards at those times. I am particularly susceptible when I am tired, immediately after a "ministry high," and when I am away from home. One friend I know always removes the aerial cable from the television if he is staying in a hotel room alone, and places it in his car until he departs. I've also found it helpful to tell my closest friend, Rob, about the biggest struggles I have in this area, and ask him to hold me accountable. Just knowing that someone else knows is often enough to stop me doing anything foolish. But I recognize that, for some, this area is one of great concern and difficulty, and that addiction to certain things is a hard habit to break. That's when we may need professional help, as well as the loving support of those closest to us.[5]

I want to be faithful to my spouse, so I will have to exercise leadership over myself in this area.

Temperate

This word means to fast or abstain from eating, and here (v. 2) refers to leaders who are able to control themselves when eating. In our food-addicted culture, with the increasing number of food-related problems,[6] it is vital that we lead ourselves well. This not only benefits our personal health and well-being, but also ensures we don't become gluttons and helps us to take seriously our response to Third World poverty.

It is about both what we eat and how much we eat. Each of us will adopt our own guidelines on this (for example, only to have one helping, to avoid junk food, to eat five bits of fruit a day, to limit puddings to only two meals a week, to fast once a week and give the money to a charity, and whatever they are, we need to stick to them. Food has a subtle capacity to become an idol or addiction, perhaps particularly so for Christians who readily avoid some of the other more widely accepted "releases" such as alcohol, other drugs or pornography. Maybe that's why chocolate is a common Christian "addiction," to the extent that when I bought three large chocolate bars at a Christian conference center the staff member leaned over the counter and, in a hushed voice, said in all seriousness, "Would you like a brown bag for those, sir?"

How is our attitude to food and fasting? What would it mean for us to become increasingly "temperate" in this area of our life?

Self-controlled

So many of the other attributes in these verses depend on self-control (v. 2). What does it mean to exercise self-control? Other references in the New Testament link self-control with alertness (1 Thessalonians 5:6; 1 Peter 1:13; 4:7; 5:8) and grace (1 Peter 1:13). These two things are like the bookends around self-control, holding the discipline in a safe place.

We need to be alert because our enemy prowls around like a roaring lion looking for people to devour (1 Peter 5:8). Seeing him helps us to resist him and decide to take control. Proverbs 25:28 puts it well: "Like a city whose walls are broken down is a person who lacks self-control." Without self-control we are open to the attack of anyone or anything that wants to walk in and destroy our life. Self-control keeps the walls of the city standing, and the gates firmly closed.

Grace is the other bookend. For Christian leaders, self-control does not come naturally or merely by hard work, but is a product of the Spirit's work in a Christian's life (Galatians 5:23; 2 Timothy 1:7). As one minister put it:

Self-control, in a biblical context, is first and foremost a work of God in the life of a self-surrendering believer. For the modern mind, to be self-sacrificing, self-effacing and self-denying is to be out of control; it goes against every natural impulse of self-preservation. Nevertheless, this is what the scriptures require of anyone who is to live a self-controlled life.

Christian leaders show their utter dependence on God through surrendering themselves to Christ, who by his Spirit bears the fruit of self-control. This is a work of grace.

Respectable

This word means "orderly, decent, one who quietly fulfils their duties." The leaders for whom I have greatest respect are the unknown ones who quietly get on with the job without any great show. One of the dangers of this book is that I tend to quote or illustrate from the lives of well-known Christian leaders. I am thrilled at what God is doing through such people and what we can learn from them, but the real stars are the ones who are being faithful and fruitful in ministry without anyone putting them on a platform or offering them a book contract.

One of my great heroes is a man called Peter Jordan. Nearly all his working life, Peter has faithfully exercised the ministry of a Christian leader in some of the toughest areas of the country. He's suffered abuse, arson, burglary, violence and countless setbacks. His family have suffered as well. Yet he has loved, cared for and served hundreds of people into God's kingdom, including, nearly thirty years ago, my colleague and friend Roger Murphy, who is an evangelist with something of a profile within the UK. Peter's "respectability" comes from his willingness quietly to get on with the job and his complete commitment to respect others, no matter what they've done in life, no matter how disadvantaged or difficult they are. It is so easy to dismiss people because they don't fit in our comfort zone or further our ministry.

The temptation to want people to know about us is one that needs to be resisted. Instead we are called to a quiet and ordered life, where we gain respect from others because we first respect them.

Hospitable

Hospitality (v. 2) may be a particular challenge for those of the younger generation. The heightened individualism of our society over the last fifty years, along with increased mobility and consumer choice, has led to a breakdown of community. At a time when we desperately need to be modeling community, we ourselves have withdrawn from a basic building block of community life—hospitability.[7] We are more concerned with improving our homes than sharing them.

In Paul's day, as Christians traveled around Europe they were welcomed into the homes of other Christians as strangers. This is the literal meaning of the word "hospitable"—one who welcomes strangers. In the early Church, hospitality was also a way in which the church grew. Christians met in small groups within homes, sharing what they had with one another. In his commentary on I Timothy, Donald Guthrie writes, "Without the willing hospitality of Christian people, expansion would have been seriously retarded."[8] I suggest that the same is true today. I know the challenge in a minister's life related to the home becoming the office, or, for the youth worker, the youth center. There are some boundaries that need to be established. But once again the pendulum may have swung too far. Christian leaders who close their front doors on the world are not exercising hospitality.

When I was an assistant minister, one of the congregation members, a single mum with a son, lost her home. The minister's family invited them into their home, which was already very full with four of their own children, and gave them the main bedroom with the suite bathroom. The pair stayed with the minister's family for many months, and it wasn't always easy, but this has stayed with me as a wonderful example of sacrificial hospitality.

Able to teach

This quality (v. 2) was an important requirement for the early church leaders as they sought to instruct, counsel and pastor people. "Able" involves having the appropriate knowledge, skills and love. Some may have the knowledge but not the skills, in which case they simply frustrate those who listen. Others may have the skills but not the knowledge, in which case they lead people astray. Others may have the skills and knowledge but lack love, in which case they berate those who listen. It is not about loving teaching, it is about loving people and serving them through our teaching. The combination of all three provides a good base for teaching, but we need to add two further ingredients—hard work and being a role model.

Leaders who lead themselves in this area will recognize the sheer hard work of study that allows greater effectiveness in teaching—study of both the Bible and the art of communication, whatever the context for teaching (congregation, small group or one to one; as a pastor, discipler or evangelist; with children, young people or adults). Study of the Bible involves breadth and depth. Reading through the whole Bible in a year, and studying a particular part of the Bible in depth over a significant period of time, both help us to be people of the book. I try to read a book on preaching/teaching each year, and to attend some training on this area every couple of years. I always try to get feedback on talks I give or training I lead, and I know that some people meet monthly with a small group of others who are regularly teaching, to chat over their sermons, talks, or youth session outlines and help one another in preparation and reflection.

We can also reflect on how we use the Bible in pastoral counseling and personal evangelism, ensuring that we are "able to teach." For example, in evangelistic conversations what we think isn't as important as what Jesus says. If we simply stress what we think, we end up in a standoff where two people are left entrenched in their own positions, both claiming that this is their belief, thought or opinion. What matters is what Jesus says, so as we talk with people we want to get out of the way and get him central to the conversation. Inevitably this leads to the Bible, not in an aggressive way, but gently and thoughtfully, shifting the focus off what we believe and on to what Jesus says.[9]

Christian leaders must also model the importance of teaching in their own life, as those who are willing to be taught, and who live out what they've learned themselves. Without this role modeling, our teaching sounds with a hollow note. Are we teachable as well as able to teach?

Not given to drunkenness

This phrase (v. 3) is not condemning alcohol itself, as consumption of alcohol was commonplace in Jesus' day, but the excessive consumption of alcohol. The phrase means "not given to much wine"—avoiding excess. What does excess look like? It's consumption at any level that involves unhealthy or unhelpful dependence. It is not the amount, necessarily, but the reason.

Bob was enjoying a season of fabulous fruitfulness as a church minister. With five children, a growing church and an increasing profile within the local community, the pressure was on. Occasionally he found it difficult to get to sleep at night, and would drink a glass of wine to help him relax. Then his mother died, unexpectedly and tragically. Everyone remarked on how well he coped—and he did, except that the occasional difficulty with getting off to sleep turned to a nightly experience, and so too did the glass of wine. Over two years, the one glass became two, three, four. Bob wasn't drunk at any point, he never drank in public, and he never suffered a hangover, but he depended on the wine to anaesthetize the pain and relieve the pressures. Slowly he came to realize what had happened, and one day corked the bottle for good. No one knew until he dared to share his pain of loss, and the fact that he'd been living life in the red zone too long, with a group of peers. He exercised leadership of himself.

Not violent but gentle

The word "violent" here (v. 3) means lashing out in rage with one's tongue or with one's body. There is so much teaching in the Bible about the tongue, and for good reason. It probably does more damage than any other part of our body, especially when we use it in temper to hit at someone. Christian leaders are to be gentle. Violence, even verbal violence, destroys people and destroys respect and trust. If we "lose it" with someone, it may take years to rebuild the trust, and if we lose it in public, the ripples will be many and long-lasting. One of the most helpful courses I've attended was on how to control anger by creating a process for spotting the warning signs and defusing the situation before it explodes. I've taught this process to a number of people through the years, and just occasionally had to use it myself. If we are aware that violent lashing out is not too far below the surface, it is worth exercising leadership over ourselves, and finding ways to keep it in check.[10]

Not quarrelsome

This phrase (v. 3) refers to stubbornness, a desire always to win the argument, not to back down. Grace and gentleness in our relationships with those we lead is a beautiful trait. One of the temptations for a leader is to misuse the imbalance of power that commonly exists between the leader and the led for personal advantage. We can hide stubbornness behind power, and appear to handle a situation well. One thing that keeps my quarrelsome side in check is a commitment to listen as much as to speak, really to make sure that I've understood what a person is saying. For me, this involves asking questions, listening carefully and trying to avoid the tendency to see conversations as an argument to be won rather than a topic to be explored. If we always have to be "right," people eventually stop telling us what they really think, and then our leadership is risky, because we may not know when we are about to get something very wrong.

Not a lover of money

The subtle, sensuous whisper of money (v. 3) constantly woos us away from our first love. Decisions are made on the basis of money rather than on a prayerful seeking of God's kingdom. We become increasingly adept at getting money through questionable means—the subtle hints, the knowing pauses. We hold on to money rather than generously giving it away, and ignore the inner prompts of God toward generosity. We long for just a little more, rather than growing in gratitude for what we have. As Jesus said, "No one can be the slave of two masters . . . You cannot be the slave both of God and money" (Matthew 6:24). In our increasingly acquisitive age, Christian leaders are called to avoid love of money, and all material possessions, so that we can faithfully serve one master.[II]

An encouragement to keep going

As we read what Paul writes to Timothy, we may feel challenged and daunted by the standards he sets, but I find encouragement in the first verse of the chapter. "If anyone sets his heart on being an overseer, he desires a noble task." Christian leadership is a noble task, one worth aspiring to. That is a good reminder when so many younger people see leadership in the Christian community as something to be avoided. What a privilege it is to be called to lead, and what an inspiring challenge to lead in a way that reflects Jesus himself.

Earlier in I Timothy, Paul explains his motive for writing: "Timothy, my son, I give you this instruction in keeping with the prophecies once made about you, so that by following them you may fight the good fight, holding on to faith and a good conscience" (I:18–19). Our fight is not against flesh and blood but the spiritual forces arrayed against us, and in order to keep going we "hold on to faith." If we lose our faith, we lose our moorings, and we will drift on the sea of life. If we lose our faith, we will lose our bearings, and no longer be sure which way to set sail to find secure harbor. Then we are no longer a safe person to follow and we "shipwreck our faith" (I Timothy I:19).

We also hold on to a "good conscience." It is perfectly possible to lead people forward and to lead people badly. Leading ourselves ensures that we can stand before our all-knowing God and offer him not only what we've done, but also the way we've done it. I was reading through my journal this morning and came across an incident a few months back—not one I'm proud of. Wanting the best for the program I lead, I was quietly manipulating a situation behind the scenes. From the outside the result looked good, but from the inside I knew the way I had done it was wrong. Journaling helped me to see that my method was wrong because my motivation was wrong. I kidded myself that I wanted the best for the program, but my real motivation was fear: I didn't want to confront a particular situation. My conscience wasn't good. Maintain a good conscience, urges Paul. Pursue righteousness, godliness, faith, love, endurance, and gentleness. Chase after the attributes of godly character with all your strength. Lead yourself well.

LEADING THOSE CLOSEST TO US

The second aspect of this leadership is leading those closest to us. "He must manage his own family well and see that his children obey him with proper respect. (If anyone does not know how to manage his own family, how can he take care of God's church?)" (1 Timothy 3:4–5), and "A deacon must be the husband of but one wife and must manage his children and his household well" (v. 12).

To modern ears these commands may seem strangely old-fashioned, suggestive of Victorian father figures as head of the household, distant and domineering. What about equality in relationships? Thankfully, we no longer live in an era where one sex is seen as better than the other, but rather complementary. The roles of men and women in marriage relationships have undergone radical change.[12] The principle clearly taught in Ephesians 5:21–33 is one of mutual submission out of reverence for Christ. The complementarity of that mutual submission is expressed in the equality of men and women before God. In marriage, it is important to work out what this means, and not to lose the vital place of leadership exercised in the home. For example, I know how easy it is for parents never to make changes in their family life because no one takes the initiative.

What about the leader who is single? The principle of leading those closest to us still applies to the single person in Christian leadership. The phrase "household" in verse 12 refers to those within a wider extended network of relationships than simply the nuclear family. Wider family, close friends and neighbors are all included. Our sisters and brothers in other parts of the world have a much better understanding of this.

To lead others closest to us involves taking the initiative to fulfill God's vision for our family and wider household. This is one of the main ways we "preside" over and "care" for them, part of the root meaning of the word translated "manage" in the NIV.

Presiding takes time

Christian leaders needs to give priority to "presiding over" their household if they are to do it "well" (v. 4). Time is the essential ingredient. Too often, Christian leaders sacrifice the leadership of their own household for the leadership of the Church. If children are to have "proper respect" for their parents, they need to have a proper relationship with them, and relationships are only developed through time. I can command my children to obey me, but rules without relationship lead to rebellion in children, be that active and aggressive or passive and regressive.[13] Respect and obedience flow out of good, healthy, vibrant, loving relationships, and children spell relationship "TIME." As Rob Parsons mentions, "It is not our *presents* children are looking for, but our *presence*."[14]

I don't accept the distinction that is sometimes made about quality and quantity time. Children, especially young children, can't switch into "quality time." They need "quantity time," and out of that, when they are ready, will flow the quality moments that are simply too important and precious to miss. The links here with living life in the red zone are clear.

Presiding involves initiative

Presiding also means taking the initiative to bring direction and change, not waiting for others to do it. I sometimes hear myself saying to Sophie after a particularly stressful week, "Don't ask me to make any decisions." Yet that is exactly what she is looking for—someone to share the important decisions about the children or the household. If I am so worn out by my work that I have no energy for creative, fun and dynamic leadership in the home, then I am working too hard.

As a couple, we share decision-making, but the temptation to become lazy and weak with my involvement in the process is constantly with me. I find it helpful sometimes to reflect on the amount of energy and time I invest in people I lead outside the home, and ask whether I am investing equivalent amounts in the home. How am I practically growing godliness in my children? At work I try to learn about how to refine my skills as a leader, so what about in the home? As a principle, I try either to read at least one book on marriage and one on parenting every year, or listen to a teaching cassette, or watch a film that engages my heart.

I want to grow in my relationships with those nearest to me, not stagnate, and that will only happen through learning and reflecting on what it means to be a son, a brother, a husband, a dad, a friend and a neighbor, taking the initiative to be the person others need me to be.

Presiding means caring

This caring takes a practical form, putting ourselves out for others. That's the nature of love. Why am I so much more willing to put myself out in the workplace than in the home? David Ferguson[15] speaks of genuine servanthood being learned in the home, where we are not on public display, where no one is going to reward us publicly. Practical caring is a mark of leading those closest to us. For me it is in the small things—making sure I load the dishwasher and washing machine each evening, and empty them both before I go to work in the morning; doing the ironing; sharing in the food shopping and cooking, cleaning and maintenance; trying to fit my work agenda around my family agenda to help out with the endless ferrying to and fro; remembering to take home gifts that say "I love you" and "thank you"; getting up to answer the phone when we are all tired; volunteering to do jobs and not waiting to be asked.

The reason for all this could not be clearer: "If anyone does not know how to manage his own family, how can he take care of God's church?" (1 Timothy 3:5). Tragically, the breakdown of Christian leaders' marriages, the estrangement of their children from the Christian faith, and the isolation from wider family and friends, are commonplace. Even as I write these words, I pray "There but for the grace of God go I." I am very aware that I am only sixteen years into ministry and marriage. I know personally those who have experienced the pain of things going horrendously wrong. But surely the reality of these difficulties makes it all the more important that we heed Paul's advice to Timothy and seek to live it out ourselves, not as a guarantee that all will go well, but as a priority commitment to fulfill God's call on our lives.

GRACE, MERCY AND PEACE

"This is a tough chapter," said a friend. "The bar for Christian leadership is set so high." He's right. But Paul begins his first letter to Timothy with the words "Grace, mercy and peace from God the Father and Christ Jesus our Lord" (1:2). A few verses later on, he says:

I thank Christ Jesus our Lord, who has given me strength, that he considered me faithful, appointing me to his service. Even though I was once a blasphemer and a persecutor and a violent man, I was shown mercy because I acted in ignorance and unbelief. The grace of our Lord was poured out on me abundantly, along with the faith and love that are in Christ Jesus. Here is a trustworthy saying that deserves full acceptance: Christ Jesus came into the world to save sinners—

of whom I am the worst. But for that very reason I was shown mercy so that in me, the worst of sinners, Christ Jesus might display his unlimited patience as an example for those who would believe on him and receive eternal life. Now to the King eternal, immortal, invisible, the only God, be honor and glory for ever and ever. Amen.

I TIMOTHY 1:12–17

For Paul, God's grace was sufficient, God's mercy was constant, and his patience was unlimited. God hasn't changed. May we know this to be true for ourselves.

FOR REFLECTION

- What do God's unlimited patience, constant mercy and sufficient grace mean for me, today?
- Where am I doing well in leading myself and those closest to me?
- What one message from this chapter most struck me? And what shall I do with it?

FIVE SCENARIOS, FIVE DIFFERENT PEOPLE'S LIVES

Monday 9:07 am. Paul walks into the church office. "Good morning," he murmurs as he strides past the administrator without looking at her, adjusting his clerical collar. He doesn't spot the tissue hastily hidden from sight, or hear the catch in the voice of the quietly whispered "Good morning" in response. Nor does he see the value statement freshly printed on the administrator's desk: "Value 1: relationships."

Tuesday 10:40 am. Ed's preparation is going well, especially as there is such a limited amount of time for it this week. Still, it should be a good youth group session. Truth is such an important issue for young people to grasp in today's postmodern mindset. The phone rings. "Not again." Snatching it up, he snaps, "Yes." It's Simon—again. The fourth time this week, and it's only Tuesday. He'll be around if he knows I'm on my own. "Simon, not now. I've got someone with me."

Thursday 2:12 pm. Meeting starts at 2:15pm. Time for a quick break. Nick enters the room with seconds to spare. Grabbing the agenda from his bag, he sits and quickly scans what's coming. Not good, he tells himself. First look at the agenda since it arrived a week ago. Hmmm. Item 6—a discussion on honesty in leadership. Interesting. Then he catches sight of his name. "Rats, I'm down to lead prayers." Sue begins, "Shall we get started? Nick, you're down to lead prayers." "Er . . . yes, of course, shall we turn to John 3 . . ."

Friday 3:27 pm. Three minutes to doors open. They won't miss me for the start of the session. Plenty of people to help. I'll just finish this bit of preparation, and then I'll be there in time for the first activity. The kids love it, and it's great to see the club grow through the year. So nice to have others helping to lead it; I'm sure they will understand if I'm a little late.

Saturday 10:45 pm. That was a great DVD; now it's time for bed. Leading worship tomorrow morning. Maybe I'll see what's on TV. NBC: The Tonight Show, my parents' favorite. PBS: another documentary about the war. AMC: I saw that movie ages ago. GSN: these game shows get more and more bizarre. MTV: what on earth are they doing? Should go to bed really. Looks interesting, though. Need to know what others are watching—keeps me in touch with young adults today.

Chapter 9

LEADERS EMBODY KINGDOM VALUES

"Try not to become a person of success, but rather try to become a person of value."

ALBERT EINSTEIN

In the last chapter we addressed the first essential leadership competency, and now we turn to the second—embodying values. Both these competencies focus inward, connecting with the character and call issues of earlier chapters. Every leader has values, whether or not they are aware of it, whether or not their values match their words, and whether or not those they lead share their values. We are a 24-hour value transmission station. We communicate our values all the time through actions, words and attitudes. These values are received by others and affect the way we lead people, and the way people are prepared to be led.

WHAT ARE VALUES?

Values are the beliefs of a person or group in which they have emotional investment.[1] For example, what do we believe about how to treat a person? If we believe that people are made by God, and we hold that belief with emotional intensity, we will value people and be upset when others treat people poorly. On the other hand, if we believe people aren't that important (quite probably because that is how we ourselves were treated in early life) and hold to that belief with some emotional investment (as a means of protecting ourselves), we won't value people and may treat them poorly.

Take another example: what do we believe about how we relate to God? If we believe that he is the creator and sustainer of the universe, and that through grace he's made it possible for us to know him and live for him, and if we hold that belief with emotional intensity, we will value prayer as a way of expressing our dependence on God in all things and growing in relationship with him. If, however, we believe he is simply a God who started the whole process up and now looks on to see what happens, and we hold that belief with emotional intensity, we are less likely to see prayer as a priority.

Values flow from beliefs, when the beliefs are held with emotional investment. For example, someone may say they believe in the Ten Commandments, but unless they hold that belief with some emotional investment they won't necessarily value the things reflected in the Ten Commandments, like fidelity, respect for others' property and faithfulness to God. The person's true emotional investment might lie in the belief of self-autonomy—so "how dare anyone stipulate how I should live my life?"

Everyone believes certain things and invests those beliefs with some emotional intensity. We hold our particular beliefs because of our choices, upbringing, emotional maturity, psychological well-being, sin, cultural background and a host of other factors. Leaders are no exception, but the influence they have over others is greater than most people's, so the implications of getting this wrong are potentially more serious. People nearly always adopt the values of those they follow, whether they are good values or not.

There are three dilemmas that face us as leaders.

When we hold the wrong values

Few Christian leaders deliberately set out to embody the wrong values, but history reminds us that many committed religious leaders have managed to do just that. In the name of Christ, people have held wrong values because they have held wrong beliefs. Slavery and apartheid are both honest recognitions of this fact. We constantly need to be checking that the values we hold reflect Christ's own values rather than the values of the culture of our day, or even of our church culture.

If values are shaped by belief, constant reflection on the scriptures and openness to the work of the Holy Spirit will serve us well as we try to formulate values that honor God. But even then we must be open to our blind spots that only others can see.

I've had the privilege of working for a short time in India, and after my second visit was able to welcome into my home, church and village several of the Indian Christians I'd met in Vellore. Having read some of Lesslie Newbigin's excellent work on culture, and the advantages of seeing ourselves through the eyes of those outside our own culture, at the end of their stay I invited the Indians to comment on what most surprised them about English Christians. They were a little taken aback, but once I'd assured them that I was genuinely interested in an honest answer, they ventured one thing: they were shocked at how little we prayed. Through my time with them in India, I knew that they prayed. We were never allowed to leave a home without praying. They prayed because they knew with a depth of intensity missing from most Western Christians that their daily bread, health and safety depended on the generosity of a God who sustains. Their comment to me was, "It is as if you almost don't believe God has any relevance to your life other than on Sundays."

What are some of the values we may need to question today? Perhaps valuing comfort more than servanthood, financial security more than trust in God, the nuclear family over the extended family, getting rather than giving, the church more than the kingdom, and young people more than old people. And for those of us living in the red zone? Valuing success more than faithfulness, achievement more than worth, our ministry more than our family, and reputation more than character.

Our beliefs are constantly being refined as we learn more about God and his purposes for his world; we need to be open and humble enough to ensure our values follow swiftly behind.

When our stated values don't match our embodied values

This is the second dilemma. Expressing values isn't sufficient. We can express them but not embody them. Leadership depends on trust, and trust is built on credibility and integrity that expresses character. Character is shaped by values. When my stated values don't match my actions, words or attitudes, I erode my credibility and people's trust.

I once heard a leader give a great speech. The words were carefully chosen, the content was stirring and inspirational, the context perfect for people to receive the message. But the speech made little impact, and the reason was simple: the people didn't trust the leader. They had heard words before, but they hadn't seen words backed up by action. Those in the audience were thinking "We've heard this before" or "When you show us you mean what you're saying, we'll start to believe you." There was a credibility gap, based on the fundamental issue of integrity.

The relationship between integrity, authenticity and credibility is sometimes confusing. Let me illustrate by using by three circles.

Integrity is at the center, and is the quality of being undivided, complete: "I am who I am, no matter where I am or who I am with."[2] Integrity flows from who we are, and builds consistency. People know what they are going to get; our values are reflected in our conduct.

Authenticity is the next layer out and is dependent on integrity. It is the quality of lack of falseness or imitation, of being fully trustworthy. Authenticity builds trust: people will follow an authentic leader a long way, but they won't follow an inauthentic leader very far at all. Authenticity is not perfection. Christian leaders don't have to get it right all the time, but they do need to admit responsibility and apologize when they get it wrong. Authenticity is not omniscience. Acting as if we know everything is a mark of the inauthentic life. We need to acknowledge the limits of our abilities and ask for help. Bill Hybels says, "Authenticity means consistency between words and actions, and between claimed values and actual priorities."[3] Jesus' criticism of the religious leaders of his day wasn't that they didn't know the truth, but that they didn't practice what they knew (Matthew 23:2–3).

Credibility is the external circle, and depends on both the inner circles. It is the quality of inspiring belief, of being believable, and it builds confidence. You can appear to be credible without actually being authentic and having integrity. For example, when a person arrives in a new job, they may look the part, sound the part and act the part: they appear credible. But if they don't demonstrate integrity and authenticity over time, confidence in their leadership and willingness to follow will quickly diminish.

Management expert Peter Drucker once said to church leaders:

The final requirement of effective leadership is to earn trust . . . To trust a leader, it is not necessary to agree with him or her. Trust is the conviction that the leader means what he or she says. It is a belief in something very old fashioned called "integrity". . . . Effective leadership is not based on being clever; it is based primarily on being consistent.

Jesus modeled this for us. His life was a seamless whole in which integrity meant he was utterly consistent, authenticity meant he was completely trustworthy, and credibility meant he was totally believable. Why else did a woman who had lived a sinful life dare to burst into a dinner party of religious leaders to break a jar of expensive perfume over his feet? (Luke 7:37–50). Why did a blind man cry out over the dismissive crowd, "Jesus, Son of David, have mercy on me?" (Luke 18:36–43). Because they both saw in him someone they could trust who, unlike so many others, wouldn't reject them. It is also why Jesus, under great stress, suffering both mental anguish and physical pain, was able to pray, "Father, forgive them, for they do not know what they are doing" (Luke 23:34). He was utterly consistent until his last breath.

In contrast, today there is a great deal of distrust of those in authority, fuelled by the regular exposing of public figures whose stated values don't match their actual values. People are looking for integrity. "Don't tell me!" they cry. "Show me." It is another reason why I long for people to see Jesus, for only there will they see the integrity they seek. I realize that most people aren't looking at Jesus, but rather at his Church or at Christians they know. They need to see in us lives where stated values and actual values match up.

This is a huge challenge to a leader, and to the church as a whole. For a leader to embody values, those values need to come from within the leader's very being, from their character. As we saw in the section on character, this is formed in the crucible of the silversmith's foundry, until others can see Jesus' face in us.

When our values are not the same as the values of those we lead

The third dilemma is when the people we lead have a different set of values from ours. We may be living by our values, we may believe they are the right values, but other people live by a different set of values and they believe they are the right ones. The values clash, and can lead to major problems.

What advice does Paul have for us in such a situation?

EMBODYING VALUES

Given these three dilemmas, what can we do to ensure we embody our values?

Know our values

To embody certain values, we need to be clear about which ones are important to us. This is true personally and organizationally. It

Values Clash ▢ ▢ ☒

Reply **Reply All** **Forward** **Print**

From: paul@fish.net
To: timothy@fish.net
Subject: Values Clash

Hi Timothy.

Following my e-mail yesterday, there is one further thing I want to say. The time will come when people won't like what you teach and what you value. Expect it. They will distance themselves from you. It won't be pleasant, it never is, but it will happen. They'll want to find those who say what appeals to them and confirms them in their own position. They'll even suggest, because so many of them are in agreement, that you must be wrong. You'll feel the pressure at times like this, the pressure to cave in, to give people what they want to hear, to join the crowd. But I urge you, don't.

When people turn away from the truth, they can only turn to myths. There is no other place to go. And believing these myths will lead them further and further away from all that our heavenly Father values and the Lord Jesus taught us. Yes, of course you must check yourself carefully; make sure you are not simply being stubborn or arrogant. Talk with Titus about it if I am no longer around; consult with Peter and the other apostles.

Take time to humble yourself before God and prayerfully discern where your heart is in all this. Do away with any attitude that doesn't honor Jesus. But if you are as sure as you can be that you're holding to the truth, endure whatever happens. They may speak against you in other congregations, they may try to steal other devoted followers to their cause, they may accuse you falsely and slander those you love. Keep your head, Timothy, endure the hardship, for Jesus told us to expect such things. In fact, he warned us to watch out if all spoke well of us.

What does "keeping your head" mean? Don't be distracted from exercising the ministry God has called you to. Keep on doing the work of an evangelist. If you lose some to false teachers, win more for the true teacher. Keep praying for those who persecute you, keep serving, avoid bitterness and unforgiveness, proclaim Jesus. I know how tough it can be, but remember the crown that awaits us on that great day.

With love
Paul[4]

can help to write a list of core values. Walter Wright identified his own personal values for leadership while President of Regent College, Vancouver. He lists them in three categories:

- **People**
  1 People have intrinsic worth.
  2 Everyone should make a commitment to the mission.
  3 People who work with us should grow.
  4 No one should take themselves too seriously.
  5 All people should be treated as contributing peers regardless of their scope of responsibility.
  6 Leadership should be empowering.

- **Work**
  1 The mission of the organization normally takes precedence over individual purposes.
  2 Participation produces ownership of results.
  3 The workplace should provide community.
  4 People should have fun and find joy in their work.
  5 We should always provide professional service in a friendly environment.

- **Relationships**
  1 Truth is found in relationship.
  2 Information is friendly.
  3 Confrontation is a sign of caring.
  4 Criticism without constructive action is destructive gossip.
  5 Honesty, integrity and trust are essential in everything we do.
  6 Forgiveness should characterize our life together.[5]

I list Wright's values not as an example for us to follow, but to illustrate someone who has clearly identified his values. I for one would be happy to work under a person with that set of values, with one proviso—that he or she truly lived them out.

Live our values

Once we know them, we need to live them. If we don't, we'll undermine our integrity.

Some friends booked a holiday in Tenerife, Spain. It was one of those time-share deals: the company provide you with free accommodation; you come to a three-hour presentation. A variety of accommodation was on offer, so my friends selected carefully, and received a letter confirming they'd been allocated their choice. On arrival, they were surprised and disappointed to be given "alternative accommodation," which had quite a lot wrong with it, including cockroaches and a broken cot. They told the holiday rep, but nothing happened.

Wednesday afternoon was presentation time. They duly turned up, and the rep was all charm and smiles. My friend said, "Excuse me, I don't wish to be rude, but why should we listen to your three-hour presentation when you gave us the wrong accommodation, haven't sorted out any of the problems with the room, and haven't checked up on us at all since we arrived?" He had a point. The rep didn't agree, became defensive and called his manager, who eventually agreed and let my friend leave without having to endure the presentation. The next day they received a letter saying that, as they hadn't attended the presentation, they had to pay for their accommodation.

The irony of this saga is that the company was trying to sell something, and couldn't see that their treatment of my friend undermined their image (glossy brochure), their vision (providing first-rate holidays at a good price) and their values (excellent service). Attitudes, words and actions need to line up if we are to embody values.

Surprisingly, it is often the little things that count most. Most competent leaders do a reasonable job of the "set-piece" stuff. They may be able to lead a good children's holiday club, preach a good sermon, and run a good meeting. At moments of crisis they steer a good course, offer good care and make good decisions. But if they don't attend to the small things that show care and concern for people on a daily basis, they quickly undermine their position.

How leaders handle correspondence, voice mail, chance encounters, anniversaries and ongoing pastoral situations matters. Too often people excuse their actions with "I'm just not a detail person." Occasionally people justify themselves on their Myers-Briggs profile. "I am an ENFP, or whatever it is, so I can't be expected to be good at the small stuff." Whether it is our preference or not, small stuff matters because people matter. Answering letters, returning calls, changing our schedule because someone is upset, remembering anniversaries, writing notes of encouragement, celebrating achievements, carrying boxes, making coffee, honoring commitments, being prompt, all matter.

There is a balance here, as leadership involves keeping the big picture, not getting too immersed in the detail and not forsaking the wider agenda for the agenda of every person we meet. But we lead through service. We start embodying our values in the small things. Without this, the big things lack credibility. If the holiday company had taken this seriously, they may have made a sale.

Share our values

One way to gain help in living out our values is to make ourselves accountable to others. This can be scary, because people may actually tell us when there is a discrepancy. If we have a set of values that only we know about, we can kid ourselves that we are fulfilling them. When we make our values public, others can look at the stated values and then look at our life. Any gaps will be obvious. It is also a dynamic thing to do, because it places relationship at the heart of good leadership. It models vulnerability.

Over the last few years, one of the teams I lead has consistently challenged me to live by my values. Every time it happens I want to defend myself, and then I want to retreat from the front line of leadership. Thankfully, I've learned to try to respond with humility and grace, to accept the challenge, to ask for forgiveness and then to change.

If we don't share our values and make ourselves accountable in this way, people's concerns and comments are expressed behind our back. That breeds dissent, gossip and dissatisfaction, prevents us from growing through feedback, and makes it harder for others to be open, honest and vulnerable. Sharing our values openly encourages both personal growth and the growth of those we lead.

Honor our values

We honor the values we hold by being quick to admit fault when we get it wrong, and by being willing to change. The longer there is discrepancy between our stated values and the way we live, the greater the erosion of other people's confidence and trust. If this continues, there comes a point when the damage is almost impossible to repair. The phrase "set in their ways" is a terrible epitaph for a leader.

Growing leaders need to admit fault quickly. Why do we struggle to do this? Mainly because we are insecure. As I write this, I am thinking, "But what about all the other reasons?" What about "I didn't have all the facts" or "I wasn't feeling well" or "I was given the wrong information" or "Someone else made the decision?" These and countless others may be good excuses, but they aren't normally the root issue for struggling to admit fault. Insecurity is the root problem. We fear what might happen to us. We fear what people might think. We fear others taking advantage of us. We fear getting it wrong.

Last night I was reading my young daughter the story of the three men coming to Abraham and Sarah in Genesis 18. One phrase in the story caught my attention. Verse 15 says, "Sarah was afraid, so she lied and said 'I did not laugh.'" She was afraid, so she didn't admit fault quickly. Why was Sarah afraid? Because she wasn't prepared to take God at his word. Fear and insecurity are linked to faith. Do we believe what God says about us, or do we take our security from what others say or think?

People who've realized how important this is are wonderfully liberated, not in the sense of freedom to do whatever they please, but being free to be themselves, to admit fault, to change. We flourish best as leaders when we take time to hear God's words about ourselves, so that we can deal well with others' words, and honor our values through acknowledging our mistakes.

Align our values

We'll be helped to embody our values if we seek places of leadership where our personal values and the corporate values align closely. I love working for CPAS because the corporate vision and values closely align with my own personal vision and values.

I feel challenged to live out my expressed vision and values every time I come to work. If we work in a context where our expressed values and those of the workplace are different, tension will inevitably occur. This can be a creative tension if we are challenged to review our values and adopt even better ones, or it can be a damaging tension if we find ourselves having to work in a way that undermines our personal values.

What about a Christian leader contemplating a position in a place where the values are not ones they share? It is wise to ascertain both the stated values and the actual values. Some churches and Christian organizations have stated values written down. If so, check them against the actual values by asking a wide group of people some questions. What do people really value around here? What do people spend their time on? What one thing would people be most concerned about changing? Then take a look at the way things are done. Often, attending a service in a church or a staff meeting in an organization will tell us a lot about the actual values as they are embodied in the life of the congregation or organization. This is the culture of the congregation or organization. It is very powerful, and forms the ways things are done, often without people realizing it.

Through questions, listening and observation, we can gain a reasonably clear picture of the actual values, stated or not. At this point the leader has a choice to make, based on a series of questions.

1. *"Is it right for me to change these values?"* The answer may be yes—for example, when the actual values go against biblical values. The answer may be no—for example, if the values have more to do with style than substance. If the answer is yes, then the next question needs to be asked.

2. *"Do I have the capacity, commitment and concern to lead this congregation or organization through the necessary process of change?"* Each part of that question is important. Capacity: do I have the right sort of skills and experience to lead well in this context? Commitment: do I sense a sufficient call to this place to see me through the difficult and tough times that may lie ahead? Research suggests that it takes two to five years to change the values of an organization. Concern: do I feel a genuine concern for these people so that I can lead them lovingly and carefully rather than angrily and aggressively? If the answer is yes again, move on to the next question.

3. *"Do I have a sufficient mandate and clear support to make these changes?"* What are the existing leaders looking for? What about those who have responsibility for oversight of the congregation or organization? Who will back me up when it gets difficult?

4. *"How open are they to the potential change I am offering?"* Some congregations are simply not open to change. Their values are clear, and one of them is "we don't change." If that is the case, it takes a very courageous, patient and competent person to proceed. More often there is a mixture of attitudes to change, with some longing for change, others unsure, and still others quite resistant.

Prayer for wisdom and discernment needs to underlie the whole of this process. I know a number of ministers who've gone into church situations where their only certain conviction was that God wanted them there, and wonderful lasting change has taken place. I also know others who have met such resistance that they've been crushed. Change doesn't take place in a congregation or organization unless we address both the vision *and* the values at the same time.[6] This subject borders on the topic of handling change, and in the notes I've included some excellent resources for those who want to explore this further.[7]

Embodying values is made easier when we align personal values with corporate values. Rarely, if ever, is there an exact match when we arrive in a new place, but the closer the alignment over time, the easier it is to maintain our values.

Keeping values aligned is the other side of this coin. Something called "value drift" occurs in churches and organizations. Over time, no matter how clearly we start, people drift from the stated values and other values creep in, becoming the actual values of the organization. "Value drift" is countered by consistently rehearsing the values, both in speech and in deed. For the Arrow Program we have a list of eight core values. When we meet as a team, the agenda has the values listed in a column on the left-hand side, and a little phrase at the bottom of the agenda says, "In this meeting we aim to seek God's will, work well together, take action for the future, and *reflect our values.*" It is one small way of rehearsing our values. We also look at one value each month and ask ourselves, "How do we best reflect this value in what we do and the way we do it?" When it comes to staff appraisal we can appraise against the stated values of the organization.

In a local church setting, we can rehearse the stated values through a sermon series; structuring the prayers of intercession around the values, perhaps one a month; constructing a prayer of confession around them; ensuring they are discussed at the annual meeting and form part of the agenda at the leadership team meetings; sharing them with newcomers through a church welcome pack and in personal conversation; displaying them prominently at the back of the church; and helping the children and young people work out what the values mean for them.

WE ALL EMBODY VALUES

Through the years I've done lots of events around the country, many of them attended by senior staff of the Church of England. In my work with Springboard we would start the day at 7:30 am, driving to a place where we would spend an hour setting up, run a conference for clergy from 10:00 am to 4:00 pm, break down for an hour, drive to the next place where we would set up for an hour, run an evening conference for 200 local church leaders from 7:45 to 9:45 pm, and then have to break down for 45 minutes after everyone had gone. We would then drive back home, arriving at 11:00 pm. The next day we would do the same all over again and continue this pattern for two to three weeks. It was exhausting. During one of these weeks, at the end of each evening, a bishop rolled up his sleeves and helped carry equipment to the car, stack chairs and pack boxes of books. We weren't too tired to notice that he embodied a value.

A speaker at a conference sat down after an excellent talk. The delivery was superb, the content stimulating, her willingness to listen carefully during the question-and-answer time exemplary. The chair of the conference invited us to respond with a song of worship. Quickly it became apparent that no one was lined up to operate the overhead projector for the words. Quietly, unassumingly, the speaker slipped into place and changed the transparencies. She embodied a value.

Twice a year my colleagues load a van full of stuff to take to the Christian Resources Exhibition. When the exhibition is finished, the van returns to CPAS, often early on a Friday evening. A few days beforehand, an e-mail goes round the office asking for volunteers to help unload. You can almost hear the corporate groan! Once I decided not to groan but to help out. I was impressed to see the society's C.E.O helping to unload the van. Apparently he was always there. He embodied a value.

We are a 24-hour value transmission system. What are we transmitting?

FOR REFLECTION

- How much does God value me?
- What are my core values, and why?
- Where do I see value clashes with those I lead, and what might I do about it?

I wanna be the leader
I wanna be the leader
Can I be the leader?
Can I? I can?
Promise? Promise?
Yippee, I'm the leader
I'm the leader

OK what shall we do?[1]

ROGER McGOUGH (B. 1937)

Chapter 10

LEADERS DISCERN, ARTICULATE AND IMPLEMENT GOD'S VISION

Articulating the vision may be the single most important responsibility that a leader has.

WALTER WRIGHT[2]

We now consider two outward-focused competencies. In this chapter we think about the leader's responsibility for discerning, articulating, and implementing vision. Leadership by definition involves leading people, and to do this well the leader needs to know the direction for the future so that others can decide whether or not to follow. Leadership without direction is meandering. Christian leaders have an additional responsibility, to help a church or organization discern where God is leading. Personal vision backed up by sheer force of personality or stubborn determination is not enough for the Christian leader. The heart of Christian leadership is paying attention to God and where he is leading his people.

Many Christians sit Sunday by Sunday in church, unsure about where they are going personally in their walk with Christ and together as a local church. The lack of corporate direction ultimately undermines any sense of personal direction. If the church doesn't move forward in its worship, discipleship, mission and evangelism, it suggests that lack of change is an acceptable position for the people of God. "As it was, is now, and ever shall be" is sadly a suitable epitaph for far too many churches, and far too many Christians.

The Christian life is about change. Walter Wright describes it clearly: "A biblical vision, according to Paul, results in changed lives in everyday living."[3] It is about being changed into the likeness of Christ, growing in holiness. Discipleship implies learning and growth through change. Local churches need to be about change, discipleship, growth and outreach. Where those responsible for leadership in the local church don't lead, churches and Christians begin to atrophy. This is why articulating and implementing vision is so vital.

For some, the language of vision sounds alien—jargon brought in from the business world to try to help an ailing church. But I suggest that even if the terminology sounds foreign, the concept is very much part of everyday church life. Nearly everyone has a vision for the local church. Unsure? Let me ask two questions. What would you like to see happen in your church over the next three years? What are the most frustrating aspects of churches you've belonged to so far?

I think all of us can answer those questions because each of us has an internal picture of what we would like church to be. This is our "vision" of church. The question isn't whether we have a vision for the church, but whether it is *God's* vision. And once we have a clear sense of where God is leading us, is that vision shared and owned? Are we making progress towards fulfilling it?

WHY DO WE NEED GOD-HONORING VISION?

On a dangerous sea coast where shipwrecks often occur, there was once a crude little life-saving station. The building was just a hut, and there was only one boat, but the few devoted members kept a constant watch over the sea and, with no thought for themselves, went out day and night, tirelessly searching for the lost.

Some of those who were saved, and various others in the surrounding area, wanted to become associated with the station and give their time and money and effort for the support of its work. New boats were bought and new crews trained. The little life-saving station grew.

Some of the members of the life-saving station were unhappy that the building was so crude and poorly equipped. They felt that a more comfortable place should be provided as the first refuge of those saved from the sea. They replaced the emergency cots with beds, and put better furniture in the enlarged building.

The life-saving station became a popular gathering place for its members, and they decorated it as a sort of a club. Fewer members were now interested in going to sea on life-saving missions, so they hired lifeboat crews to do this work. The life-saving motif still prevailed in the club's decoration, and there was a liturgical life-boat in the room where the club initiations were held.

One day, a large ship was wrecked off the coast, and the hired crews brought in boatloads of cold, wet, half-drowned people. They were dirty and sick and some had black skin and some had yellow skin. The beautiful new club was in chaos, so the property committee immediately had a shower house built outside the club, where victims of shipwrecks could be cleaned up before coming inside.

At the next club meeting, there was a split in the membership. Most of the members wanted to stop the club's life-saving activities, arguing that they were unpleasant and a hindrance to the normal social life of the club. Some members insisted upon life-saving as their primary purpose—they pointed out that they were still called a life-saving station—but they were finally voted down and told that if they wanted to save the lives of the various kinds of people who were shipwrecked in those waters, they could begin their own life-saving station down the coast. So they did.

As the years went by, the new station experienced the same changes that had occurred in the old. It evolved into a club, and yet another life-saving station was founded. History continued to repeat itself and, if you visit that sea coast today, you will find a number of exclusive clubs along the shore. Shipwrecks are frequent in those waters, but most of the people drown.[4]

Churches and organizations have a natural tendency to move from being a mission to a movement to a monument to a mausoleum. The pressure of day-to-day concerns, the constant battle with resources and the ease with which we opt for the comfortable option all work against forward-thinking change. Leighton Ford captures it well: "Circumstances change. Values decay. People age and get fatigued. Systems become rigid. Purposes get lost."[5] Vision helps leaders keep the blood flowing in the arteries of the body of Christ, the mind engaged, the heart beating, the limbs working, the will complying and the imagination sparking. Vision is one way of opening up an important "next step." It also addresses the deep desires and needs of people that are currently not being met.

Vision identifies where God is leading this group of people

Vision differs from church to church. Take St. Peter's and St. Paul's. They are two miles apart in Manchester. St. Peter's is a church plant on a tough council estate. It's been there five years and has just had a change of minister. The congregation is 45 adults and twelve children, all from the estate. The church is growing. St. Paul's is a thriving congregation of 250 adults, 80 children and 60 teenagers in a prosperous suburb. People commute quite a distance to attend St Paul's. There is a staff team of five and an annual budget of $150,000. The church is in decline. Both these churches are parts of the body of Christ; both are committed to fulfilling the great commandments and the great commission; both share similar values based on their reading of the Bible. The point at which they differ is vision—where God is leading them over the next period of time. This is influenced by their *context*[6]—their story so far (what God has done throughout the church's history, and the particular story of where they are now); their setting (the physical and social mix of the area they are in); and their spirituality (the particular nuances of how this local congregation encounters God and nurtures relationship with him). Each of these elements is different for the two churches. So too is the *character* of the leaders and the congregation.[7] The appropriate direction for one congregation at this point will be different from the other's. That's the point of vision—discerning where God is leading *this church at this moment* in time.

Vision captures imagination

While working for Springboard, a colleague and I helped to develop an evening for local church governing board members. Great crowds of them, often hundreds at a time, would come to an event designed to help them reflect on what a church board is and the place of evangelism in the church. The vast majority arrived unsure what to expect, and often not wanting to be there. It was a church business event, after all, and they knew what that meant—dull, boring and full of dreary business. Even worse, it was on evangelism—hardly an intoxicating combination. What astounded us was how they left. So many walked out commenting, "It's given me a whole new way of seeing the church board"; "Thank you for painting a picture of the church I'd like to see become a reality"; "I've never seen evangelism like that before"; "You've given me hope." That is the power of vision, of helping people see things differently. They realized that their deep sense of dissatisfaction didn't have to remain, that change was possible, that there was another way. Many people are prepared to change if they are given a vision that captures their imagination.

Vision helps decision-making

Vision is the final goal or standard by which all decisions are evaluated. When trying to decide where to invest limited time and resources, knowing that God is leading you in a certain direction helps to focus the issues. Too many churches lurch from one scheme to another in a desperate bid to try to encourage more people into the Christian faith or deepen the faith of those already present. Energy and effort are expended on each new scheme until eventually no one believes it is worth investing any further effort or energy, because none of the schemes are completed. They don't work, not necessarily because they aren't any good but because they aren't fully implemented. Discerning God's way forward helps you to leave aside the good for the sake of his best.

Vision gives meaning to those who are part of a congregation

Vision creates a sense of togetherness and accomplishment. People like to belong. One of the uses of the word "fellowship" in the New Testament is "to partner with a purpose." A clear vision helps people to know where they are going and work out the part they might play. The sense of "being in it together" is very important.

Vision generates resources

Resources follow vision, not the other way round. Vision helps to determine what not to do and so frees up other resources. People are willing to give to a vision that inspires them. "It's the energy that creates action. It's the fire that ignites passion of followers. It's the clear call that sustains focused effort year after year, decade after decade, as people offer consistent and sacrificial service to God."[8]

A PROCESS FOR DISCERNING GOD'S VISION

Our task is not to dream up visions and develop strategies but to see God's vision for a church or organization and follow where he leads. There are a number of ways of discerning such vision, and below I've outlined one that we've used to discern God's way ahead for the Arrow Program. It is only one method, and will need adapting for your context. If you already have a clear vision, whether it is written down or not, this process may provide some prompts to fine-tune what already exists.

There are two ways of approaching this process, an explicit formal approach or a more implicit informal approach. The more explicit and formal process needs clear and consistent management, and makes greater demands on the people involved. For the purposes of this book I've chosen to describe the explicit and formal approach because it enables me to explain the process clearly. If you want to make the process implicit and informal:

- Don't make a big thing about it, by announcing, "We're looking to discern God's vision for the future." Instead enter the process informally, making the various stages part of the ongoing life of meetings and events that already occur. Keep the process in the background.
- Don't use any jargon words like "mission" or "vision." Instead use the questions that define each of the words (see Resource Section 5).
- Don't make a big announcement when the process is complete. Rather, permeate the life of the church or organization with the conclusions in a variety of ways over a period of time.

In a local church setting, this implicit, informal approach is often the better way. Whichever approach we choose, we're looking for a clear idea of where God is leading us at this time. This is likely to need writing down.

The initial idea for this process came from a comment by Steven Croft: "The process is best seen as very simple. At the heart of any process of defining, refining and communicating vision is this simple dynamic of comparing reality with an emerging ideal."[9] There are eight stages to the process, and these will form the framework for the rest of the chapter.

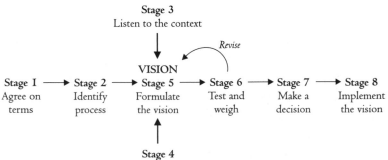

STAGE 1: AGREE ON TERMS

Much is written on the subject of vision, mission, values and strategic plans in both secular and Christian literature. In such material, words are often used interchangeably, with, for example, some people defining mission as others would define vision and vice versa. Experience also shows that in any given context, church or organization, people will understand these words differently. Thus, the first stage in the process is agreeing terms.[10]

The Bible uses the concept of vision in a number of different ways, with a wide range of subtle meanings. Rather than trying to twist texts to fit the modern-day understanding of vision, like the often quoted "Where there is no vision, the people perish" (Proverbs 29:18, KJV), we need to take the concept of vision as a vital facet of leadership, and ensure it is shaped by biblical values and kingdom vision. We cannot adopt current business terminology without critical reflection on the values behind it, values that may not be appropriate for Christian leaders. Nor should we dismiss it all as commercial, worldly and not of the kingdom of God, for we may be fooled into thinking that vision and values don't exist in the church, when they plainly do, whatever terminology you care to put on them.[11]

Once terms are agreed, everyone will know what we mean when we use certain words. Unless we are clear what we are talking about, it is very hard to decide how we are going to do it, which is the next stage. Defining terms immediately begins to set expectations with the group about what is going to come out of the process, and helps people to jettison unrealistic expectations (see question 1 under stage 2 for further explanation of this). It also ensures that leaders have a clear rationale for embarking on the process of change.

STAGE 2: IDENTIFY PROCESS

What is the particular way that we are going to seek God's vision? Six preliminary questions may help.[12]

1. *Is this the right next step for our church/organization?* Discerning vision as an explicit formal process is a risky path to follow. Sometimes people try to proceed down this path because of particular problems or difficulties, *but* (and it is a big but) if there are problematic areas within the life of a church or organization, we need to be clear whether these problems are related to vision issues or other matters. For example, if the real problem is the frustration people feel when decisions are made and aren't implemented, clarifying vision won't help. It will probably only make matters worse. The problem is not vision-related, and needs to be tackled directly, before identifying vision.

2. *How many people are we going to involve in the process?* The fewer people involved, the simpler the process is to manage; but the more people are involved, the greater their ownership of the end product. By the time we communicate the vision, we've lost most of the ways of gaining ownership, so including people as much as possible in the discernment process is a good thing. Inevitably different people will be involved at different levels, but wherever we can, it is worth involving people, and deciding what that involvement is going to be right from the outset. The minimum is to involve those who lead in the church or organization, and this does not necessarily mean the formal leadership structure. Who actually leads? They are the ones you want to gather together. A leader may come as a representative of a particular group (such as a children's leader) or as someone who exercises leadership without any particular role. And in a local church context there is one group that is nearly always completely left out of the process—children and young people. Including them will bring a whole different perspective.

3. *How far ahead are we looking?* Vision needs destination, so what timescale are we working on? In the past, people have talked of five years, but with the rapidly changing nature of society

and church, two to three years is probably a better timescale. This makes it a lot easier to identify a realistic plan of what you are actually going to do.

4. *How long will we spend discerning the vision?* Set a realistic time limit, and stick to it. This will depend on answers to the previous questions, but two to four months are helpful parameters. Any longer and it all becomes too much effort; any shorter and it is likely to be unrealistic.

5. *What resources will we use?* There is a cost attached to the process, and the time of those involved will always be the major cost. Do we need to release anyone from other responsibilities to oversee the process? There may be financial costs. Do we want to visit other places, go on conferences, or involve an external consultant? Will there be printing or design costs?

6. *What are we aiming to produce as a result of the process?* This is often the hardest question to answer, and we may not be able to answer it before we start. The end product could be numerical, qualitative or reputational. For example, one church produced a vision that included specific figures for what they believed God wanted to do; another described their vision in terms of qualities they wanted to work towards. Objectively we're looking for something future-oriented that, through the grace of God, is a possibility. Subjectively we're looking for something that inspires and excites people. One way to get ideas is to look at some church or organization websites.

There are three common models used for the process of discerning vision. The *individual model* particularly appeals to the rugged, entrepreneurial, pioneering type. It is the "Moses" model: go up on the mountain, discern what God is saying, then come back and tell the people. The results tend to be fairly revolutionary, and those who connect with the model tend to be the ones who write books on the subject! Its strengths are that, in a time of crisis or difficulty, the process is fairly quick and the implications fairly immediate. Its weaknesses are the difficulty of getting people to own the vision and the transition of the vision when the leader leaves.[13]

The *team model* is a process of corporate discernment, where the key is a leadership team. People sometimes decide against this method because they think it will lead to a "lowest common denominator" sort of vision. That isn't the case at all. Involving people in the process doesn't mean that everyone gets their way. At some point the leadership team will need to sift material and make a decision on the way ahead, but the likelihood is that, through the process, not only will more people feel they own the end product, but the end product will be considerably improved because more people are involved. Its weaknesses are that it takes more time and, if not handled well, leads to even greater frustration than before the process started.

A third model is the *individual who takes a discerned vision to a team for consultation.* This combines elements of both the above. It begins with someone prayerfully discerning God's vision for the future, perhaps through prolonged prayer and Bible study, perhaps as a momentary insight. However it comes, the individual brings it to the leadership team for reflection. Often the individual receives the blessing and backing of the leaders, and the vision is adopted by the whole church or organization as God's way forward, or the individual is encouraged to see it as a more specific vision for themselves. Sometimes the leaders decide not to back the individual's vision, and then the individual has to decide whether to pursue it as something really from God, or not.

The one golden rule is to be clear about which model you're using and, in the initial stages, stick to it. If you change half way through, everyone becomes confused and disillusioned. That's not to say that later on, when the situation has changed, our approach won't need to change too. Using different approaches over time is a strength, but in the middle of one approach it is normally best to stick with it until that part of the process is complete.

STAGE 3: LISTEN TO THE CONTEXT

If vision is to be found in the gap between the emerging ideal and the present context, the next stage in our process is to listen to the context. Where are we now? What are things really like? It is all too easy for leaders to lose touch with reality. This is why listening is so important. Here are a few ideas to help us avoid losing touch.

- Become one of your "shop floor" people for a week. View everything from their perspective.
- Conduct a questionnaire among three groups of people—leaders within the church, members of the church, and the community you serve.
- Invite someone within the community who knows nothing about your church to come along on a Sunday morning and give you honest feedback on the experience.
- Have your church leadership team (local church board, elders, deacons), select six people from the congregation who are slightly on the fringes, and ask them to share their views about the church. Include children and young people.
- Buy copies of the local newspaper and, over six weeks, identify the common issues raised that are concerns for the community.
- Purchase a church audit resource and systematically work through it.[14]
- Invite a consultant to come in and conduct an audit process.[15]

We need to discern what things are really like, not what do we think things are really like. As someone who no longer has responsibility for leading a local church, I've spent the last ten years worshipping in my local church and working in dozens of others all over the country. I would lead a local church very differently as a result of this experience, as it is so different being a member of a church rather than the leader. In my role as a team leader, there are regular occasions when someone in the team will say something that I disagree with because I don't think they understand the truth of the situation. I am slowly learning at those points of disagreement really to listen and not simply react, because others often see more clearly than I do.

STAGE 4: NURTURE THE IDEAL

Nurturing the ideal means looking at what we sense God is calling us to be. If we know what we're meant to be and we know what we are, then the gap is the place of vision, the work we need to focus on.

For a local church, this includes nourishing our impoverished ideal of what it means to be church through the study of the scriptures and prayer. This can be done in sermons, small groups, and individually. Without it we may not have any sense of what God is calling us to be, and therefore we will either flounder without any direction or we will have a variety of ideas pulling us in different directions.

One way to do this is to select a variety of key passages on the church from the Bible, and print them off on paper with lots of white space around them. Give them out to those involved in the process and ask them to meditate on the passages and write a response to the following questions. How does this passage inform our understanding of church? In what ways do we currently capture this picture of church and make it a reality? Where are we falling short?

Discerning the gap between the reality and the ideal isn't always easy, so here are a few suggestions for creative exercises that might get the juices flowing in other contexts as well as a church—for example, a youth group or a Christian organization. Remember, the aim of all this is to hear God.

- Gather a group of people and ask them to describe the church as a color, an animal and a simile. Get them to do the same exercise for their best experience of church, and for their perception of what church should be like.

- Imagine that in three years' time the local newspaper has heard so much about what is happening, it wants to write an article on your local church. What do you think God would like the headline to read? Now write the article.
- Imagine you're delivering a leaflet about your church to every home in the area in three years' time. Design the brochure, draw the photos and write the content.
- Imagine writing a book of the life of your church, and identify the chapter headings so far. What are the next four chapter headings covering the next three years?

STAGE 5: FORMULATE THE VISION

Part of the process of discerning vision will be formulating it. This stage is linked with the next as we go round a loop of writing the vision down, testing and weighing it, rewording it, testing and weighing it again, and reformulating it. After three years of running Arrow, we took some time to discern where God might be leading us next. These two stages (5 and 6) took about two months. Each time the vision was clarified and sharpened. Throughout, we kept praying and asking God to keep us open to him. We found it useful to have someone completely outside the loop to help us with words. When we are intimately involved with the process, it is easy to make assumptions in the way we formulate ideas and concepts. A fresh pair of eyes at this stage asks the awkward but necessary questions.

STAGE 6: TEST AND WEIGH

We can test and weigh the vision by involving the leadership team overseeing the process, a wider audience of those potentially affected by the vision, and a group totally outside the situation. The aim is to check that we are seeing God's vision and not just something we've dreamed up.

Everyone involved in the process is shaped by not only their Christian faith, but also values and ideas gained from general life that may or may not be helpful. At this stage the leadership team can ask reflective questions to help weigh if the vision reflects God's kingdom values.[16]

1. *What are the horizons of the vision?* For a church, vision is ultimately for the blessing of the whole world. The horizon is the kingdom of God, not just a local congregation. It cannot be inward-looking, purely for the benefit for those already involved.

2. *Whose vision is it anyway?* The church has a responsibility not simply to generate its own ideas or invent something, but to discover the vision that God has for the whole church and, in particular, this local congregation. Secular vision is generally self-generated.

3. *What's below the surface?* In the biblical tradition there is an emphasis on what is unseen and immeasurable—hidden qualities. What is outwardly successful may be inwardly impoverishing. For example, well attended and effective worship services mean little if people aren't embodying Christian values in their everyday lives. The vision must not simply reflect external, measurable qualities.

4. *In what ways is the vision shaped by gospel perspectives?* Secular approaches may focus on protecting personal interests or extending their influence, "saving their life and gaining the world." The heart of the Christian gospel is death and resurrection. Our vision must be shaped by gospel perspectives—the importance of truth; the priority of the poor, disadvantaged and weak; and the second coming of Christ.

5. *What is the underlying understanding of growth?* A secular view often works on the ideal of continuous growth and development. The model at the heart of a church is a more agrarian model, with seasons of growth within the life of the church.[17]

Involving the group who will be affected by the final vision, as well as the leadership team, continues to be important. We can share the vision with some or all of them, keeping them informed about where we are in the process, and inviting them to specific times of prayer and fasting. Anything that helps people to be involved will increase their sense of ownership.

Finally, when we enter the last stages of the vision discerning process, we can share it with those completely outside our immediate context. At this stage in the Arrow process, we sent the document to a range of people and consulted with them, carefully listening to what they thought. The feedback was not only overwhelmingly positive, but also full of wisdom and insight which helped to reshape the final version.

STAGE 7: MAKE A DECISION

After testing and weighing the vision, decision time comes. We act prayerfully, sensitively and yet definitely. A wise colleague reminded me at this stage in the Arrow process that we could never be sure we'd got it right, and there would always be little things we could change, but having tried to the best of our ability to discern what God might want, we needed to ask whether we were sufficiently confident that we'd got there. If so, we should go for it.

Checking out people's level of commitment can help. People can say "I agree" or vote "yes" and mean very different things, such as, "OK, if we have to"; "I'm for it, but don't want any further involvement"; "I'll do something about it, once or twice, if I have time"; or "I'll do anything to ensure this happens." If we don't ascertain the level of commitment, we may launch a vision that doesn't actually have the necessary backing of the leadership. When this happens, the whole process collapses at the first sign of opposition or sacrifice.

At this stage, people think all the hard work is done, whereas in reality it has only just begun. Although the discerning process may seem long and complex, it is far easier in most circumstances than implementing the vision—a crucial responsibility for the Christian leader, to which we now turn.

STAGE 8: IMPLEMENT THE VISION

The process of implementation involves three interconnected elements: capturing the vision in a memorable way, communicating it clearly, and connecting it with everything we do.

Capture

We need to capture the vision in words, clearly. People who write for a profession will be a great asset at this stage. We are looking for something that is:

- Straightforward enough to be understood
- Startling enough to be exciting
- Specific enough to give direction
- Simple enough to be remembered

Clever slogans that actually don't reflect the fullness of God's vision are not helpful. People are helped to remember and grasp the vision if it uses a mental image or picture, something they can see in their mind's eye.

Ensure that the words are well presented. A graphic designer can do wonders with how the words look, and a printer can give the whole thing the right feel (or a potter or painter or some other creative artist). Once we've captured the vision in the best possible way, we are ready to continue the process of communication. I say "continue" because ideally people should have been informed all the way through the process and know something, if not everything, of what is to come.

Communicate

The process of communication is complex, and there will be progress only if the vision is communicated in a way that people understand. This may mean breaking it down into small chunks, released a bit at a time, rather than giving it all at once.

The single most effective means of communicating vision is to live it out, so that people literally see it. That is why it helps to have total backing for the vision within the leadership of a church or organization. Then everyone is praying and working towards the same vision, living it out and modeling it for others. Like many other things, vision is caught as much as it is taught. Often people really grasp the vision only after six to nine months, when they begin to see the tangible results.

As an evangelist, I've worked with many local churches over the last ten years and I am often invited to speak at evangelistic events. I remember two men's events particularly well. At each of these events the church leader who'd invited me to speak brought along contacts who weren't Christians, from his own network of relationships. One leader played squash at a local club and filled a table with men who weren't Christians. The other had joined the local birdwatching club, because that was what men did in his town. In fact, in a short time he'd become something of a local expert. He too invited a bunch of his friends. It is no surprise to me that, at both those events, there was a higher proportion than normal of those who weren't yet Christians, as most of the Christian men attending had brought someone along. The leaders lived out part of God's vision for their churches; the other men caught it.

Influencing others is a process, not an event. We need to be wise about the process, communicating with the relevant people at the relevant time in the relevant way. I've found this communication train a helpful resource to understand the process.

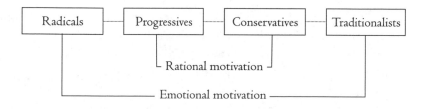

- Radicals (track layers) want everything to change *now*. They function more like a track-laying vehicle than an engine, always disappearing over the horizon of change, often careless as to whether anyone is following on behind them.
- Progressives (engine drivers) feel positive about change, but are aware that it needs skill, wisdom and patience to see it through, so they work more selectively and thoroughly. They often get their ideas from the Radicals, but think about how the Conservatives will respond.
- Conservatives (fare paying passengers) are wary of change, but can be persuaded (most likely by Progressives) to be positive; especially if they feel that their concerns and feelings are taken seriously.
- Traditionalists (brake operators) think ("fear"?) that all change is for the worse and, in some way, erodes the rich heritage from the past.

Radicals and Traditionalists are energized by emotions, so respond to passion, enthusiasm and vision. Progressives and Conservatives are motivated rationally, so require clear arguments as to why something should be done—or stopped. Key to influencing people are the middle-ground people who have a moderate approach to change, are pretty quiet, not great encouragers, who offer support by doing and are the internal opinion makers.

When I arrived in my first church, I got this hopelessly wrong. I thought that the key people were those who made the right noises and seemed most supportive. They were the Radicals who were often so far ahead of others that they were dismissed by the majority as "weird." Sadly, I didn't realize that the real opinion makers were the quiet people whom I hardly recognized. Identifying these people, probably about 10 per cent of any given congregation or organization, and quietly working with them, is a valuable investment of time. Influencing people takes time, and helping others to share in the process has great effect.

It is also important to avoid thinking that communication is primarily about what we say. Giving notices is one small part of communication, and not a very effective one at that. We have to employ every means possible to help people grasp the vision. We need to tell as many as we can, as much as we can, as soon as we can, as often as we can, and in as many ways as we can. And when we've done this once, we have to start all over again, because existing members will forget it and new people won't know it. The leader's role is to keep raising people's eyes to see why we're doing what we're doing, where we've come from, and where we are going. Without this people will lose focus, direction and motivation. Missions turn into mausoleums frighteningly quickly.

Connect

Bishop Mike Hill once commented, "Much is written about casting a vision. Much less is written about maintaining one." The last part of implementing the vision is connecting it into everything that is going on in the life of the church. Vision without action is merely a dream. Action without vision is merely passing the time. Vision and action together can change the world.

Huge amounts of energy are expended on gaining a vision statement, and then it hangs gathering dust on a wall. This is tantamount to leadership suicide. If we've sought God's leading and then don't follow, we are not only potentially being disobedient, we are almost certainly being foolish. People become disillusioned very quickly, and understandably so if all the effort merely turns out to be hype or froth.

To help us connect the vision into everything we do, we can develop a strategic plan and action plan. These next steps help us to ensure that every area of the church or organization's life is connected to the overall vision. How do we know when this is achieved?

Imagine visiting a church building on a Saturday morning. As you enter, you spot an elderly lady arranging flowers at the front. She smiles and continues with her work until you draw alongside her on your tour of the building. After various pleasantries you inquire if she always does the flowers. She replies, "Oh yes, I do them to help people feel warm and welcomed when they come to the service, especially the guests. It can be such a strange experience if you haven't been before. And then we take them to the confined and the elderly on Monday to show them a little love and care. It gives us a lovely opportunity to talk and pray with them." Somewhat surprised by her response, you ask her if she has always seen flower arranging in that way. "Oh no, I used to be on the rota. I didn't mind doing them once in a while, I quite enjoy flowers. But a few years ago our new minister got us to think about our church, what we're here for, what God might be asking us to do, and I began to realize . . ."

There is a church that's connected their vision. That's why leaders not only articulate God's vision, but also work to implement it. This is best done through developing people, often in teams, where each person is encouraged to play to their strengths. The average church doesn't have the resources of a big business, but the average business doesn't have the resources of the Holy Spirit. If we are to achieve God's vision for his church, we'll need to involve others, and that's what we consider in the next chapter.

FOR REFLECTION

- God in his grace longs to lead his people. How do I feel about this?
- Where is God leading us at the moment?
- How can I play my part in discerning and implementing God's vision?

NIGEL (63), MINISTER

The school assembly went well this morning. Yet when I look out across that sea of faces, I wonder what life is going to hold for them. It's all so different today from when I was a boy. I still remember my teacher at primary school, Miss Harman. She was great and gave such a lot of encouragement to me. Then there was Mr. Jackson, Mr. Clitheroe and Mr. Hepworth at secondary school. Each of them helped me in my faith and, I suppose, gave me the first taste of leadership. Then there was that wonderful couple who took me into their home when I was abroad. They taught me so much through how they lived their lives. They welcomed me as a precocious teenager into the church they led. And if I follow the thread further, there was Graham at university who discipled me, my first pastor who mentored me, Karen who coached me through so many life issues, Alastair who lovingly helped me grow as a Christian, deepening my spiritual life, and Mike, Odante, and Joe, colleagues whom I've had the privilege of working with.

Lord, as I look back on nearly forty years of leadership in your church, I thank you for all those who've developed me along the way. Thank you for what they gave to me, for their time and honesty, their love and concern, their strength and willingness to challenge. Please help me give as much, and may all those children at school have people who will give to them in the same way that others have given to me.

Chapter 11

LEADERS DEVELOP PEOPLE

A good leader is one who leaves behind women and men who possess the conviction and the will to carry on without them.

BARONESS LYDIA DUNN

Chapter 10 considered the place of articulating and implementing vision as the first essential outward-looking leadership competence, and in this chapter we consider the second: *leaders develop people.* Jesus clearly knew his Father's vision for his life, and as he set about it he drew around himself a small group of people. Reading through the Gospel accounts, it is noticeable how much time and energy he invested in a relatively small number of people—seventy or so in his wider group, twelve in his immediate group, and within those twelve a smaller group of three. Why didn't he just get on with what he had to do? Why don't we? We all know that investing in people is time-consuming, emotionally costly and frequently frustrating, but, as Walter Wright suggests, "Leadership is a relationship that cares enough to walk patiently with people towards a shared purpose. Leadership is not about leaders; it is about the people we lead."[1]

Through the years, a wide variety of people have developed and grown me as a leader, for which I am deeply grateful. When I mentioned this during a training session, one of the participants commented that no one had ever done that for him. Others nodded in agreement. Of course it is perfectly possible to grow and develop without the help of others—possible, but not preferable. For when leaders choose to develop people, they will see three things happen as a result.

- *Investing in others expresses the value of people.* People matter, and how we treat people matters hugely. As leaders we cannot treat people as a means to our own end, as pawns on the chessboard to be sacrificed for the grand plan. Instead, we see people as God sees them—of infinite value, created for a purpose and with potential for growth. One of our roles as a leader is to help people discover their value before God, discern God's purpose for their life and develop the potential he has placed within them.

- *Investing in others improves the quality of the job.* When we work in partnership with others, the old acronym for "team" can be true: Together Everyone Achieves More. No one Christian leader has all the gifts necessary to complete the job perfectly. God has deliberately designed his church as a body where everyone is needed and everyone has a part to play (see I Corinthians 12–14).

- *Investing in others ensures that the work continues.* There is no success without a successor. Jesus needed to leave behind people who would further the work of the kingdom, and so do Christian leaders today. There is no shortage of work to be done, but there is a shortage of workers, and part of our responsibility as those who lead is to grow more leaders at every level—in their families, among their peers at school and university, on the factory floor and in commerce, in children's groups and in churches.

For these reasons, Jesus took time to develop people. We can summarize Jesus' philosophy of ministry in the phrase "for the sake of many, invest in a few" and the rest of this chapter explores how he did that, based on Mark 3:13–19.

JESUS DISCERNED WHOM TO INVEST IN THROUGH PRAYER

Some time into Jesus' public ministry, he took a break from the crowds and "went up on a mountainside" (Mark 3:13) to spend time apart with God. Although Mark doesn't mention it specifically, in his parallel account Luke writes, "One of those days Jesus went out to a mountainside to pray, and spent the night praying to God. When morning came, he called his disciples to him . . ." (Luke 6:12–13). Jesus was about to make a significant decision, so he talked with his Father all night before making it. To lead faithfully, he himself had to be led. When choosing people to develop, we'll need to do the same. As a young assistant minister, I got this very wrong. My choice was made on what I perceived through limited understanding, and it was largely dependent on external factors. I've learned the importance of prayerfulness and of reflecting on what one is looking for in someone to lead.

I wonder what Jesus was looking for. We simply don't know, other than hearing his Father's voice confirming that a particular person was the right choice. That might be why his choice was so surprising. When deciding who to develop as leaders, we need to be very aware of our own filters and prejudices, such as gender, class, physical appearance, educational background, disability, accent, skin color, voice, age, intellectual ability and previous experience. If we allow these things to govern our choice, we may miss out on God's choices, which is why we need to start with prayer. We need to think not just in terms of mature adults, but children, teenagers and senior citizens. We need to think not just in terms of middle class but people from all backgrounds and cultures; not just extravert, male, strong natural leaders but leadership of both genders and many different styles.

It is also easy to judge on the basis of people's apparent talent for leadership, rather than on whether God is calling them and the quality of their character. To counteract these tendencies, David Ferguson identifies four things to consider:[2]

- Listen for humility, for someone who isn't caught up with themselves but is genuinely humbled by what God is doing.
- Listen for faith, for someone who trusts that God is involved in his world.

- Listen for gratitude, for someone with a sense of the privilege of being called.
- Listen for servant-heartedness, for someone who serves people through their gifts, rather than enslaving people or glorifying themselves.

As we decide whom to develop, prayer will keep us open to God's choice, wisdom will help us to see potential, and experience will help us to learn from our mistakes.

JESUS CALLED THOSE HE WANTED

"Jesus . . . called to him those he wanted" (Mark 3:13). Jesus immediately opened himself up to the charge of favoritism. So too will we if we take seriously the development of people. Others begin to gossip behind the leader's back: "Well, she has her favorites"; "He never has time for me—always spends his time with them." Of course we must avoid exclusivity and the danger of an unhealthy dependence developing in either direction or, even worse, manipulation of others for our own ends, but fear of what others say shouldn't prevent us from following the Master's example.

As the Gospel account continues, we see that Jesus did have time for others outside his immediate circle; indeed, the disciples sometimes felt they got a rough deal on Jesus' time (Mark 3:20; 6:30–44). He did teach the crowds, heal the sick, love the poor, challenge the religious leaders, answer people's questions and perform miracles. If he'd only spent time with his close band of twelve and those in his immediate support group, he wouldn't have fulfilled his Father's will. However, he balanced this "public" ministry with the development of those he'd called, and invested a disproportionate amount of time in them. Paul did the same with Timothy and a few others, proactively developing them to carry on the work of the gospel. What about us? Whom are we developing?

JESUS APPOINTED THEM TO BE WITH HIM AND GO FOR HIM

Jesus drew people to himself so that they should be with him and could be sent out by him. When we ask what helps leaders grow, we can follow through Mark's Gospel the way Jesus fulfilled these two priorities.

Role model

Jesus wants his disciples to "be with him" (Mark 3:14). He spends a huge amount of time with his disciples, sharing life and ministry with them. This challenges the modern Western compartmentalization of life. The neat boundaries between work and home never existed in first-century Palestine. If people only ever see us in one environment, they are only going to see one aspect of who we are. Growing leaders involves letting them into the whole of our life, the bits we like and bits we may not be so proud about. They need to see us tired and hungry, angry and sad, at play and at work. Individualism in Western society tends to heighten a sense of privacy in leaders' lives. Professionalism in Christian ministry puts a sense of distance between leaders and led. By contrast Jesus called people to be with him, and shared his life with them. Paul, following his Master, did the same: "We loved you so much that we were delighted to share with you not only the gospel of God but our lives as well, because you had become so dear to us" (1 Thessalonians 2:8).

Someone in our congregation recently left to go for ordination training at an Anglican "minister factory." She is a single woman. Reflecting on her two years as a pastoral assistant in our church, I heard her speak so positively of the experience that I wondered what had made it such a good time. Exploring a little further, it was the way the minister and his family had welcomed her into their family. She regularly ate with them; they did fun things together, they cried together; when she moved into her theological college it was her boss who carried heavy boxes up many flights of stairs. They shared their family life with her, and it made all the difference.

The disciples observe Jesus at work. They see him sort out priorities (Mark 1:35–39), hear him handle the critical religious leaders (2:1–12), listen to his teaching and have the opportunity to question him about it away from the crowd (4:1–20). They see how he reacts in a crisis (4:35–41), in a spiritual battle (5:1–20), and at a point of apparent hopelessness (5:21–43), and they witness those closest to him rejecting him (6:1–6). Those we seek to develop will benefit if we share our lives and ministry with them. Medical missionary Albert Schweitzer said, "Example is not the main thing in influencing others . . . it is the only thing."

Appropriate and growing experience

Jesus also appoints them "that he might send them out to preach and to have authority to drive out demons" (Mark 3:14–15), and this actually happens a little later (Mark 6:6–13). They had observed enough at this point to have a go themselves. Asking those we lead to try something that is way beyond their current capability or "comfort zone" is not helpful. Ideally we take a "next step" approach, giving those we develop tasks that are stretching, challenging and daunting, but not completely beyond them. For example, inviting them to do the same as us, without the years of training and experience that we've had, is inappropriate, and expecting them to do it as well as us is simply unrealistic.

Jesus wanted his disciples to be his representatives, with appropriate authority. Leadership without authority is crippling; authority without power is weak; and power without love is dangerous. Jesus gave his disciples authority and power, and constantly challenged them to use it in a loving way. Too often, Christian leaders fear sharing the work, and when they do their manner is begrudging and without full support. Empowering others requires giving away authority and power, a relational act based on trust. Delegation is the key tool in this act of giving away authority. It involves right attitudes towards those who are receiving the responsibility, right skills on behalf of the one delegating, and right benefits for both parties. I've found a simple model helpful when considering delegation.

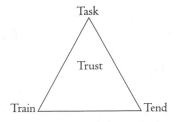

We need to identify the *task* clearly, and ensure that we give the task to the right person. The task ideally provides a suitable challenge and opportunity for an individual to grow and develop. In the giving of the task, there needs to be commensurate authority and a willingness to take risks,[3] as well as good communication. The person needs to know what is to be done, but not how to do it. If we tell them how to do it, we will squash their creativity and may miss out on new ways of getting the task done. Then we ensure they have appropriate *training* for the task in hand. This is about investing in people, providing resources that will grow them. Third, we *tend* them through the process rather than abandoning them. Delegation is not abdication of responsibility. Encouragement, affirmation, review and accountability are the tools of tending. When we delegate in this way, we can *trust* them to get on with the job without constantly worrying about how they are doing, confident that they have the necessary clarity about the task, skills to take it on, and support to complete it.

Without appropriate and growing experience given through delegation, people will stagnate. With such experiences, people develop, increase in confidence and are able to take on greater responsibilities.

Time for reflection and feedback

Upon their return, the disciples report back to Jesus and he says, "Come with me by yourselves to a quiet place and get some rest"

(Mark 6:31). I wonder what those words meant to the disciples. They were just back from a mission, excited by what God had done, and no doubt a little weary. So many people were coming and going that they didn't even have time to eat (do we know days like that?), and Jesus looked at them and said, "Let's get out of here. I want to spend time with you, I want you to rest." I imagine them smiling with appreciation. Yet if I was them, I think a part of me would have responded, "That's sounds nice, Jesus, but look at all the people, all the stuff we've got to do. We can't afford to take time out. Let's grab a quick sandwich and get back out there." Time out is not time wasted. Time spent with Jesus, reflecting and resting, is time well spent. If we are to grow leaders, we will need to model the priority of rest in our own lives, and find ways of taking people away with us so that they can reflect on ministry.

"So they went away by themselves in a boat to a solitary place" (Mark 6:32). Imagine the conversation on that boat trip. The opportunity to reflect on an experience brings perspective, encouragement, challenge and insight. If we're to do this today, we need to give those we develop feedback in the way that they are best able to receive it. I've only recently recognized the importance of the way we give feedback. I've known for a while that most people need to hear four specific encouragements to every constructive criticism. I know too that we need to be aware of our own personality, because that may well influence the type of feedback we feel most comfortable giving. What I hadn't realized was the importance of giving feedback in the way that makes it easiest for the other person to receive.

Some people, immediately after they have given a talk, want to switch off and aren't ready to receive feedback until a few days later. If we give them immediate feedback, they feel threatened. Others are really frustrated if they don't receive feedback as soon as the talk is finished. If they don't get any feedback, they think no one cares. Some prefer feedback to be written, so that they have time to ponder it quietly and then talk it through. Others prefer it verbally, and want to interact there and then. The easiest way to find out people's preferences is to ask them, and then act upon their advice.

Reliable input

People need reliable input to keep growing, and Jesus consistently provided it for his disciples. Even when a crowd of people interrupted their quiet retreat, he used the interruption as an opportunity to teach them important lessons about compassion for people and dependence on God (Mark 6:33–44). To grow leaders, we will need to make a priority of consistently investing in them. Steven Croft points out that the way most churches work is exactly the opposite of Jesus' model. We tend to give high initial input and low ongoing support, whereas Jesus gives low initial input and high ongoing support. We invest a lot in establishing a children's work leadership team. We meet with them and provide initial training and resources, send them off on their work, check up on them for the first few months and then let them "get on with it." Ongoing reliable input feeds people. Without it, they starve.

Peer support

The disciples had one another. They were not developed on their own, but in a community. Growing leaders is often done best in groups where people have support from one another in the process. Ultimately those in leadership need this context as well—a place where we are on a par with others, to prevent us from only ever living in our leadership role. It's a place where we are brought back to earth, where we aren't allowed to take ourselves too seriously, where we can share struggles and joys, where we are Bob, Jo, Mary or John and not "the leader, the minister, the boss." Peer support provides a healthy context for ongoing personal development.

As I read through these pages, I find myself thinking, "I haven't got time to do all this. There's a job to be done." But what is the job? For Jesus, the job isn't simply to achieve a task, but also to develop people. One of the easiest ways to do this is to follow Jesus' example and take people with us whenever we can. I've just come back from taking a team of six people from my local church on a mission. Only one of them had done anything like it before, and they were all very daunted. We spent two evenings together beforehand and then went for it. What a week! I was excited not only by what they did during the week, but also by how they grew personally. Those of us in leadership can take people with us in a variety of ways—for example, when visiting someone enquiring about baptism; when asked to preach in another church; when going to a conference or leading a training session; when leading children's work; when helping on a summer camp; when taking a Bible study; and when praying with someone.

JESUS DESIGNATED THEM

In Mark 3:14, we see that Jesus "appointed twelve—designating them apostles." Jesus was very specific in both number and title. From this moment on, not only the disciples but also everyone else knew that these twelve men were now the apostles. In a sense they had their job description. In Christian circles, we are sometimes in danger of "fuzziness" about what we are asking people to do. We don't issue them with a clear job description; we don't review their progress or clarify their objectives for the year ahead; we don't proactively seek to develop their talent, skills or knowledge; we don't thank them for work well done or say goodbye appropriately when they move on. Yet all these are important. In-depth guidelines are beyond the remit of this chapter, but in the notes I've recommended a number of resources to help in these areas.[4]

Developing people was a priority for Jesus, so it needs to be a priority for us as well. One of the ways this is increasingly recognized within Christian circles is through mentoring. Jesus was mentoring his disciples—a word to describe a range of ways leaders can invest in the lives of others.

MENTORING TODAY

There is a door of a little terraced house in the East End of London that closes behind me three times a year. As I stand on the street, there are two overwhelming feelings: what a privilege to have a man like that invest in my life, and what a joy to be challenged to mature in Christ. I leave the house so deeply affirmed as a human being that I feel I could take on the world, and so deeply challenged as a follower of Christ that I dare not remain the same. That's the value of mentoring.

It was a difficult time. I knew I was in a situation where my experience, knowledge and skills ran out. I didn't know what to do. I arranged a couple of meetings with a management consultant. He asked probing questions and listened carefully. He engaged with the issues, pushing me to see what the real issues were and how to tackle them. I left his house seeing things from a different perspective, able to identify a way through the mess, and with confidence to proceed. That's the value of mentoring.

On one occasion, when I was a young Christian, I'd got myself into a mess. I'd become confused about the Holy Spirit, I'd entangled myself in an inappropriate relationship, and I'd stopped giving time to prayer and reading the Bible. I wasn't sure whether I wanted help, and I certainly didn't know where to look for it. A Christian couple spotted me; one of them was a minister. They loved me, cared for me, welcomed me into their home and lives, and for seven months invested in me. I left their home freed from sin, nurtured in faith, and with a sense of God's call on my life to be a leader. That's the value of mentoring.

Mentoring isn't a fad, but something that has been a part of the church from the time of Christ onwards. What is new is some of the helpful insights that the focus on mentoring has exposed as we seek to be like Jesus and develop people.

What is mentoring?

It is informative to consider the relationship between mentoring and apprenticeship, which was the predominant training model in the UK until the last century. Traditionally an apprentice stayed under the master's control until the master decided to allow access to the final secrets of his trade. This made it hard to know when to break from the master's influence, and difficult to go beyond the master's skill. The master tended to keep his inner secrets to himself as long as possible, often taking them to the grave. Then the Industrial Revolution came, and the large numbers of apprentices swamped the masters, leaving little room for personal attention.

By contrast, mentoring is about enabling the mentoree to go beyond where the mentor is, freely investing in them everything we have to offer. It is highly personal.

My favorite definition of Christian mentoring is the following: "Christian mentoring is a dynamic, intentional relationship of trust in which one person (mentor) enables another (mentoree) to maximize the grace of God in their life through the Holy Spirit, in the service of God's kingdom purposes, by sharing their life, experience and resources." This definition highlights a number of factors:

- *Relationship:* mentoring is highly relational, and therefore demanding on both those involved.
- *Dynamic:* change is at the center of a mentoring relationship; growth is involved.
- *Intentional:* there is a clear purpose, with clear direction and expectations.
- *Mentor:* the mentor is one who knows or has experienced something. Generally the mentor is older than the mentoree.
- *Enabling:* the mentor's agenda is the other person's growth, so his/her role is to strengthen the mentoree's capacity to grow, develop and change.
- *Mentoree:* someone who desires to receive from a mentor and is willing to change.
- *The grace of God:* this is the foundation to all growth and service in the Christian life.
- *The Holy Spirit:* all Christian mentoring is dependent on what God does in a person's life through his Spirit.
- *Service of God's kingdom:* the focus is on God's kingdom purposes, not on selfish gain or influence.

- *Sharing:* this needs to be done at an appropriate time and in an appropriate way.
- *Life:* being with people and inviting them to be with us.
- *Experience/resources:* sharing from what the mentor has learned so far in life, as well as the practical resources that may develop the mentoree.

As John Mallison points out, "Jesus Christ is the real and decisive agent in Christian mentoring. We cannot bring about change in our mentorees, yet we can influence them to be changed by Jesus Christ."[5]

Mentoring covers a variety of ways to develop people, and I've found it helpful to use a diagram to describe the different types of mentor roles. You can find this in the Resources Section 6.

Mentoring needs today

We've seen that mentoring was a part of Jesus' ministry. It was used in the Old Testament (Moses and Joshua: see Deuteronomy 31:1–8) and by the early church (Paul and Timothy). Throughout history it has been a crucial way to develop people, and today there are some specific issues that highlight its need.

- *Increased mobility:* As people move away from their extended family, those who might have acted as mentors in the past have virtually no contact with their family members. In many contexts, grandparents, aunts and uncles are no longer present to guide and influence the younger generation.
- *Parenting issues:* We have increased family breakdown, and one consequence of this is the huge increase in absentee parents. One in eight children no longer have any contact with the parent that moves out of the home (normally the father) within two years of their departure. Research consistently shows that children, boys in particular, who are raised by single parents are more likely to struggle with academic studies, and are more emotionally insecure.[6]

- *Later maturity:* "Teenagers" are a creation of the 1950s. Before then, boys left school at 13 or 14 to enter their father's profession. Here they were grown into men through a variety of rites of passage. The introduction of the teenage years means that children mature emotionally at a later date. The process of maturation is extended and, combined with a loss of rites of passage, many young adults are still living adolescent lives.
- *Rapid change:* Old certainties of the past are fading, so people need help to chart the new waters. Tom Wright, theologian and bishop, speaks of us experiencing "more change in the last year than in the previous ten years, more in the last ten years than in the previous hundred years, and more change in the last hundred years than in the whole of the previous millennium."[7] With the speed, depth and breadth of change, leaders need help to find some fixed compass points to guide them along.
- *Pressures of public life:* A cynical spirit, individualism and competitive behavior all close down opportunities for people to learn creatively from one another. Independence is the virtue: "Don't rely on anyone else"; or "It's a dog-eat-dog world out there."
- *Abuse paranoia:* Sadly, the necessary emphasis on appropriate guidelines to prevent abuse means that many informal mentoring relationships no longer exist. For example, a key time for boys to have a mentor is between the ages of 12 and 18. When I was at school, two teachers acted as my mentors, helping me through the ups and downs of the adolescent years. Today, many teachers, youth workers and younger ministers avoid becoming too closely involved with those they lead for fear of being accused of abuse. For girls too, research shows that an important part of their development is hampered if there is no close significant male influence in their lives, but again men shy away from this influence for fear of accusations of abuse.

In such a society, more and more young people enter adulthood without the basic building blocks of their identity, security, self-worth and significance in place. Spiritually many lack the essential disciplines that have helped countless generations of Christians to maintain a vibrant and growing faith through their adult life. Mentoring is one way to address these chronic shortages, to help people come to a maturity of faith and life "so that we may present everyone perfect in Christ" (Colossians 1:28). For young people, mentors help to feed and focus their dreams, and enable them to fulfill their dreams. For decades, Christian organizations like CPAS have run summer camps for children and young people—eight days of fun activities, Bible teaching and worship.[8] Central to the way they work is that each child or young person is allocated a leader who mentors them. Many of the outstanding Christian leaders of our time were helped to come to faith on camps like these, grown in discipleship and nurtured in Christian leadership. This style of mentoring needs to explode out of the camp context and into the everyday life of the church.

If you are a younger leader, you may find it really hard to identify someone to mentor you, but don't give up. It took me seven years to find the right spiritual director. Be proactive; don't wait for people to offer. Prayerfully identify what you'd like to explore, ask who might be able to help, let others know what you're looking for, and then take your courage in your hands and ask people if they would be prepared to mentor you.

A colleague of mine came to a moment of deep personal self-realization while listening to some teaching on the relationship between Paul and Timothy in 2 Timothy. The speaker asked his audience, "Who has invested in you?" My friend realized that the answer was "no one." His childhood was very tough, with an alcoholic mother and an absent father. His earliest memories are of fending for himself, and that early experience became the pattern for his life. Now in his early 40s, what is he to do with the realization that no one has invested in him? What if you are a midlife leader and your realization is the same? My colleague chose to break the pattern, to look for people to invest in his life, partly to ensure that he didn't become one of those leaders who glorifies in having made it on their own. Christian leaders need to model interdependence, not independence, to the generation of emerging leaders. He also chose to use his negative experience and turn it into something positive, to make sure emerging leaders around him would not be in the same position as him in twenty years time. He chose to invest in others.

If you are an older leader, please mentor others, and realize that it is never too late to be mentored yourself. Leaders develop people. For the sake of the many, let's invest in a few.

FOR REFLECTION

- What is Jesus using at this time to grow me in discipleship and leadership?
- When I think about developing people, what am I looking for in a person?
- Is there somebody I might offer to mentor at this time?
- What mentoring needs do I have, and how could they be met?

PART SIX

GROWING LEADERS LEAD IN COMMUNITY

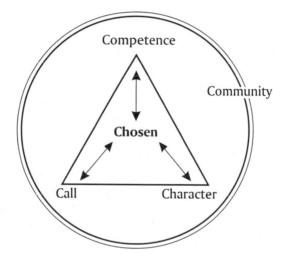

In the final part of this book, we consider the context for Christian leadership. *Growing Leaders* has so far focused on issues primarily related to individuals. We've considered the importance of knowing we're chosen by God, the priority of discerning God's call on our life and developing Christ-like character. We've explored four competencies at the heart of Christian leadership. Part Six identifies that leadership in the New Testament is plural, and that therefore the right context for any exercise of leadership is community (the circle around the rest of the diagram).

MARK (47), MINISTER: JOURNAL ENTRY

Yesterday I felt a rising sense of envy. It was after the main service and in one of those rare moments when no one had approached me for anything; I looked around at people having coffee. Some were deep in conversations, others laughing, some fixing up plans for the week ahead. I realized that although I could put a name to nearly every person, I am not sure I would call any of them my friends. I wonder if any of them really knows what goes on inside me. With the recent tough decisions I've had to make, I know I've alienated some, and that the conversations rumble on behind my back. I feel isolated, and envious of those who have close friends within the church.

I remember years ago, before I was ordained, my minister talking of the loneliness of leadership, and I now know what he meant. It is so different from being an assistant minister with a colleague. What is the way forward? I'll always carry the burden of responsibility, but surely there must be a better way to share the tasks of leadership. It would be great to be part of a team, but the thought of trying to establish one makes me feel exhausted. I am busy enough as it is, and where on earth would I find time to create a leadership team? So I guess I just press on. Perhaps that is the way it is.

Chapter 12

TEAM TALK

*Christ's concern is for both the saving of
individuals and the forming of community.
He is Savior and Shepherd.*

GILBERT BILEZIKIAN[1]

Growing leadership occurs best in community. Christian leadership is not meant to be a solo operation, but a team experience where the gifts of the team complement and balance one another. Theologically this corporateness reflects the nature of the body of Christ and of God himself as Trinity. Two reasons convince me that we must return to leadership in community if we are to grow leaders today.

THE NATURE OF LEADERSHIP WITHIN THE CHURCH

Leadership in the New Testament is always plural. Theology professor Gilbert Bilezikian comments, "Throughout the New Testament, church leadership is presented as a collective ministry. Even when the indefinite term 'leader' is used in the context of Christian community, it receives a plural reference (Hebrews 13:7, 17)."[2] Another biblical scholar, Gordon Fee, argues that Western Christians struggle to see the reality of what the New Testament is saying on this issue because of the tension between individual and corporate life "where Western Christians in particular are trained from birth to value the individual above the group, whereas in the New Testament perspective the community is still the primary reality, and the individual finds identity and meaning as part of the community."[3] He suggests that rather than the clergy being a separate group from the laity, the leaders were simply an identifiable part of the whole people of God.

Thus leadership in the New Testament people of God is never seen as outside or above the people themselves, but simply as part of the whole, essential to its well being, but governed by the same set of "rules." They are not "set apart" by "ordination"; rather their gifts are part of the Spirit's work among the whole people.[4]

Fee suggests that the essential nature of the Church was plural, which is why the epistles are addressed to churches, leaders are rarely singled out,[5] and the imperatives in the epistles are primarily corporate in nature, addressing individuals only as part of a community. The "one another" verses are one expression of this corporateness (for example, Romans 12:10, 16; 13:8). He concludes that leadership in the New Testament was of two kinds— itinerants like Paul and Timothy who founded churches, and elders (only ever referred to in the plural), composed of overseers and deacons.

The elders were to build the people of God for works of service (Ephesians 4:11–13), exercising their particular gifts as part of the people of God, just as everyone else was expected to exercise their gifts. Gordon Fee longs to see the reemergence of a community of people with leaders emerging from within. He writes:

[The single-person model] tends to focus both authority and ministry in the hands of one or a few persons, who cannot be so gifted as to fill all the needs of the local community . . . For me the great problem with single leadership is its threefold tendency to pride of place, love of authority, and lack of accountability. Whatever else, leadership in the church needs forms that will minimize these tendencies and maximize servanthood.[6]

The model of church and leadership outlined here challenges deeply most people's experience. If we are to become the Church that the New Testament presents—an Acts 2 Church—then growing leaders in the context of the faith community is a priority not only for the health of the leadership but also for the effectiveness of the Church's mission.

For the growth of healthy leadership

In Acts 2 we see the early Christians expressing community in daily life. They devote themselves to the apostles' teaching, to fellowship, to prayer, sharing a common life to provide for one another as people had need. They met together for corporate worship in the temple, and broke bread together in homes. In the following chapters we see the emergence of leadership within this fledgling community, as the apostles teach (Acts 3:12–26), heal (3:1–11; 5:12), defend the faith before the Sadducees (4:1–13) and organize their collective life (4:32–37). Those in leadership are a part of the community, benefiting from its provision, care, and prayer as they serve as leaders. The interconnectedness of leadership within the community is expressed well when the problem of food distribution is raised. The twelve gather all the disciples, and together the group solves the issue (Acts 6:1–7), choosing seven men and presenting them to the apostles for prayer and the laying on of hands.

Healthy leadership accepts the responsibility of leadership and exercises it within the context of the caring community, sharing a common purpose, worshipping a common Savior. This is the best context for leaders to grow.

For effective mission

One of the results of the disciples' community life was that "the Lord added to their number daily those who were being saved" (Acts 2:47; see also 4:4; 5:14, 42). The focus of their leadership and community life wasn't internal. Unity wasn't their aim. They sought to honor God in their corporate life and looked outward to others, effectively sharing in God's mission to his world. Growing leaders facilitate such mission.

The nature of leadership within the church needs to reflect the church's life as community. This is the first reason for returning to a more biblical model of leadership in community. The second is our current experience.

THE EXPERIENCE OF LEADERS WITHIN THE CHURCH

Loneliness is a killer. According to recent studies, it is a growing epidemic among people in the UK. In particular, young men suffer from the isolation of loneliness. Loneliness doesn't mean having no contact with people, it means having no meaningful relationships. As rock star Freddie Mercury said just before his early death, "You can have everything in life and still be lonely."

Tragically, loneliness is just as common in the church. Part of the focus of my work is with men, and on occasions I ask them how many friends they have, defining friends as those with whom we share our deeper thoughts, feelings and concerns. The answer is nearly always "None." Some church men are more isolated than those outside church. Church activities make great demands on their time; they don't get the chance to make deep friendships either inside or outside the life of the church. Sadly, Christian leaders often model this sort of relational poverty.

In the past, much church leadership was male, and one model of leadership was that of competence and toughness. When things got difficult you pushed your way through, without expressing emotion or vulnerability. Military metaphors dominated teaching about leadership, and incredible adventures dominated the stories told of leaders. Then came the confusion over male roles fuelled by the feminist movement and a rapidly changing world. The nurturing '90s and the idea of the "new man" encouraged a different approach to masculinity. This was combined with the emergence of new roles for women in Christian leadership. Now we experience a reaction that calls for men to be men again, getting in touch with their "warrior spirit," reclaiming their masculinity. What is the result? A great deal of confusion and continuing loneliness among Christian leaders, especially men.

Combine this with a model of leadership that places an individual in a position that highlights their separateness from others within the church, along with many church members who are happy to see this model sustained, and we perpetuate the undermining of fundamental theological truths about the God we know and the Church we serve.

In the Arrow Program, we gather twenty-four Christian leaders between the ages of 25 and 40. It is surprising to find how many of these relatively young leaders already feel isolated and long to find a different context for expressing their leadership—one of community, team, interrelatedness and interdependence. They aren't naïve—they know that there is a necessary "first among equals" in leadership—but they long for the "equals" bit as well as the "first" bit.

How is the situation going to change? By developing a clearer understanding of community, and by modeling that in teams within the way we lead.

COMMUNITY AS FELLOWSHIP

Christian community is a place of fellowship—but "fellowship" is a much-maligned concept. Images of insipid smiles and superficial relationships abound, and fellowship is weakened to something akin to belonging to a club. I belong to a squash club. I attend regularly and know quite a few people there. When I enter the changing rooms, I get a warm welcome. I pay a subscription each year for membership, and receive notice of the annual general meeting and updates on what is happening in the life of the club. Yet when I don't show up for a few weeks, it doesn't make any difference to anyone. The only time anyone chases me up is when my subscription is due. In reality, I am a customer, and I don't belong in any true sense.

If we see the church as a club, it robs fellowship of its true meaning. There is a little commitment, no real caring, and connection only at the level of what suits me. This is not the picture of fellowship we receive from the New Testament, which uses the word "fellowship" in three ways.

- Fellowship means *sharing the same lifeblood.* We don't become Christians in an individualistic way; we become Christians in a deeply personal but also fully corporate way. I become part of the family of God, in which "each member belongs to all the others" (Romans 12:5) with Christ as our head. We share the same values as those who are part of his body.
- Fellowship means *caring connection* and intimacy (Acts 2:42). This caring connection is expressed in practical ways—love for one another, sharing with those in need, living in harmony with one another, and a whole range of "one another" actions, to be found throughout the New Testament (see Resources 1 for a full list).
- Fellowship means *partnering together with a purpose* (Luke 5:10). This body has a purpose, governed by its head, Christ. We are called to share in that purpose and play our part within it. We don't simply meet to make ourselves feel good; we meet together to fulfill the great commandments and the great commission.

Therefore, within the Christian community we discover a place of *forgiveness.* When you break the rules of a club, you're out. Don't pay the membership fee; your membership is terminated. Don't care for the facilities; you're asked to leave. Abuse the staff; you're banned from entering. Churches are called to be different. They are based not on rules but on relationships. Love is the defining mark of Christian community (John 13:34–35), forgiveness the natural result of love. If forgiveness is not part of our culture, we will restrict growth in leadership and discipleship. Leaders grow when they know they can make mistakes and *not* be thrown out. The defining moment for a church or organization is not when things are going well, but when their leaders let them down or make a mistake. How will we respond at that moment?

The Christian community is also a place of *friendship.* Without meaningful friendships, a Christian leader will continue to lead in isolation, and loneliness will be a constant companion. If we see "leadership" as plural, and "leading" a community task, then we need to develop healthy relationships to share the burden and blessing of this responsibility. Bill Hybels comments, "I have learned over the years that I am not strong enough to face the rigor of church work alone."7 None of us is. Friendship always carries risk, and in some senses friendship among leaders carries more risk than most, as we not only share life together but also work together. But without friendship we are in a vulnerable position.

The choice is clear. We either choose to be vulnerable and find support, accountability and encouragement to help us on the way; or we choose to be alone, and end up vulnerable to living in the red zone, and to sin, loneliness and breakdown.

One of the gifts Arrow offers to those who attend is the other participants who understand the dynamics of leadership and loneliness, and who can become close friends. As a leadership team, we work hard to create the context in which loving, wholesome and mature relationships can develop. We've learned that the following ingredients are essential for growing a community.

- *Authenticity:* take the masks off, and be yourself. Stop pretending.
- *Mutuality:* don't develop dependency in relationships, but rather grow together in interdependence.
- *Humility:* don't think less of yourself, but think of yourself less.
- *Vulnerability:* be willing to let others in and help you even in the most sensitive parts of your life.
- *Confidentiality:* reassure people that they are in a safe place.

Growing leaders will express their commitment to community by submitting themselves to learn from others. This includes learning from those whom others would discount—for example, children, and people who are disadvantaged or disabled.8 It will involve learning from those outside our context, finding people who can invest in our lives to help shape us as leaders. We will also learn from peers who are traveling on a similar journey, including colleagues and companions outside our context with whom we hold a mutual accountability and encouragement.

This commitment to community is ultimately expressed through worshipping and working together, and one way leaders can model this is through teams. Teams are a safe place to grow as a leader, where the temptation to abuse power or go it alone can be held in check, rough edges are smoothed, and pride is reduced through the sharing of results.

LEADERSHIP AS A TEAM

When Jesus selected his team of twelve, he had a particular reason for choosing them. There was a job to be done and he wanted them to join him in achieving that job. It was a leadership team.

There is little in the Bible about teams *per se*, although of course there is lots of wisdom about the human relationships that are at the heart of any effective team. Teams are a natural expression of the biblical priority of leadership as plural; they are a powerful context in which to express the reality of the biblical concept of community; and they are a God-honoring way of fulfilling God's purposes for his Church.

Some of my most exhilarating experiences of ministry have occurred as part of a team, as have some of my most painful experiences. Great teams are amazing: the potential for good is huge. Bad teams are appalling: the potential for harm is frightening. That's one of the reasons why people are so divided about teams. Part of the difficulty is that we are often unclear about what a team actually is.

Team talk

I want to define a Christian team as a number of interdependent people committed to a common purpose, who choose to cooperate in order to achieve exceptional results for the glory of God.

Teams are made up of people willing to be in *interdependent relationships*. This is much more than just getting a job done. Such relationships challenge deeply the inherent tendency to individualism, and they provide the safest context for gifts to thrive through mutual accountability.

Teams are committed to a *common purpose*. This is the reason for the team's existence. You don't start with people but with purpose, which needs to be clear, shared and owned. Bees can show us something about this. On a warm day, about half the bees in a hive stay inside beating their wings while the other half go out to gather pollen and nectar. Because of the beating wings, the temperature inside the hive is about 10 degrees cooler than outside. The bees rotate duties, and the bees that cool the hive one day are honey gatherers the next. They are committed to the common purpose.

Team members *choose to cooperate* in order to achieve exceptional results. This choice to cooperate must be based on the belief that together everyone will achieve more. If the team doesn't experience the benefit of such cooperation—exceptional results—their commitment to team will diminish, and the team will degenerate into a group.

Christian teams operate for the *glory of God* and the furthering of his kingdom. Christian teams need to apportion the glory to God constantly, and this is helped by the realities of team life. Exceptional results are achieved at considerable physical cost, through considerable relational pain, and with considerable emotional energy. These things force you both to rely on God and ultimately to recognize his grace at work in anything good that comes from a fallen bunch of people trying to work for kingdom purposes. We capture this on my current team with a liturgical response: "God is good"; "It's just as well."

There is a difference between a team and a group. In churches we often use the terms interchangeably or wrongly call a group a team, and that is why we create confusion. The following table outlines these differences.

GROUPS	TEAMS
Focus on individual results	Focus on team results, a common purpose
Focus on individual effort in group setting, independence	Focus on interdependence
Talk about "contribution"	Talk about "cooperation"
Focus on individual accountability	Sense of mutual accountability
Focus on collective results: $1 + 1 = 2$	Focus on synergistic results $1 + 1 = 3, 4, 20$
If one fails, s/he fails	If one fails, all fail

In a local church context there is often a variety of groups. For example:

- A home group (4–12 people). This group may meet to study the Bible, to pray, to support one another and to enjoy each other's company. It isn't a team because it doesn't have a common external purpose and its membership is not selected for gifts and skills to fulfill this purpose.
- A Church Council or eldership (6–20 people). This group meets to share leadership of the church in accordance with certain parameters. This group is unlikely to be a team because its members are elected rather than selected.
- The youth team (2–? people). This group may be called a team but not function as one. Often the group flounders at the level of appropriate roles. They function as a group with a common purpose but there is no internal structure to ensure that people are really working together towards that common purpose.

I am not suggesting that groups are wrong, or necessarily that teams are better. It is simply helpful to know which we need for what function in the life of a church or Christian organization. Clarity fuels commitment and cooperation. However, Jesus drew together a leadership team, the early church exercised leadership as plural, and although groups are appropriate at all sorts of levels, I think we need leadership *teams* to lead the church.

Over the last few years of working in good teams and in bad teams, the following six things have crystallized as insights into the make up of leadership teams.

1 Not every group is a team, and not every team is the same. Teams function at different levels.[9]

2 Teams don't just happen; they require effort and commitment. Teamwork is not a project, but a process that demands lots of practice; not a program but rather a philosophy. Teams, like any living thing, need a climate conducive to growth.

3 Teamwork is more than an activity; it is a relationship. Status and teamwork don't fit together comfortably. Each member needs a servant attitude.

4 The best teams are *not* made up of similar people. People are recruited because they bring something to fulfill the common purpose that no one else on the team has.[10]

5 Teamwork does not make your ministry easier, but it does make it more fruitful. The purpose of the team is to accomplish an objective at "exceptional" levels. Ultimately, the success of a team will be judged by the end results.

6 The benefits of developing higher levels of teamwork must be felt and visible. If you don't see tangible ministry results over time, it is highly unlikely that you will invest the time needed to develop a more effective team.

In Resources Section 6 there are some reflective questions to use when reviewing a team's life. I now want to offer some thoughts on stages in team development as a practical tool for helping leaders develop teams. Teams progress through clear stages in their development, and knowing where we are helps us to guide the process.

STAGES IN TEAM DEVELOPMENT

Why am I here?

This is the individual focus. Each person on a team needs to know exactly what their role is, and ideally needs that role both to work towards fulfilling the common purpose of the team, and to flow out of their SHAPE.[11] Last week I was talking with someone about joining a team I lead, who kept asking "Why do you want me on this team?" I realized I hadn't explained the basis of the person's joining clearly enough. As team leader I need to keep on affirming people and their contribution.

Who are you? Why are you here?

This is the group focus. Building relationships is part of being a team. I am more a project-oriented person than a people-oriented person, so this is the stage of team life that I am in danger of skipping. I focus on getting the job done. If I am not very careful, the way I relate to people, the way I set an agenda and the way I conduct a team meeting reflect my focus. Helping people to get to know one another, building trust and meeting people's needs are crucial to teamwork. We've found that it helps to do the following:

- Build relational time into each team meeting.
- Eat together.
- Go away together, meeting away from our normal context, preferably overnight.
- Do fun things together.
- Celebrate significant events, both personal and corporate, together.
- Laugh together . . . lots!

Teams are built on shared experiences, both the formal ones of the common purpose, and the informal ones that celebrate the life of the team. Without this element, the team will remain polite, cautious and uncertain. Teams also go through cycles in their group life, sometimes called forming, storming, norming and performing.[12] After the initial period of "forming," where basic expectations are set about the way the team operates, the team enters the "storming" stage. Things chug along in a particular pattern until something happens to create a "storm." This may be the first real conflict within the team, or a failure on someone's part, or an external factor that brings added pressure. At this point team members can fear that everything is falling apart, and quickly revert to operating as individuals within a group, protecting themselves rather than working for the team. Good leadership is crucial at this point. You don't fully become a team until this sort of thing happens. As I reflect on some of the "storming" times we've encountered (and there will be more than one), they have shaken us to our roots. Yet through honesty, vulnerability and a commitment to make the team work, we've come through the storms, and the roots are far deeper as a result.

What shall we do?

This is the task focus. Most teams have a tendency to get off track. Distractions abound. It is the team leader's role to ensure that the purpose, vision and strategic plan of the team are constantly at the forefront of what the team does. I try to do this through constantly connecting what we are doing today to the big picture of where we are going and why we exist. I also like to have the team values on the agenda to remind us of how we are meant to operate as we go about our business.

How shall we do it?

At this stage we focus on roles, giving creative initiative to each person. The team defines what needs to be done; individuals take that definition away and work on the best way to achieve it. The team plays a part in shaping those plans, and then recognizes and rewards effort and achievements.

Beware the idea of the dream team: it doesn't exist. Great teams exist, but they are made up of fallible people. A great team is one that focuses on the results and develops people through honest relationships. An even better team is one where the level of mutuality and commitment means that people share in its leadership. This doesn't mean that there isn't an overall leader, just that the overall leader doesn't do all the leading.

Apparently, when geese fly in a "V" formation they do so for very pragmatic reasons. As each bird flaps its wings, it creates an uplift for the bird immediately behind it. By flying in this way, the whole flock adds 71 per cent greater flying range than if each bird flew on its own. Whenever a goose falls out of formation, it suddenly feels the drag of trying to go it alone, and quickly gets back into formation to take advantage of the lifting power of the bird immediately in front. This is a great image of "Together Everyone Achieves More." But that isn't the end of the analogy, for when the lead goose gets tired, he falls back in the "V" and another goose flies the point. The remaining geese honk from behind to encourage those up front to keep up their speed.

Such teamwork is a reflection of the community nature of the Church, which in itself reflects the community at the heart of God. It is costly, but it is a priority. In a world longing for community and ultimately communion with its Father, the Church has a great opportunity to lead the way.

LIFE TOGETHER

I am committed to leadership in community despite my natural tendency to run away from it and hide. Life *together*[13] is the Christian life; there is no other way. But I want to end by quoting at length from Dietrich Bonhoeffer, who warns against bringing to community life a "wish dream"—unrealistic ideals of what community *should* be like. "Every human wish dream that is injected into the Christian community is a hindrance to genuine community and must be banished if genuine community is to survive."[14]

Wish dreams are never fulfilled: they can't be, for they are castles in the air. "But God's grace speedily shatters such dreams. Just as surely as God desires to lead us to a knowledge of genuine Christian fellowship, so surely must we be overwhelmed by a great general disillusionment with others, with Christians in general, and, if we are fortunate, with ourselves."[15]

It is only when the dream is dispersed that we can see the solid foundation of all Christian community—that God has bound us together as one body through Jesus Christ. We enter into our common life not as demanders or dreamers but as thankful recipients.

Thus the very hour of disillusionment with my brother or sister becomes incomparably salutary, because it so thoroughly teaches me that neither of us can ever live by our own words and deeds, but only by that one Word and Deed which really binds us together—the forgiveness of sins in Jesus Christ. When the morning mists of dreams vanish, then dawns the bright day of Christian fellowship.[16]

This is the reality of leadership in the Christian community, utterly dependent on Christ and his work of forgiveness in our lives. This is also the wonderful joy, for that same Jesus is alive today and reigns over his community, the Church. As leaders, we are only ever under-shepherds in the hands of the master Shepherd. In him can we trust.

Christ *has* died, Christ *is* risen, Christ *will* come again.

FOR REFLECTION

- How do I feel about leadership as an expression of community?
- What has been my experience of teams so far?
- Where could I see a team developing, and what might my part be in it?

CONCLUSION

In this book we've explored the heart of Christian leadership in knowing we are chosen by Christ to be in relationship with him, and recognized the tragic ease with which we can lose our first love. We've identified the importance of knowing God's secondary call on our lives to help us daily to discover his priorities for our time and energies, rather than simply responding to urgent needs, and living life in the red zone. We've seen how central a holy life is, as people long to see integrity, authenticity and credibility in Christian leaders. We've grappled with four of the essential leadership competencies: leading ourselves and those closest to us so that we reflect something of the beauty of Jesus; embodying Christian values so that we honor Christian belief; discerning, articulating and implementing God's vision so that we can lead people in God's direction; and developing people so that we grow more leaders to continue gospel work. We've acknowledged the place of community at the heart of our understanding of church and leadership, expressed in leadership teams. It is a daunting task.

Throughout, I've tried to stress that although Jesus constantly calls us to holiness, commitment and faithfulness, he does so as the one who loves, forgives and restores. Apart from him we really can do nothing. But with him . . . "I tell you the truth, if you have faith as small as a mustard seed, you can say to this mountain, 'Move from here to there' and it will move. Nothing will be impossible for you" (Matthew 17:20–21).

Where might we go from here? Continued reflection on the content of the chapters with friends and colleagues may provide further stimulation. Making use of the Resource Section at the back of the book may give some ideas not only for yourself but also for those you lead. Some may want to explore the possibility of participating in the Arrow Leadership Program (see www.arrowleadership.org), or some other leadership course. Others may want to start a course in their local church to grow leaders. My hope is that whatever we choose, we'll be committed to growing as leaders for the long haul, until that day when we too may receive the crown that is prepared for us.

My concern to grow leaders is not to make better leaders, but to make better servants. Focusing on leaders is a dangerous activity, particularly when we begin to talk about personal development. If we're not very careful, we enter a consumer activity where people are looking for what they can get out of it for their own sake, rather than an investment activity where people are looking to receive in order to give to others. If, as a result of this book, leaders are purely focused on getting more for themselves, I've done them a grave disservice.

Leadership in the kingdom of God is not an end in itself. It exists to serve a greater end—the mission of God. Kingdom leadership is about others, not ourselves; it is about service, not self-development; it is about God making me a better leader so that I may fulfill *his* purposes, not mine. Jesus reinforces this for us in John 15:16 when he says, "I chose you . . . to go and bear fruit—fruit that will last." Only kingdom fruit will genuinely last.

To continue to grow as leaders and to grow more leaders is a daunting task, but it is for a great commission. May we be those who are led more by Jesus, lead more like Jesus, and lead more *to* Jesus.

EPILOGUE

Here is a delicious irony. Over the last eight days, I've broken just about all the lessons I've learned over the last five years, many of them contained within this book. I set a deadline for writing this book that turned out to be unrealistic. It was a mistake. I've worked every hour of every day and night for eight days to try to complete it on time. It is already two days late. I'm back in the red zone, with early mornings, late nights, little time for the family, poor sleep, and a paltry prayer life. I knew things were bad when Sophie looked at me on day six and said, "You look as bad as you did three years ago!"

I'm not proud of the fact that I've got it wrong, but it does remind me how fallible I am, how often I make mistakes, and how much I need God's forgiveness and wisdom to live a better way. It also urges me on to live God's way and lead God's way. The standard is high—Jesus never sets any other—but as I run the race I don't wish to join a different track, but to thank him daily that he is the author *and* perfecter of my faith.

Over these last eight days, Sophie and my children have been amazing. I cannot thank them enough for their support, prayer and love. When I left home early yesterday evening to return to the computer, my six-year-old gave me a hug. He then said, "Daddy, can I pray for you?" I smiled and said, "Yes." He closed his eyes and prayed: "Dear God, please help my Daddy finish his book. Amen."

It's done. May it serve to grow leaders.

RESOURCE SECTION

REFLECTING ON THE "ONE ANOTHERS"

Listed below are all the "one another" references from the New Testament that relate to our life as Christians together. They can be used for meditation and reflection on what it means for us to be part of the body of Christ, called to live in community together.

Love one another. As I have loved you, so you must love one another. By this all people will know that you are my disciples, if you love one another.
JOHN 13:34–35

Be devoted to one another in brotherly love. Honor one another above yourselves.
ROMANS 12:10

Live in harmony with one another.
ROMANS 12:16

Let no debt remain outstanding, except the continuing debt to love one another.
ROMANS 13:8

Therefore let us stop passing judgment on one another.
ROMANS 14:13

Accept one another, then, just as Christ accepted you.
ROMANS 15:7

I myself am convinced, my brothers and sisters, that you yourselves are full of goodness, complete in knowledge and competent to instruct one another.
ROMANS 15:14

Greet one another with a holy kiss.

ROMANS 16:16; I CORINTHIANS 16:20; I PETER 5:14

I appeal to you, brothers and sisters, in the name of our Lord Jesus Christ, that all of you agree with one another so that there may be no divisions among you and that you may be perfectly united in mind and thought.

I CORINTHIANS 1:10

Serve one another in love.

GALATIANS 5:13

Be patient, bearing with one another in love.

EPHESIANS 4:2

Be kind and compassionate to one another.

EPHESIANS 4:32

Speak to one another with psalms, hymns and spiritual songs.

EPHESIANS 5:19

Submit to one another out of reverence for Christ.

EPHESIANS 5:21

Forgive whatever grievances you may have against one another.

COLOSSIANS 3:13

Let the word of Christ dwell in you richly as you teach and admonish one another with all wisdom.

COLOSSIANS 3:16

Therefore encourage one another and build each other up.

I THESSALONIANS 5:11

Encourage one another daily.

HEBREWS 3:13

Let us consider how we may spur one another on toward love and good deeds. Let us not give up meeting together, as some are in the habit of doing, but let us encourage one another—and all the more as you see the Day approaching.
HEBREWS 10:24–25

Love one another deeply, from the heart.
I PETER 1:22

Live in harmony with one another.
I PETER 3:8

Offer hospitality to one another.
I PETER 4:9

Clothe yourselves with humility toward one another.
I PETER 5:5

We have fellowship with one another.
I JOHN 1:7

We should love one another.
I JOHN 3:11

Love one another as he commanded us.
I JOHN 3:23

Let us love one another, for love comes from God.
I JOHN 4:7

We also ought to love one another. No one has ever seen God; but if we love one another, God lives in us and his love is made complete in us.
I JOHN 4:11–12

I ask that we love one another.
2 JOHN 1:5

DISCERNING YOUR SPIRITUAL GIFTS

Helping people discern their spiritual gifts is one aspect of local church leadership.

If Jesus actively leads his local church by the gifts of the Spirit, then leaders have a vital role in helping each member to be open to the Spirit, to know how he has gifted them, to encourage and train them to use gifts wisely, maturely and in faith, and to order and structure the life of the church so as to free each one to make their contribution.[1]

These gifts are given to every believer. "But each person has their own gift from God; one has this gift, another has that" (I Corinthians 7:7), irrespective of their age or their length of time as a Christian.

HOW DO WE DISCOVER OUR GIFTS?

The following is a practical exercise to help people identify what gifts God may have given to them.

Look up

Ask God to show you what your gifts are. Be prayerful as you consider your gifts, and flexible as you explore his leading.

Look at

Read through a list of spiritual gifts from the Bible. The one below is not exhaustive, but may act as a good starting point. Using a pencil, assess yourself on each one as follows:

A = definitely my gift
B = probably my gift
C = unsure whether this is my gift or not
D = definitely not my gift

Leave the list for a few days, and then see if you agree with your initial assessment. Change where necessary.

- Administration (I Corinthians 12:28)
- Apostle (Ephesians 4:11)
- Discerning spirits (I Corinthians 12:10)
- Evangelist (Ephesians 4:11)
- Exhortation (Romans 12:8)
- Faith (I Corinthians 12:9)
- Giving (Romans 12:8)
- Healing (I Corinthians 12:9, 28)
- Helps (I Corinthians 12:28; Romans 12:7)
- Interpretation of tongues (I Corinthians 12:10)
- Knowledge (I Corinthians 12:8)
- Mercy (Romans 12:8)
- Miracles (I Corinthians 12:10, 28)
- Pastor (Ephesians 4:11)
- Prophecy (I Corinthians 12:10; Romans 12:6)
- Leadership/ruling (Romans 12:8)
- Teaching (Romans 12:7)
- Tongues (I Corinthians 12:10)
- Wisdom (I Corinthians 12:8)

Look back

Think about the past. Where would you identify God's blessing on you? Where have you seen unusual fruit in ministry? What have you enjoyed doing as a Christian? What have you found energizing? When have you heard other people mention you're good at something, or are excited about something?

Look in

As you look into yourself, what do you feel passionate about? What really excites you? If you were guaranteed success, the resources and gifts to achieve it, what one thing would you most like to do for God?

Look out

Ask other people to suggest what they think your gifts are. Choose some people who know you well, and choose some who only know you a little. Be sure they are people who want the best for you, encourage them to be honest and truthful. Don't be surprised if you get contradicting opinions. You'll need to weigh their insights carefully. Spiritual gifts are recognized and confirmed by other people, so if no one thinks you've got a gift you believe you have, you may need to reassess your position. Insert their assessment of your spiritual gifts on a list, graded A to D.

Look around

As you consider your church, what needs exist? What openings are there for exercising gifts? Do any of these opportunities interest or excite you even if you don't feel qualified or skilled? If you could choose one area of involvement in your church, what would it be? Then ask if you can have a go at some of these things as a way of experimenting with whether you have a gift.

HOW DO WE USE OUR GIFTS? (1 CORINTHIANS 12)

We are called to use our gifts in a way that glorifies the giver, builds the body and extends the kingdom.

- *Remember the source:* "There are different kinds of gifts, but the same Spirit" (v. 4). We can't boast or be proud, we can only humbly and gratefully receive them as gifts.

- *Develop a right attitude:* "There are different kinds of service, but the same Lord" (v. 5). Gifts are not about status but service. Sadly, churches are riddled with people seeking status, which is why we must model ourselves on the servant character of Christ.

- *Recognize your dependence on God:* "There are different kinds of working . . ." (v. 6). Each gift is given through grace and used in God's strength. That's why Paul only ever boasts about his weakness.

- *Focus on the common good:* Gifts are not about self-glorification but building the body (vv. 7–11).

- *Function as a body:* Verses 18–20 are a watershed in this passage. Verses 14–16 identify the problem of those who downplay their gifts, verses 21–24 the problem of those who deny others' gifts. Verses 18–20 stress the interconnectedness of the body, welded together by love. We need everyone to use their gifts if we are to function well as the local church.

DEFINING TERMS

It is important not to get too hung up on terminology, but because so much terminology is used interchangeably we need to define terms like "vision" and "mission" so that we know what we mean when we use them. Often the process of discerning God's direction is hampered because people use the same words and invest them with different meaning.

Here is what I mean by certain words.

IDENTITY

"Identity" answers the question "Who are we?" Knowing who we are helps to shape belonging and involvement. For the local church, the Nicene Creed provides us with a statement of our belief, including our identity. This identity is a given in the church: we are an organism, not just an organization. Often, problems occur later in the process of discerning God's way forward because we haven't grasped our identity clearly enough. If we are an organism, part of the one, holy, catholic and apostolic Church, it will mean that certain things about the way we function differ from the way other organizations function.

MISSION OR PURPOSE

These terms answer the question "Why do we exist?" A mission statement is an enduring statement that doesn't change. It is likely to be short, and may be captured in a pithy slogan or tag line. Local churches can spend far too long trying to work out their mission statement, when actually, if we take seriously the identity issue above, it is mainly a given.

Not everything is up for change. Because the church is rooted in a vision and purpose that in some sense exists outside of time and above culture, not every aspect of its growth and development is subject to constant change. There is adaptation and embellishment, but there is a core story that remains unchanging and unchanged. This significantly impacts the creation of vision and mission statements, which cannot simply respond to cultural conditions and market forces, but must also take account of eternal concepts: an ethos often alien to secular leadership thinking.[2]

We don't decide the purpose of the Church; God does. It is given in the great commandments and the great commission, and is reflected in the Acts 2 description of church. It may take some time to decide how to phrase that purpose, to ensure that it communicates well in our specific context, but the content is, in essence, the same whatever part of the world we're in.[3] Capturing our purpose or mission is important, though, because it helps to shape everything else the church does.

VALUES

"Values" answer the question "What guides how we do things?" Values affect our behavior, driving us to do things in ways that reflect kingdom priorities. Again I suggest that, for a church, most of our values are given through our identity and a careful reading of the scriptures. Values make the church distinctive from some other organizations: for example, the church is in essence a non-profit-making environment.

VISION

"Vision" answers the question "Where are we called to go?" Vision looks to a destination, and needs to be clear, compelling and caught. A vision statement will be longer than a mission statement. Vision changes as the circumstances of the organization or church change, as individuals change, and as the vision is realized. Ideally it needs a time frame, probably 1–3 years, 3–5 years, or 5–10 years. After one year, however, the vision will need to be reviewed and refined because of changing circumstances. Vision often uses a refrain, or a mental image, or a word picture to capture the imagination, and needs to have a sense of "Wow!" If you can do it without God, it is unlikely to be his vision.

STRATEGIC PLANNING

Strategic planning involves targets or aims answering the question "What do we need to do to fulfill the vision?" How do we intend to realize the vision in a way that fulfils our mission and values? What areas of our activity will need to change? Ideally there will be four to eight major aims that need to be achieved to get us from where we are to where we want to be. These aims still represent the "big picture," and it helps to phrase them with destination language.[4]

ACTION PLANNING

Action planning involves tasks or goals/objectives answering the question "How are we going to do it?" These are practical steps that identify the focus of what we do this month rather than next month, as well as what we are going to do over the whole year and so on. They can broken down into priorities, plans, action, responsibilities and timing. Ideally they need to be SMART (Specific, Measurable, Achievable, Relevant, and Timed).

EVALUATION

"Evaluation" answers the question "When will we know we're there?" Through evaluation and review, we can assess how we are

doing in terms of both progress and process. This helps us to fulfill the vision in line with our mission and values, and to learn, develop, improve and grow. Sadly, this is a much-neglected part of
the process, but it is really important if we are to make healthy
progress. It also helps us to mark significant points on the journey,
preferably with some form of celebration.

THE MENTORING MATRIX

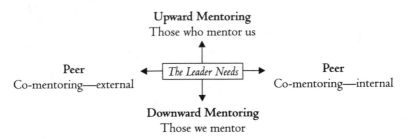

Intensive	Occasional	Passive
Discipler	Counselor	Contemporary
Spiritual Guide	Teacher	Historical
Coach	Sponsor	

Upward Mentoring
Those who mentor us

Peer		Peer
Co-mentoring—external	*The Leader Needs*	Co-mentoring—internal

Downward Mentoring
Those we mentor

Intensive	Occasional	Passive
Discipler	Counselor	Contemporary
Spiritual Guide	Teacher	Historical
Coach	Sponsor	

THE INTENSIVE PART OF THE MATRIX[5]

- *Discipler:* enables a person to grow in the basics of following Christ. On a number of occasions when men have come to Christ, I've met with them every two weeks over a 12- to 24-month period to help ground their newfound faith in basic Christian teaching and practice.

- *Spiritual guide:* offers accountability, direction, insights for commitments and decisions affecting spirituality and maturity. Finding a spiritual guide or director can be very hard, but when you find a good one they are wonderful. Often it is best to use someone outside your own tradition, as they will bring insights into a relationship with Christ with which you are not familiar.

- *Coach:* provides motivation, skills and application to meet a task or challenge. While trying to handle a process of change, I met with someone who coached me through the things I was struggling with, applying his experience and expertise in a way that brought me clarity and confidence in what I needed to do.

THE OCCASIONAL PART OF THE MATRIX

- *Counselor:* provides timely advice and correct perspectives on viewing self, others, circumstances and ministry. On a number of occasions, I've realized that there were things inside me that were having a major effect on how I related to people or a situation. I've met with a counselor to try to process those issues, and have found it gloriously liberating.

- *Teacher:* offers knowledge and understanding of a particular subject. Some years ago, we asked someone with grown-up children to spend an evening with us, exploring some issues in our parenting of our own three children. It was an invaluable time as they taught us some new skills in parenting that we desperately needed.

- *Sponsor:* provides career guidance and protection as one changes roles. I've been very fortunate to have a number of people who have sponsored me through various organizational changes. They have had the contacts and the clout to open doors for my ministry that would otherwise have remained closed.

- *Peers (internal and external):* offer support, encouragement, challenge and fun on your life journey. Internal peers are direct colleagues, external ones are people outside our immediate working environment.

THE PASSIVE PART OF THE MATRIX

- *Contemporary:* a living, personal model for life, ministry or profession who not only exemplifies the values one holds but also inspires emulation. I've never met Bill Hybels, never talked with him or written to him, but he has had a major influence on my life. I've read everything he's written, I've listened to many tapes, and I've talked with people who do know him.

- *Historical:* a person from the past who models dynamic principles and values for life and ministry. A number of such people are my passive models—perhaps David Watson above all. He helped me to come to faith as a teenager, and I constantly return to his books and talks for inspiration and help.

We can use this matrix to reflect on mentoring from a personal perspective. What are our mentoring needs at this time? Which type of mentoring do we find ourselves drawn to? Whom are we currently mentoring?

ESTABLISHING A
MENTORING RELATIONSHIP

Much mentoring is done on an informal basis, but if you want to establish a formal mentoring relationship some guidelines might help.

GETTING STARTED

If someone approaches us and asks if we would mentor them, or we've identified someone to mentor, we need to establish an initial meeting to discuss the possibility of mentoring, without any commitment on either side to the relationship actually going ahead. At that meeting there are three things to cover. First, get acquainted. Find out about the person's current situation, their story so far, and what excites them in life. Take time to get to know them a little as a person before talking about their current specific needs. Second, identify needs. What are they looking for in a mentoring relationship? Why now, and why you? Third, pray together. Christian mentoring is never a two-way relationship. It is always a three-way relationship with Jesus at the center.

The only commitment at this stage is to meet once to explore the possibility of establishing a mentoring relationship. From personal experience I know the danger of entering the meeting with an assumption that it will go ahead. There are very good reasons why it might not proceed, and both parties need to be genuinely open to these possibilities.

First, the mentor may not be able to offer what the mentoree is looking for. This may be discerned by either party. I once approached a person to mentor me, and after the initial meeting my gut instinct was that the person wasn't going to be tough enough with me. I know myself well enough to realize how easy it is to manipulate a situation, and I wanted someone who would be strong enough not to let me "control" things. I should have gone with my gut reaction. The relationship didn't work well, and because I was rather naïve and didn't know how to do anything about it, we rumbled on for nearly two years until it eventually fizzled out. He was a really good guy; he had lots to offer; he was prayerful and wise. The issue wasn't his competence; it was just that he wasn't the right person for me at that time.

Second, the "chemistry" may not work. Our experience through Arrow is that if there isn't some level of connection on the chemistry front, it is hard to sustain a good mentoring relationship. We are not expecting the other person to be a lifelong friend, but we do need to be able to spend time with him or her without having to fight off negative thoughts the whole time.

At the initial meeting, set a time to pray over and reflect on the conversation and a date when you will contact one another to let each other know your thoughts. If either one doesn't want to proceed, they need to be free to say so without fear of the other asking why.

DEVELOPING THE RELATIONSHIP

If both parties agree that it would be good to proceed, the next meeting needs to establish clear parameters. Experience shows that this is where most mentoring relationships falter. If clear parameters are not set from the start, the mentor or mentoree later becomes dissatisfied because something they expected isn't happening.

- *Clear expectations:* What are the mentoree's needs? How does he/she want them met? What can the mentor offer?
- *Clear commitment:* What is the level of commitment to the relationship? Can meetings be rescheduled? What if the mentor asks the mentoree to do something and they don't do it?

- *Clear communication:* What are the limits of our communication? Will there be any off-limit areas? What sort of contact will there be between meetings? What is the level of confidentiality?
- *Clear demarcation:* Establish the boundaries. How often will you meet and for how long?
- *Clear timeframe:* For how long are both parties committing themselves to the relationship?
- *Clear evaluation:* When is evaluation of the relationship going to take place? How will the agreement be modified to fit the reality of the mentoring situation? How will we know it is time to end? How will we end well?

After this meeting, invite the mentoree to write down their understanding of what you've agreed. This provides a check to make sure good communication has occurred.

WHAT A MENTOR PROVIDES

- *Affirmation:* Most leaders regularly receive criticism. What they need is genuine affirmation that builds them up. This isn't to make them big-headed or proud, but rather to constantly help them to see themselves as Christ sees them.
- *Perspective:* A mentor is outside the situation, and can offer perspective on whatever is happening in the mentoree's life. Mentors need to respond to the raw material of the mentoree's life, and not dismiss it as irrelevant. It sets the agenda.
- *Feedback:* Mentors offer honest, loving and helpful feedback to those they mentor—a very rare commodity in life.
- *Challenge:* Your aim as a mentor is to challenge people to become more like Christ (not to fall into the trap of trying to get them to become more like you). Attached to this challenge, the mentor can offer accountability by following up issues with further questions and insight, to ensure change takes place. A colleague who has met twice with a mentor says, "The thing that impresses me is her willingness to challenge me on the things I say.

Not many people have ever done that, but it's exactly what I need."

- *Prayer:* The mentor prays for the mentoree, believing that God alone can effect change in people's lives, and that the most loving way to care for someone is to pray for them.

KEY SKILLS FOR THE MENTOR

The key skills required are asking good questions and listening. Questions need to be open, direct, reflective and developmental. For example:

- *Developmental questions:* "If we were to cover something today that would make the biggest difference in your life or ministry, what would it be?"
- *Reflective questions:* "If you could . . . ?"
- *Character-based questions:* "What might be your next step towards Christ-likeness?"
- *Value questions:* "If you were to be known for one thing, what might that be?"
- *Relationship questions:* "What one thing would transform your closest relationship?"

Listening takes time and requires concentration. When we listen, we do so with our eyes, heart and spirit, listening for emotion, fears, silence and expectations. Thankfully, there are a number of books full of good questions to use in a mentoring relationship, and advice on how to mentor, such as John Mallison's excellent practical training guide, *Mentoring to Develop Disciples and Leaders*, Scripture Union, 1998.

CHARACTERISTICS OF EFFECTIVE TEAMS

A team in formation must answer a number of key questions and resolve some important issues as it creates a climate that engenders high levels of cooperation. If these issues are not resolved satisfactorily, they can sabotage the team effort at any point along the way. However, it is worth remembering, "Your attitudes are far more fundamental to your success in team building than any skills or techniques."[6] The following questions can help a team leader reflect on how the team is developing.

A TEAM CYCLE

Common purpose (the reason for cooperation)

The key question is alignment.[7] Is everybody focusing in the same direction? Do their goals match the team's goals? Do we have unity of purpose? If not, to what degree are we out of alignment, and why?

Appropriate roles and division of labor
(the strategy for cooperation)

It is not good for one or two people to work harder than everyone else. Are all team members clear on their roles? Do they know who does what? Are the right people doing the right jobs? Are things not being done that should be? Are things being done that shouldn't be? To what degree is the team interdependent, and in what areas? Are there reasons why we hesitate to become too interdependent—for example, lack of trust? Are there some obvious areas where greater levels of interdependence would bring added synergism to the team?

Accepted leadership (the structure for cooperation)

Good leadership provides structure and prevents floundering. The main reason for leadership to be challenged in a team is that the style of leadership is wrong, and one can tell whether or not leadership is being accepted, for example, by how quickly team members respond to decisions made. The leader also needs to maintain the balance between the task of the team, the individual needs of those on the team, and the life of the team.

Is it clear who is the leader in a given situation or on specific issues? Does the team leader effectively facilitate key team processes such as maintaining a spiritual focus, running effective meetings, problem-solving, planning and decision-making? (These can be delegated to other members of the team.) Are the team members proactive, taking initiative and supporting the team leader?

Effective plans and methods (the process of cooperation)

Is there an effective, systematic method of making high quality decisions? Is the team generally good at executing various strategies and action plans? Are we regularly reviewing progress, discovering and implementing better ways to do things? Are team meetings efficient, yet warm and characterized by effective communication?

Solid relationships (the climate for cooperation)

Are our relationships characterized by high levels of trust and respect? Do we appreciate the unique contributions of each team member? Do we accept the differences and diversity each member brings to the team? Does each member understand the goals, interests, strengths and weaknesses of the other members?

Excellent communication (the means of cooperation)

Is interaction among team members characterized by open, clear and honest communication? If not, it's important to explore why people find it difficult to communicate. Does the team work effectively to resolve interpersonal conflicts and differences that hinder team results?

RESOURCES LIST

The following resources are listed in relation to the sections of this book. Some are no longer in print but may well be available from your Christian friends, or from Amazon.com as a second-hand purchase. Obviously I don't necessarily agree with the content of all these books, but they are all worth reading.

PART 1: LEADERSHIP TODAY

What is Christian leadership?

Walter Wright, *Relational Leadership*, Paternoster, 2000
Henri Nouwen, *In the Name of Jesus*, Crossroad, 1989
Leighton Ford, *Transforming Leadership*, IVP, 1991
Derek Tidball, *Builders and Fools*, IVP, 1999
Bill Hybels, *Courageous Leadership*, Zondervan 2002
Michael Jinkins, *Transformational Ministry and the Way of the Cross*,
    St. Andrews Press, 2003
Jin Collins, *Good to Great*, Random House, 2001
Max DuPree, *Leadership Jazz*, Bantam Doubleday, 1993

The leadership challenge

Viv Thomas, *Future Leader*, Paternoster, 1999
Bob Jackson, *Hope for the Church*, Church House Publishing, 2002
Graham Tomlin, *The Provocative Church*, SPCK, 2002
Michael Moynagh, *Changing World, Changing Church*, Monarch, 2001
Eddie Gibbs and Ian Coffey, *Church Next*, IVP, 2001
Rick Warren, *The Purpose Driven Church*, Zondervan, 1996

PART 2: GROWING LEADERS KNOW THEY'RE CHOSEN

Philip Yancey, *What's So Amazing About Grace?* Zondervan, 1997
Dallas Willard, *The Divine Conspiracy,* Harper SanFrancisco, 1998
Henri Nouwen, *The Way of the Heart,* Harper SanFrancisco, 1991
John Piper, *Desiring God: Meditations of a Christian Hedonist,* IVP, 1996
Robert Warren, *An Affair of the Heart,* Highland Books, 1994
Patrick Klingaman, *Finding Rest When the Work is Never Done,* Cook, 2000

PART 3: GROWING LEADERS DISCERN GOD'S CALL

Pamela Evans, *Driven Beyond the Call of God,* Bible Reading Fellowship, 1999
Os Guinness, *The Call,* Nelson, 2001
Rick Warren, *Purpose Driven Life,* Zondervan, 2002
John Adair, *How to Find Your Vocation,* Canterbury Press, 2000
Stephen Covey, *Seven Habits of Highly Effective People,* Simon & Schuster, 1991
Mick Isbister and Martin Robinson, *Who Do You Think You Are?* Zondervan, 1999

PART 4: GROWING LEADERS DEVELOP CHRIST-LIKE CHARACTER

Dallas Willard, *The Spirit of the Disciplines,* Harper San Francisco, 1996
John Ortberg, *The Life You've Always Wanted,* Nelson, 2003
Richard Foster, *Celebration of Discipline,* Harper San Francisco, 1980
Gordon MacDonald, *Ordering Your Private World,* Nelson, 1988
Gordon MacDonald, *Renewing Your Spiritual Passion,* Thomas Nelson, 1989
Eugene Petersen, *Working the Angles: The Shape of Pastoral Integrity,* Eerdmans, 1990
Bill Hybels, *Making Life Work,* IVP, 1998

PART 5: GROWING LEADERS CULTIVATE COMPETENCE

Leaders discern, articulate, and implement vision

Steven Croft, *Transforming Communities*, Orbis Books, 2001
Aubrey Malphurs, *Developing a Vision for Ministry*, Baker, 1999
George Barna, *The Power of Vision*, Regal Books, 2002

Developing people

Paul Stanley & Robert Clinton, *Connecting*, NavPress, 1992
John Mallison, *Mentoring to Develop Disciples and Leaders*, SU, 1998
Ted Engstrom, *The Fine Art of Mentoring*, Trinity Press, 1989
Keith Anderson and Randy Reese, *Spiritual Mentoring*, Eagle, 2000
Paul Fenton, *Someone to Lean On*, SU, 1998
James Houston, *The Mentored Life*, NavPress, 2002

Leadership and handling change

Gilbert Rendle, *Leading Change in the Congregation*, Alban Institute, 1997
Michael Fullan, *Change Forces*, Falmer Press, 1993
Spencer Johnson, *Who Moved My Cheese?* Vermillion, 1999
Lee Bolman and Terence Deal, *Reframing Organizations*, Jossey-Bass, 1997

PART 6: GROWING LEADERS LEAD IN COMMUNITY

Dietrich Bonhoeffer, *Life Together*, SCM Press, 1954
Gilbert Bilezikian, *Community 101*, Zondervan, 1997
Steven Croft, *Transforming Communities*, DLT, 2001
Jean Vanier, *Community and Growth: Our Pilgrimage Together*, Paulist Press, 1999
J. R. Katzenbach and D. K. Smith, *The Wisdom of Teams*, Harper-Business, 2003
R. Meredith Belbin, *Management Teams*, Heinemann, 1996
Patrick Lencioni, *The Five Dysfunctions of Teams*, Jossey-Bass, 2002

**ARROW LEADERSHIP
INTERNATIONAL MINISTRIES**

THE ARROW LEADERSHIP PROGRAM

Arrow Leadership International Ministries believes that leaders that shake the Kingdom and the world cannot be mass-produced; they are sharpened and polished one by one into effective "arrows" that fulfill their God-given calling. Arrow's passion and purpose is to identify and significantly invest in the lives of proven, emerging Christian leaders who have a clear anointing and calling by God. Arrow looks to pour into the lives of a select few who are Kingdom seekers, not empire builders; proven leaders with potential, not potential leaders; anointed, not interested; gifted, not average; authentic, not superficial; relevant, not cliché; teachable, not just knowledgeable. While assisting leaders to cultivate the right mix of calling, character and competency, Arrow seeks to develop leaders who are led more by Jesus, who lead more like Jesus, and who lead more to Jesus. For information and resources on how to mentor emerging leaders, contact:

Arrow Leadership International Ministries
Suite 201A-19232 Enterprise Way
Surrey, BC
Canada V3S 6J9
Email: info@arrowleadership.org
Telephone: 604-576-5613 or 1-877-262-7769.
Web: www.arrowleadership.org

THE CHURCH PASTORAL AID SOCIETY (CPAS)

CPAS is an evangelical Anglican mission agency and community that exists to inspire and enable churches to reach everyone in their communities with the good news of Jesus. For more information about CPAS, contact:

CPAS
Athena Drive, Tachbrook Park
WARWICK CV34 6NG
United Kingdom
Email: info@cpas.org.uk
Telephone: 01926 458458.
Web: www.cpas.org.uk

NOTES

Introduction

1. Church Pastoral Aid Society is an Anglican home mission agency; Springboard is the Archbishops of Canterbury and York's initiative for evangelism.

2. The other marks listed in *Growing Healthy Churches*, a Springboard publication available from www.springboard.uk.net, are (1) an energizing faith, (2) an outward-looking focus, (3) finding out what God wants, (4) facing the cost of change and growth, (5) having a participative laity, (6) being a loving community, (7) seeing faith as a lifelong journey, (8) practicing what it preaches, (9) doing a few things well. For further reading see Christian Schwarz, *Natural Church Development*, Churchsmart Resources, 1996.

3. NCD Newssheet 18.

4. Leighton Ford, *Transforming Leadership*, IVP, 1991, p. 14.

5. Chris Edmondson, *Fit to Lead*, DLT, 2002, p. 14.

6. See Kent and Barbara Hughes, *Liberating Ministry from the Success Syndrome*, Tyndale, 1992, chapter 17, for an excellent analysis of the pressures upon ministers.

7. Carl Lee and Sarah Horsman, *Affirmation and Accountability*, The Society of Mary and Martha, 2002.

8. Colin Buckland and John Earwicker, *Leaders Under Pressure*, on behalf of the Evangelical Alliance, the Care for Pastors Network, Care for the Family, the Claybury Trust, CWR and InterHealth. See the Evangelical Alliance website for a helpful summary of their findings (www.eauk.org); see also Yvonne Warren, *The Cracked Pot*, Kevin Mayhew, 2002.

Chapter 1

1. Walter Wright, *Relational Leadership*, Paternoster, 2000, p. 7.

2. One of the most common positions of leadership, of course, is not "given" but rather chosen when we become parents.

3. Marcus Buckingham and Donald Clifton, *Now, Discover Your Strengths,* Simon and Schuster, 2001, chapter 2. Inevitably the talent can also be our Achilles' heal. See also Marcus Buckingham and Curt Coffman, *First Break All the Rules,* Simon and Schuster, 1999, www.gallup.com, and the work of Beverley Alimo-Metcalfe (Professor of Leadership Development at Leeds University) and her Transformational Leadership Questionnaire (www.lrdl.co.uk).

4. See Buckingham and Clifton, 2001, p. 48.

5. Paul Simpson, in an article in *Personnel Today,* June 2001, "So Are Leaders Born or Made?"

6. John Adair, *How to Find Your Vocation,* Canterbury Press, 2000, p. 133. I've slightly adapted his terminology.

7. Graham Cray, *Tools for the Job,* CPAS, 1990, p. 39.

8. "If spiritual gifts are manifestations of the grace of God, they are not to be precisely identified with natural or creation-given abilities. They amount to more than a local church talent list. Some are indeed natural abilities empowered by the Spirit through the call of Christ, but not all spiritual gifts are 'anointed talents' and certainly not all natural talents become spiritual gifts." Graham Cray, *Tools for the Job,* CPAS, p. 40.

9. I'm grateful to participants in the Arrow Leadership Program for their insights into this question.

10. Steven Croft, *Ministry in Three Dimensions,* DLT, 1999.

11. This time of change is reflected in secular thinking about leadership, and the abundance of books written on the subject. "In 1975 two hundred books were published on the subject of managing and leadership. By 1997 that number had more than tripled. Over the last twenty years 9000 different systems, principles and paradigms have been promoted to help explain the mysteries of management and leadership." Marcus Buckingham and Curt Coffman, *First Break All the Rules,* p. 53.

12. "Kingdom seekers are leaders marked by loyalty, for they seek another's cause; by fidelity, for they tell another's truth; by humility, for they accept another's results; by constancy, for they await another's time; and by expectancy, for they dream of another's glory." Leighton Ford, *Transforming Leadership,* IVP, 1991, pp. 97–98.

13. "If we strive to become great we become driven not humble; we lose sight of faith, while defending position; we become central, not servants." David Ferguson, *Relational Leadership,* ILM, 1999, p. 9.

14. Steven Croft, *Ministry in Three Dimensions,* DLT, 1999, pp. 45–46.

15. Graham Cray, *Tools for the Job*, CPAS, 1990, p. 49.

16. Stacy Rhinehart, *Upside Down, The Paradox of Servant Leadership*, Navpress, 1998, p. 28.

17. See 2 Corinthians 1:1–11. This vital aspect of Christian leadership is beautifully and brilliantly explored in one of the most helpful books on leadership I've read: Michael Jinkins, *Transformational Ministry, Church Leadership and the Way of the Cross*, Saint Andrew Press, 2002.

18. See the Teal Trust website www.teal.org.uk/styleind.htm; and Bill Hybels, *Courageous Leadership*, Zondervan, 2002, Chapter 7.

19. The "one anothers" are written out in Resource 2. As an exercise, either prayerfully work through the list one a day, pondering how you could better fulfill this "one another" in life and ministry, or take the list and share them with those you work with and ask how you could better reflect these as a team.

20. Viv Thomas, *Future Leader*, Paternoster, 1999, p. 32.

Chapter 2

1. See Grace Davie and David Martin, Religion in Britain Since 1945: *Believing Without Belonging*, Blackwells, 1994; G. E.Veith, *Guide to Contemporary Culture*, Crossway Books, 1994.

2. See Peter Brierley, *The Tide is Running Out*, Christian Research, 2000.

3. For example, one of the larger dioceses needs a 25 per cent increase in giving in the next year, or it will have to make redundant 80 stipendiary ministers, representing a cut in the workforce of 17 per cent.

4. Patrick Dixon, *Futurewise*, Profile Business, 2002, p. 11.

5. Graham Cray and Paul Simmonds, *Administry How to Guide: Being Culturally Relevant*, Administry, 2001, p. 8.

6. Beyond the scope of this section is the issue of growing leadership among children and young people. Research suggests that most leadership development occurs before the age of 25. To address the crisis in leadership, we need to work with children and young people to grow leadership in them—not a greenhouse atmosphere where fast growth in a specific climate leads to plants that can't cope outside their greenhouse environment, but a concern to think creatively about growing leaders of a young age, to identify such leaders and nurture them, to affirm their rightful place as children and young people in the family of God, and to give appropriate leadership responsibility within caring relationships as the years go by.

7. Pete Ward, *Are We Wasting Our Valuable Resources?* CEN, March 13 2003.

8. "Inherited ways of being church" and "new ways of being church" are terms pioneered by Robert Warren to refer to the distinction between churches that continue to function as they have done for decades, even centuries, and those who explore different ways of operating to connect with people disassociated from the church. See Robert Warren, *Being Human, Being Church: Spirituality and Mission in the Local Church,* Zondervan, 1995.

9. Richard Foster, *Celebration of Discipline,* Harper San Francisco, 1988, p. 97.

10. Foster, 1988, p. 102.

11. Foster, 1988, p. 100.

12. Some research discovered that "lack of or inadequate ongoing training" was one of the eight reasons ministers gave for leaving church leadership.

13. SHAPE stands for Spiritual gifts, Heart's desire, Abilities, Personality, Experience. See Chapter 5 for a detailed explanation.

14. Various assessment tools can give insights into this, for example, Leadership Practices Inventory (LPI) available from www.amazon.com; or DiSC available from International Training and Development Associates, www.itda.com or www.inscapepublishing.com.

15. The most helpful resource I've come across is Douglas Stone, Bruce Patton and Sheila Heen, *Difficult Conversations, How to Discuss What Matters Most,* Penguin, 2000. See also Jim Collins, *Good to Great,* Random House, 2001, chapter 3.

16. Chapter 11 focuses on developing people.

Chapter 3

1. Oswald Chambers, *My Utmost for His Highest,* Barbour Books, 2003, January 18.

2. Quoted during my ordination service.

3. Quoted in Paul Beasely-Murray, *Dynamic Leadership,* Monarch, 1990, p. 200.

4. The title of Pamela Evans' very helpful analysis of addictive patterns of living, *Driven Beyond the Call of God,* BRF, 1999.

5. A term taken from Transactional Analysis. For further information, see www.itaa-net.org.

6. Pamela Evans identifies five common problem areas that lead to addictive patterns of behavior: (1) Self esteem problems; (2) Identity problems; (3) Physical effects; (4) Psychological features; (5) Spiritual bankruptcy.

7. Basing his work on a study of John's Gospel, Christian psychiatrist Frank Lake suggested that in Jesus' life there was a rhythm of ongoing input that led to appropriate output. Lake's work is not without controversy, but I think the cycle of grace itself stands as a helpful tool in understanding the opposite of the cycle of grief.

8. Viv Thomas, *Future Leader*, Paternoster, 1999, p. 17.

9. Philip Yancey, *What's So Amazing About Grace?* Zondervan, 1997, p. 70.

10. Henri Nouwen, *In the Name of Jesus*, DLT, 1989, p. 30.

11. Richard Foster, *Celebration of Discipline*, Harper San Francisco, 1988, pp. 1–2.

12. John Ortberg, *The Life You've Always Wanted*, Nelson, 2003, pp. 52–53.

13. See Ortberg, 2003, p. 47.

14. John Ortberg, *The Life You've Always Wanted*, Nelson, 2003; Foster, *Celebration of Discipline*; Dallas Willard, *The Spirit of the Disciplines, Understanding How God Changes Lives*, IVP, 1996. There are excellent materials and resources on this subject on the Renovare website, www.renovare.org.

15. Most Anglican dioceses have a person who coordinates spiritual direction and has a register of spiritual directors.

16. Ortberg, 2003, p. 62.

Chapter 4

1. Henri Nouwen, *In the Name of Jesus*, Crossroad, 1989, p. 10.

2. Bill Hybels spoke on four of these gauges at the WCA Conference, Cardiff 1998. I've adapted his material.

3. Stephen Covey, *First Things First*, audiotape, abridged edition, Sound Ideas, 1999.

4. For a more detailed exploration of calling, see Os Guinness, *The Call*, Nelson, 2001.

5. See Guinness, 2001, p. 4.

6. "You have to know where you are going to understand what to do now." David Andrew, "Time and What to Do With It," *The Briefing*, May 2002, p. 17.

Chapter 5

1. "Those who cross the sea change only the climate, not their character," Horace.

2. David Runcorn, *Choice, Desire and the Will of God*, SPCK, 2003, p. 53.

3. Bill Hybels, *Courageous Leadership*, Zondervan, 2002, p. 248.

4. David Andrew, "Time and What To Do With It," *The Briefing*, May 2002, p. 17.

5. See Stephen Covey, *Seven Habits of Highly Effective People*, Simon and Schuster, 1999. See Habit 3, pp. 145–82, for an excellent tool to help discern between what is important and what is urgent.

6. If we are in complete crisis, things must be cancelled, help sought (both pastoral and medical), and immediate action taken. How will we know if we are at that point? One way is if all five gauges are in the red and have been for some time. Other serious warning signs may include suicidal thoughts, persistent inability to sleep, continuous illness, relationships on the edge of breakdown, or panic attacks.

7. Rick Warren, *A Purpose Driven Life*, Zondervan, 2002, chs. 30–32.

8. The Willow Creek *Network Course* is available from the Willow Creek Association at www.willowcreek.org; a Spiritual Gifts Diagnostic Inventory is available from Lead Consulting, Raleigh, North Carolina, USA, tel: 919 783 0354, fax: 919 783 0354. The following websites also list other tools and comment on their usefulness:

www.acts17-11.com/gift_inventory.html

http://sundayschool.ag.org/Training_and_Helps/Articles/a_recru_0302discvrgft.cfm

You can use online tools at: www.buildingchurch.net/g2s.htm

www.cforc.com/sgifts.html

www.churchgrowth.org/cgi-cg/gifts.cgi.

9. Rick Warren, 2002, p. 237.

10. An industry standard psychometric inventory is 16 Personality Factors (16PF5). Catherine Date of Character Dynamics is a qualified Christian consultant in psychometric inventories, and offers personal consultancy and church consultancy in this area: catherine.date@btinternet.com.

11. Quoted in Rick Warren, 2002, p. 247.

12. See Rick Warren, 2002, p. 247.

13. Oswald Chambers, "Man's Weakness—God's Strength," *Missionary Crusader*, December 1964, p. 7, quoted in Kent and Barbara Hughes, *Liberating Ministry from the Success Syndrome*, Tyndale House Publishers, 1992, p. 137.

14. "We are not so much human beings as human becomers. We are creatures in process—growing, changing and developing. Our lives will always be unfinished." David Runcorn, 2003, p. 103.

15. Taken from Bobb Biehl, *Asking to Win*, available from Masterplanning Group, www.masterplanning.com.

16. I'd be really pleased to receive your ideas on how to develop a life statement, as well as a copy of your life statement as an example that I can use with others. Please send them to James Lawrence, CPAS, Athena Drive, Tachbrook Park, Warwick, CV34 6NG or e-mail on jlawrence@cpas.org.uk.

Chapter 6

1. Kent and Barbara Hughes, 1992, p. 87

2. John 8:36; 2 Corinthians 3:17; 1 Peter 2:16.

3. I once heard John Stott say, "We have been set free from the *penalty* of sin, are being set free from the *power* of sin, and will be set free from the *presence* of sin."

4. Joseph Luft, *Group Processes; an Introduction to Group Dynamics*, National Press Books, 1970.

5. Feedback isn't only helpful on character issues, it is also vital in other areas of leadership. Here are a few examples. (a) *Invite feedback after every talk.* Gather a little group who regularly help improve your preaching and teaching. (b) *Invite feedback at the end of meetings.* Years ago, Church Consultant and Trainer John Truscott (www.john-truscott.co.uk) taught a group of us to put "review of the meeting" as an item on the agenda. Sadly I've only recently taken the advice, and what a difference it makes. (c) *Invite feedback at key leadership moments,* preferably before an important decision is made. I've learned now to check out such decisions with people before making them. I ask not only about the decision, but also about the process of implementing the decision.

6. I have Carson's permission to tell this story.

7. For the full text of their agreement, go to: www.christianitytoday.com/le/2003/001/17.3.html.

8. Another way of considering these marks would be to use Galatians 5:22 as a basis for a meditation on the fruits of the Spirit.

9. "Everything about Jesus' life shouts service. And the ultimate expression of his servanthood was the cross." Kent and Barbara Hughes, 1992, p. 50.

10. "Are we living lives that are obedient to the Scriptures? The question is a valid one because, while professing to obey God's word, we inherently possess an amazing capacity to do otherwise." Kent and Barbara Hughes, 1992, p. 40.

11. See E. L Worthington, *Five Steps to Forgiveness*, Crown, 2001.

12. Warren Bennis, *On Becoming a Leader*, Addison Wesley, 1994, p. xiii.

13. See Bennis, 1994, p. xiv.

Chapter 7

1. I think these are from Bill Hybels (source unknown).

2. For details about the *Lectio Divina*, see either www.valyermo.com/ld-art.html or Margaret Hebblethwaite, *The Way of Ignatius, Finding God in All Things*, Fount, 1998.

3. Colin Buckland, *Liberated to Lead*, Kingsway, 2001, Chapter 2 on Journaling; John Ortberg, *The Life You've Always Wanted*, Zondervan, 2003; Brother Ramon, *Seven Days of Solitude*, Hodder and Stoughton, 2000; Joyce Huggett, *Open To God*, Eagle, 1997.

4. Mike Yaconelli, *The Door*, May 1991.

Chapter 8

1. Bill Hybels, *Courageous Leadership*, Zondervan, 2002, p. 184.

2. Quoted in John Maxwell, *Develop The Leader Within You*, STL, 1998, p. 163.

3. If you are unsure whom to approach, see www.christianitytoday.com/leaders/features/classics.html. See also Gordon MacDonald, *Rebuilding Your Broken World*, Nelson, 1988.

4. The most compelling of these arguments is Gilbert Bilezikian's excellent book *Community 101*, Zondervan, 1997.

5. For an excellent series of articles on this, go to: www.christianitytoday.com/le/classics/war1.html and follow the links to additional articles on sexual issues.

6. Again I am very aware of the immense difficulties for those who suffer from eating disorders. The following resources may be of help. Helena

Wilkinson, *Puppet on a String*, Zondervan, 1998; *Beyond Chaotic Eating*, Impulse Sales and Marketing. See also The Kainos Trust, e-mail enquiries@kainostrust.co.uk.

7. It's interesting to note that one of the keys to the effectiveness of the Alpha course is the meal, a time where community is built.

8. Donald Guthrie, *The Pastoral Epistles*, Tyndale, 1990, p. 92.

9. For further insight into this approach, see James Lawrence, *Lost for Words*, BRF/CPAS, 1999, or visit the CPAS website (www.cpas.org.uk) for details of the Lost for Words pack, three courses to run in a local church to help adults, young people and children share faith naturally.

10. For an introduction to managing anger, see Bill Hybels, *Making Life Work*, IVP, 1998, chapter 11.

11. See Richard Foster, *Money, Sex and Power*, Harper San Francisco, 2000.

12. See James Lawrence, *Men: the Challenge of Change*, CPAS, 1997.

13. For an excellent insight into this, see Ross Campbell, *How to Really Love Your Children*, SP Trust, 1994.

14. Rob Parsons, *The Sixty-Minute Father*, Hodder, 1995, p. 95.

15. *Relational Leadership* course available from Intimate Life Ministries, P.O. Box 201808, Austin, TX 78720, Phone: 1-800-881-8008.

Chapter 9

1. I am aware that any definition of values is complex. Indeed, one Christian dictionary of ethics begins its section on values, "A widely used term, though often without clear meaning . . ." For Christians, I hold our values to be rooted in our beliefs about God. For example, love is a value that most people espouse. Christian beliefs about God shape our understanding of love and therefore the sort of love we value. Values fit within the broader categories of ethics and morality (each word having its root in a word which means "customs").

2. John Maxwell, *Developing the Leader Within You*, Nelson, 2001, p. 34.

3. Bill Hybels, *Dare to be Different*, Marshall, 1994, p. 12.

4. 2 Timothy 4:1–5.

5. Walter Wright, *Relational Leadership*, Paternoster, 2000, pp. 134–37.

6. "Organizational culture is a powerful force in all of our churches and organizations. It is a force that leaders must understand and address, because

leaders create and reinforce organizational culture." Walter Wright, *Relational Leadership*, Paternoster, 2000, p. 125.

7. See Gilbert Rendle, *Leading Change in the Congregation*, The Alban Institute, 1997; Lee Bolman and Terence Deal, *Reframing Organizations, Artistry, Choice and Leadership*, Jossey-Bass, 1997; Michael Fullan, *Change Forces*, Falmer Press, 1993.

Chapter 10

1. *100 Poems on the Underground*, Cassell, p. 87.
2. Walter Wright, *Relational Leadership*, Paternoster, 2000, chapter 3.
3. Walter Wright, 2000, p. 66.
4. This story is not original to me. I believe it was written by Thomas Wedel in the 1950s.
5. Leighton Ford, *Transforming Leadership*, IVP, 1991, p. 278.
6. See the diagram in Resource Section 5.
7. Robert Warren terms this the "angel" of the church.
8. Bill Hybels, *Courageous Leadership*, Zondervan, 2002, p. 31.
9. Steven Croft, *Transforming Communities*, Orbis Books, 2002, chapter 3.
10. I've defined my terms in Resource Section 5.
11. "Whatever else faith groups are, they are organizations: bodies or networks of people moving towards a common goal or goals. As such they share common characteristics with other organizations—even if their goals (and values) may differ." Gerard Kelly, *Learning for Leadership*, p. 3 on www.cafe-net.org.uk.
12. These are loosely based on some material from church training consultant, Bryn Hughes.
13. See Jim Collins, *Good to Great*, Random House, 2001, chapter 3.
14. Paul Morris, *Gearing Up For Mission*, CPAS, 1995; John Finney, *The Well-Church Book: a Practical Guide to Mission Audit*, SU, 1991 (available second-hand on Amazon); several Anglican Dioceses have audit processes.
15. Try John Truscott: www.john-truscott.co.uk; or Bryn Hughes on 01474 854774, who offer training and consultancy in personal and organizational development.
16. This section is based on Steven Croft, *Transforming Communities*, DLT, 2002, pp. 38–41.
17. See Christian Schwarz, *Natural Church Development*, Churchsmart Resources, 1996.

Chapter 11

1. Walter Wright, *Relational Leadership*, Paternoster, 2000, p. 148.

2. David Ferguson, *Relational Leadership Course*, ILM, 2000.

3. "The secret lies in assessing and managing the risk, not trying to remove the possibility altogether." Bryn Hughes, *The Leadership Tool Kit*, Monarch, 1998, p. 99.

4. See Hughes, *The Leadership Tool Kit*, chapters 3, 4, 7, 10; also Wright, 2000, chapters 2, 6, 7.

5. John Mallison, *Mentoring to Develop Disciples and Leaders*, Scripture Union, 1998, p. 39.

6. Anthony Clare, *On Men: Masculinity in Crisis*, Chatto and Windus, 2000.

7. Tom Wright, *Restoring Hope for the Church video*, CPAS and others, 2003.

8. For further information, visit www.ventures-online.com.

Chapter 12

1. Gilbert Bilezikian, *Community 101*, Zondervan, 1997, p. 131.

2. See Bilezikian, 1997, p. 165.

3. Gordon Fee, *Listening to the Spirit in the Text*, Eerdmans, 2000, p. 124.

4. See Fee, 2000, p.132.

5. Fee notes the one exception of Philippians, and argues that Timothy and Titus are addressed to colleagues serving as apostolic delegates in Ephesus and Crete and therefore, in that sense, not local church leaders.

6. Fee, 2000, p. 145.

7. Bill Hybels, *Courageous Leadership*, Zondervan, p. 248.

8. If we are not prepared to learn from children, Jesus has some stern words for us. See Matthew 25:34–40; Mark 9:33–37.

9. See J. R. Katzenbach and D. K Smith, *The Wisdom of Teams*, Harper-Business, 2003, chapters 4 and 6.

10. See the work of R. Meredith Belbin, *Management Teams, Why They Succeed or Fail*, Butterworth-Heinemann, 1996, on team roles. Belbin also produced a fairly simple questionnaire to help people identify what roles they play on a team. Psychometric consultant Catherine Date of Character Dynamics can help church teams use this material. Contact her at catherine.date@btinternet.com.

11. Pat MacMillan, *The Performance Factor*, Broadman and Holman, 2001.

12. Identified by Bruce Tuckman in the 1960s.

13. The title of a book by Dietrich Bonhoeffer.

14. Dietrich Bonhoeffer, *Life Together*, SCM Press, 1954, p. 15.

15. See Bonhoeffer, 1954, p. 15.

16. See Bonhoeffer, 1954, pp. 169–70.

Resources section

1. Graham Cray, *Tools for the Job*, CPAS, p. 49.

2. Gerard Kelly, *Learning for Leadership*, p. 9 on www.cafe-net.org.uk.

3. Example 1: To be a community of believers in Jesus Christ who are devoted to loving God, loving others, making disciples.

Example 2: The Christian community of St James' Church seeks to worship God and to further his kingdom through (1) Our praise and prayer (2) Our care and protection for God's creation (3) Our willingness to be open to others, sharing God's love through word and deed (4) Our commitment to nurturing our relationship with God and each other in Christ (5) Our daily lives lived in service.

4. They can also be framed in a SMART way: see the next point.

5. Taken and adapted from Robert Clinton and Paul Stanley, *Connecting*, NavPress, 1992.

6. John Adair, quoted in Steve Chalke, *Making a Team Work*, Kingsway, p. 25.

7. Pat MacMillan, *The Performance Factor*, Broadman and Holman, 2001.